IFIP Advances in Information and Communication Technology 464

Editor-in-Chief

Kai Rannenberg, Goethe University Frankfurt, Germany

Editorial Board

IFIP – The International Federation for Information Processing

IFIP was founded in 1960 under the auspices of UNESCO, following the First World Computer Congress held in Paris the previous year. An umbrella organization for societies working in information processing, IFIP's aim is two-fold: to support information processing within its member countries and to encourage technology transfer to developing nations. As its mission statement clearly states,

> IFIP's mission is to be the leading, truly international, apolitical organization which encourages and assists in the development, exploitation and application of information technology for the benefit of all people.

IFIP is a non-profitmaking organization, run almost solely by 2500 volunteers. It operates through a number of technical committees, which organize events and publications. IFIP's events range from an international congress to local seminars, but the most important are:

- The IFIP World Computer Congress, held every second year;
- Open conferences;
- Working conferences.

The flagship event is the IFIP World Computer Congress, at which both invited and contributed papers are presented. Contributed papers are rigorously refereed and the rejection rate is high.

As with the Congress, participation in the open conferences is open to all and papers may be invited or submitted. Again, submitted papers are stringently refereed.

The working conferences are structured differently. They are usually run by a working group and attendance is small and by invitation only. Their purpose is to create an atmosphere conducive to innovation and development. Refereeing is also rigorous and papers are subjected to extensive group discussion.

Publications arising from IFIP events vary. The papers presented at the IFIP World Computer Congress and at open conferences are published as conference proceedings, while the results of the working conferences are often published as collections of selected and edited papers.

Any national society whose primary activity is about information processing may apply to become a full member of IFIP, although full membership is restricted to one society per country. Full members are entitled to vote at the annual General Assembly, National societies preferring a less committed involvement may apply for associate or corresponding membership. Associate members enjoy the same benefits as full members, but without voting rights. Corresponding members are not represented in IFIP bodies. Affiliated membership is open to non-national societies, and individual and honorary membership schemes are also offered.

More information about this series at http://www.springer.com/series/6102

Luc Claesen · Maria-Teresa Sanz-Pascual
Ricardo Reis · Arturo Sarmiento-Reyes (Eds.)

VLSI-SoC: Internet of Things Foundations

22nd IFIP WG 10.5/IEEE International Conference
on Very Large Scale Integration, VLSI-SoC 2014
Playa del Carmen, Mexico, October 6–8, 2014
Revised and Extended Selected Papers

 Springer

Editors
Luc Claesen
Hasselt University
Diepenbeek
Belgium

Ricardo Reis
Federal University of Rio Grande do Sul
Porto Alegre, Rio Grande do Sul
Brazil

Maria-Teresa Sanz-Pascual
Electronics Department
INAOE
Tonantzintla, Puebla
Mexico

Arturo Sarmiento-Reyes
Electronics Department
INAOE
Tonantzintla, Puebla
Mexico

ISSN 1868-4238   ISSN 1868-422X (electronic)
IFIP Advances in Information and Communication Technology
ISBN 978-3-319-38734-5   ISBN 978-3-319-25279-7 (eBook)
DOI 10.1007/978-3-319-25279-7

Printed on acid-free paper

Springer International Publishing AG Switzerland is part of Springer Science+Business Media
(www.springer.com)

Preface

This book contains extended and revised versions of the highest-quality papers that were presented during the 22nd edition of the IFIP/IEEE WG10.5 International Conference on Very Large Scale Integration (VLSI-SoC), a global System-on-Chip Design and CAD conference. The 22nd conference was held at Iberostar Hotel in Playa del Carmen, Mexico (October 6–8, 2014). Previous conferences have taken place in Edinburgh, Scotland (1981); Trondheim, Norway (1983); Tokyo, Japan (1985); Vancouver, Canada (1987); Munich, Germany (1989); Edinburgh, Scotland (1991); Grenoble, France (1993); Chiba, Japan (1995); Gramado, Brazil (1997); Lisbon, Portugal (1997); Montpellier, France (2001); Darmstadt, Germany (2003); Perth, Australia (2005); Nice, France (2006); Atlanta, USA (2007); Rhodes, Greece (2008); Florianopolis, Brazil (2009); Madrid, Spain (2010); Kowloon, Hong Kong (2011), Santa Cruz, USA (2012), and Istanbul, Turkey (2013).

The purpose of this conference, which was sponsored by IFIP TC 10 Working Group 10.5, the IEEE Council on Electronic Design Automation (CEDA), and by IEEE Circuits and Systems Society, with the In-Cooperation of ACM SIGDA, was to provide a forum for the exchange of ideas and presentation of industrial and academic research results in the field of microelectronics design. The current trend toward increasing chip integration and technology process advancements has brought new challenges both at the physical and system design levels, as well as in the test of these systems. VLSI-SoC conferences aim to address these exciting new issues.

The quality of submissions (103 regular papers from 18 countries, excluding PhD Forum and special sessions) made the selection processes a very difficult one. Finally, 33 were accepted as full papers and 11 as posters. Out of the 33 full papers presented at the conference, 12 papers were chosen by a selection committee to have an extended and revised version included in this book. The selection process of these papers considered the evaluation scores during the review process as well as the review forms provided by members of the Technical Program Committee and session chairs as a result of the presentations.

The chapters of this book have authors from China, Denmark, France, Germany, Hong Kong, Italy, Ireland, Korea, The Netherlands, Switzerland, and USA. The Technical Program Committee comprised 112 members from 28 countries.

VLSI-SoC 2014 was the culmination of the work of many dedicated volunteers: paper authors, reviewers, session chairs, invited speakers, and various committee chairs. We thank them all for their contribution. Special thanks to Prof. Roberto Murphy for his invaluable help in the cumbersome tasks of local organization, finances, and registration.

This book is intended for the VLSI community, mainly those who did not have the chance to attend the conference. We hope you will enjoy reading this book and that you will find it useful in your professional life and for the development of the VLSI community as a whole.

August 2015

Luc Claesen
Maria-Teresa Sanz-Pascual
Ricardo Reis
Arturo Sarmiento-Reyes

Organization

The IFIP/IEEE International Conference on Very Large Scale Integration-System-on-Chip (VLSI-SoC) 2014 took place during October 6–8, 2014, in the Iberostar, Playa del Carmen, Mexico. VLSI-SoC 2014 was the 22nd in a series of international conferences, sponsored by IFIP TC 10 Working Group 10.5 (VLSI), IEEE CEDA, and ACM SIGDA.

General Chairs

Arturo Sarmiento-Reyes   INAOE, Mexico
Ricardo Reis   UFRGS, Brazil

Technical Program Chairs

Luc Claesen   Hasselt University, Belgium
María Teresa Sanz   INAOE, Mexico

Special Sessions Chair

Salvador Mir   TIMA, France

Local Arrangements Chair

Gabriela López   INAOE, Mexico

Publication Chair

Lorena García   UNIANDES, Colombia

Publicity Chair

Michael Hübner   Karlsruhe I.T., Germany

Registration Chair

Roberto Murphy   INAOE, Mexico

Finance Chair

Roberto Murphy   INAOE, Mexico

PhD Forum Chairs

Srinivas Katkoori   USF, USA
Reydezel Torres   INAOE, Mexico

VLSI-SoC Steering Committee

Manfred Glesner   TU Darmstadt, Germany
Matthew Guthaus   UC Santa Cruz, USA
Salvador Mir   TIMA, France
Ricardo Reis   UFRGS, Brazil
Michel Robert   University of Montpellier, France
Luis Miguel Silveira   INESC ID/IST - University of Lisbon, Portugal
Chi-Ying Tsui   HKUST, Hong Kong, SAR China

Technical Program Committee

Analog and Mixed-signal IC Design

Michiel Steyaert   KU Leuven, Belgium (Chair)
Jerzy Dabrowski   Linköping University, Sweden (Chair)
Haralampos Stratigopoulos TIMA Laboratory, France
José M. de la Rosa   IMSE-CNM, Spain
Piero Malcovati   Università degli Studi di Pavia, Italy
Jean-Michel Redoute   Monash University, Australia
Elvis Pui-In Mak   University of Macau, SAR China
Filip Tavernier   KU Leuven, Belgium
Pawel Grybos   AGH University of Science and Technology, Poland
Rashad Ramzan   University of Computing and Emerging Sciences,
                           Pakistan

Physical Design and 3D Integration

Ian O'Connor   Ecole Centrale de Lyon, France (Chair)
Youngsoo Chin   KAIST, Korea (Chair)
Taewhan Kim   Seoul National University, Korea
Saqib Khursheed   University of Liverpool, UK
Terrence Mak   Chinese University of Hong Kong, SAR Hong Kong
Pascal Vivet   CEA-LETI, France
Martha Johanna Sepulveda   University of Sao Paulo, Brazil
Eby Friedman   University of Rochester, USA
Tsung-Yi Ho   National Cheng Kung University, Taiwan
Olivier Sentieys   Inria, France

SoC Design for Variability, Reliability, Fault Tolerance, and Test

Matteo Sonza Reorda	Politecnico di Torino, Italy (Chair)
Seiji Kajihara	Kyushu Institute of Technology, Japan (Chair)
Satoshi Ohtake	Oita University, Japan
Luis Entrena	Universidad Carlos III de Madrid, Spain
Fernanda Kastensmidt	UFRGS, Brazil
Ozgur Sinanoglu	New York University, Abu Dhabi, United Arab Emirates
Swaroop Ghosh	University of South Florida, USA
Erik Larsson	Lund University, Sweden
Li-C Wang	University of California Santa Barbara, USA
Shyue-Kung Lu	National Taiwan University of Science and Technology, Taiwan

New Devices, MEMS, and Microsystems

Wenjing Rao	University of Illinois at Chicago, USA (Chair)
Libor Rufer	TIMA Laboratory, France (Chair)
Dennis Wang	Broadcom, USA
Joshua En-Yuan	City University of Hong Kong, Hong Kong, SAR China
Man Wong	Hong Kong University of Science and Technology, Hong Kong, SAR China
Igor Paprotny	University of Illinois at Chicago, USA
Swarup Bhunia	Case Western Reserve University, USA
Csaba Andras Moritz	UMass Amherst, USA
Rasit Onur Topaloglu	IBM, USA
Skandar Basrour	University of Grenoble, France

Digital Signal Processing and Image Processing SoC Design

Peilin Liu	Shanghai Jiao Tong University, China (Chair)
Sergio Bampi	UFRGS, Brazil (Chair)
Liang Tang	University of New South Wales, Australia
Chun-Jen Tsai	National Chiao Tung University, Taiwan
Dajiang Zhou	Waseda University, Japan
Hassan Ghasemzadeh	Washington State University, USA
Lingzhi Liu	Intel, USA
Ilker Hamzaoglu	Sabanci University, Turkey
Urs Frey	RIKEN QBiC, Japan
Vijaykrishna Narayanan	Penn State University, USA

Prototyping, Validation, Verification, Modeling, and Simulation

Laurence Pierre	Université de Grenoble, France (Chair)
Horácio Neto	INESC-ID, Portugal (Chair)

Graziano Pravadelli	Università di Verona, Italy
Cristoph Grimm	TU Kaiserslautern, Germany
Andreas Veneris	University of Toronto, Canada
Ian Harris	University of California Irvine, USA
Marc Boulé	École de Technologie Supérieure, Canada
Alper Sen	Bogazici University, Turkey
Laurent Maillet-Contoz	STMicroelectronics, France
Wendelin Serwe	Inria-Grenoble Rhône-Alpes, France

Embedded Systems and Processors, Hardware/Software Codesign

Yajun Ha	National University of Singapore, Singapore (Chair)
Lan-Da Van	National Chiao Tung University, Taiwan (Chair)
Muhammad Shafiqe	Karlsruhe Institute of Technology, Germany
Jigang Wu	Tianjin Polytechnic University, China
Heng Yu	Audaque Corporation, China
Andrea Acquaviva	Politecnico di Torino, Italy
Philip Brisk	UC Riverside, USA
Yu Pu	Qualcomm Research, USA
Tien-Fu Chen	National Chiao Tung University, Taiwan
Jason Xue	City University of Hong Kong, Hong Kong, SAR China
Sri Parameswaran	University of New South Wales, Australia

Processor Architectures and Multicore SoCs

Yun Pan	Zhejiang University, China (Chair)
Andreas Burg	EPFL, Switzerland (Chair)
Wei Zhang	Hong Kong University of Science and Technology, Hong Kong, SAR China
Jie Han	Technology University of Alberta, Canada
Chih-Tsun Huang	National Tsing Hua University, Taiwan
Anupam Chattopadhyay	RWTH Aachen, Germany
Zhiyi Yu	Fudan University, China
Jiang Xu	Hong Kong University of Science and Technology, Hong Kong, SAR China
Davide Rossi	University of Bologna, Italy
Bevan Baas	UC Davis, USA

Logic and High-Level Synthesis

Masahiro Fujita	University of Tokyo, Japan (Chair)
Philippe Coussy	Université de Bretagne Sud, France (Chair)
Giuseppe Di Guglielmo	Columbia University, New York, USA
Taemin Kim	Intel Labs, USA
Elena Dubrova	Royal Institute of Technology, Sweden
Preeti Panda	Indian Institute of Technology Delhi, India
Jason Anderson	University of Toronto, Canada

Luciano Lavagno   Politecnico di Torino, Italy
Deming Chen   University of Illinois at Urbana-Champaign, USA
Virendra Singh   IIT Bombay, India

Low-Power and Thermal-Aware Design

Ping Luo   University of Electronic Science and Technology,
                           China (Chair)
José L. Ayala   Universidad Complutense de Madrid, Spain (Chair)
Sherief Reda   Brown University, USA
Armin Tajalli   EPFL, Switzerland
Mirko Loghi   Università di Udine, Italy
Baker Mohammad   Khalifa University, United Arab Emirates
José M. Moya   Universidad Politécnica de Madrid, Spain
Marco D. Santambrogio   Politecnico di Milano, Italy

Reconfigurable SoC Systems for Energy and Reliability

Dirk Stroobandt   Ghent University, Belgium (Chair)
Jürgen Becker   Karlsruhe Institute of Technology, Germany (Chair)
Michael Hübner   Ruhr-Universität Bochum, Germany
Philip Leong   University of Sydney, Australia
Joao Cardoso   Universidade do Porto, Portugal
Koen Bertels   TU Delft, The Netherlands
Pascal Benoit   LIRMM - University of Montpellier 2, France
Disonisios Pnevmatikatos FORTH-ICS, Technical University of Crete, Greece
Anh Tran   Xpliant, USA
Qiuling Zhu   Google, USA

Contents

Dynamic Programming-Based Lifetime Reliability Optimization in Networks-on-Chip

Liang Wang[1]([✉]), Xiaohang Wang[2], and Terrence Mak[1,2]

[1] Department of Computer Science and Engineering,
The Chinese University of Hong Kong, Shatin, N.T., Hong Kong
{lwang,stmak}@cse.cuhk.edu.hk
[2] Guangzhou Institute of Advanced Technology,
Chinese Academy of Sciences, Guangzhou, China
xh.wang@giat.ac.cn

Abstract. Technology scaling leads to the reliability issue as a primary concern in Networks-on-Chip (NoC) design. Due to routing algorithms, some routers may age much faster than others, which become a bottleneck for system lifetime. In this chapter, lifetime is modeled as a resource consumed over time. A metric lifetime budget is associated with each router, indicating the maximum allowed workload for current period. Since the heterogeneity in router lifetime reliability has strong correlation with the routing algorithm, we define a problem to optimize the lifetime by routing packets along the path with maximum lifetime budgets. A dynamic programming-based lifetime-aware routing algorithm is proposed to optimize the lifetime distribution of routers. The dynamic programming network approach is employed to solve this problem with linear complexity. The experimental results show that the lifetime-aware routing has around 20 %, 45 %, 55 % minimal MTTF improvement than XY routing, NoP routing, and Oddeven routing, respectively.

Keywords: Reliability · Networks-on-Chip · Routing algorithm · Dynamic programming

1 Introduction

Networks-on-Chip (NoC) is emerging as an efficient communication infrastructure for connecting resources in many core system. NoC is composed of routers interconnected through a network. NoC provides communication fabrics for data transmission among cores. The data transmission is in the form of packets, which are divided into flits and routed by routers. In NoC, routing algorithm provides a protocol for routing the packets. In other words, the pathways of the packets are determines by a routing algorithm. Generally, routing algorithms are classified into deterministic routing and adaptive routing. Deterministic routing algorithm provides a fixed path given source and destination. Compared to deterministic routing algorithm, adaptive routing algorithm is more flexible. The pathway of a packet can dynamically adapt to NoC traffic or other conditions. In this chapter,

© IFIP International Federation for Information Processing 2015
L. Claesen et al. (Eds.): VLSI-SoC 2014, IFIP AICT 464, pp. 1–20, 2015.
DOI: 10.1007/978-3-319-25279-7_1

we exploit an adaptive routing algorithm to optimize the lifetime reliability of NoC.

With shrinking feature size and increasing transistor density, reliability issue is becoming a primary concern for chip design. The failure rate of electronic components increases 316 % as the features size decreases 64 % [27]. Along with shrinking feature size, power density of chips increases exponentially, leading to overheat. High temperature also greatly reduces the lifetime of a chip. Dynamic thermal management (DTM) techniques such as dynamic voltage and frequency scaling (DVFS) [13], adaptive routing [2] are employed to address the temperature issues. The temperature is maintained below a limit to ensure the reliability of a chip. Dynamic reliability management (DRM) is first proposed in [26], aiming at ensuring a target lifetime reliability at better performance.

The reliability of NoC depends on the routers. The lifetime reliability of a router has strong correlation with the routing algorithm because the lifetime reliability is relevant to operating conditions and temperature, which are affected by the routing algorithm. We conduct a case study to show the distribution of routers reliability under two different routing algorithms, XY and Oddeven. The case study is evaluated in 8 × 8 2D mesh NoC. The detailed description of simulation setup is referred to Sect. 5. The lifetime, measured in MTTF metric (mean time to failure), is normalized to the maximum one. The results are presented in Fig. 1, which shows the number of occurrences in different MTTF ranges. For both routing algorithms, there is a heterogeneity observed among the routers. Especially for Oddeven routing, the minimum MTTF of router is even less than 20 % of the maximum one. It suggests that the minimum MTTF router is aging more than 5 times faster than the maximum MTTF router. The unbalanced lifetime distribution would become a bottleneck for the lifetime of system. Furthermore, the two distribution functions differ in slop for XY and Oddeven, indicating the correlation of router reliability and routing algorithms.

The above example indicates routing paths can be a control knob to optimize the router reliability. In this chapter, we apply dynamic reliability management to NoC and propose a lifetime-aware routing to optimize the lifetime reliability of NoC routers. Lifetime is modeled as a resource consumed over time. A lifetime budget is defined for each router, indicating the maximum allowed workload for current time. We define a longest path problem to optimize the router lifetime by routing packets along the path with maximum lifetime budgets. The problem is solved by dynamic programming approach with linear time complexity. The key idea is to use lifetime budget as the cost for dynamic programming. Moreover, a low cost hardware unit is implemented to accelerate the lifetime budget computation at runtime.

This chapter is an extension of previous work [28] by adding more detail descriptions, substantial analysis and modified experiments. The main contributions of this chapter include:

(1) Define a lifetime budget for each router, indicating the maximum allowed workload for current period.

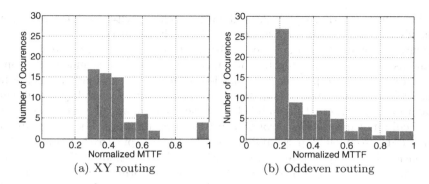

(a) XY routing   (b) Oddeven routing

Fig. 1. A case study for motivation. In 8×8 NoC, the Normalized MTTF of routers is evaluated under different routing algorithms

(2) Define a problem to optimize the lifetime by routing packets along the path with maximum lifetime budgets.
(3) Propose a lifetime-aware routing algorithm, which solves the problem through a dynamic programming approach with linear time complexity.

The remainder of the chapter is organized as follows. Section 2 briefly introduces the related work. Section 3 discusses the DRM and defines the lifetime budget for a router. Section 4 presents the adaptive routing, including problem formulation and routing algorithm. Section 5 analyzes the experimental results and Sect. 6 concludes this chapter.

2 Related Work

There are two kinds of failures in ICs: extrinsic failures and intrinsic failures. Extrinsic failures are caused by manufacturing defects and occur with a decreasing rate over time. Intrinsic failures are related with wear-out and are caused due to operation conditions within the specified conditions, e.g. temperature, current density, *etc.* In this chapter, we focus on long-term reliability management of routers, and only consider intrinsic failures. The failure mechanisms for intrinsic failures include electro migration (EM), time-dependent dielectric breakdown (TDDB), stress migration (SM), Negative Bias temperature instability (NBTI) and thermal cycling (TC). A reliability model named RAMP is proposed in [26], which combines various failure mechanism models using Sum-of-failure method.

In the failure mechanism models, lifetime reliability is highly related to temperature. Most prior studies consider thermal issues, with the objectives to balance the temperature or to take temperature as a constraint [2,13,23]. Mulas *et al.* [23] employed a task migration approach to redistribute power dissipation such that the temperature of multiprocessor system is balanced. Hanumaiah *et al.* [13] adopted DVFS to maintain the temperature of multiprocessor system under a constraint. Al-Dujaily *et al.* [2] proposed to balance the temperature of NoC by a thermal-aware routing algorithm. However, the thermal techniques neglect other factors on reliability, such as switch activity, operating frequency, *etc.* The lifetime could not be effectively balanced.

Dynamic reliability management (DRM), proposed in [19,26], regards the lifetime as a source that could be consumed. Reliability management is mainly studied for single-core processor or multi-core processors through various solutions, such as task mapping [14], frequency control [25], reliability monitoring and adaptation [22], *etc.* Hartman [14] proposed to dynamically manage the lifetime of chip multiprocessors through run-time task mapping. The task mapping obtains data from on-chip reliability sensors and adapts to changing lifetime distribution in the system at run-time. Shi *et al.* [25] explored DRM for both single-core and multi-core processors. The overall performance expressed as frequency policies is maximized under soft thermal constraint. Mercati *et al.* [22] proposed a DRM policy based on a two level controller. The controller monitors system reliability on a long time scale and adapts operating conditions on a short time scale. The multi-core system adapts operating conditions with DVFS such that a predefined target lifetime is satisfied.

Since NoC is becoming more important for multi-core system interconnection, reliability management in NoC domain is attracting increasing attentions. Some studies make attempt to improve the NoC reliability through microarchitecture design. A wear-resistant router microarchitecture is designed in [17] to improve reliability of routers. However, they did not consider the routing algorithm impacts on the router lifetime. Task mapping is another solution to improve NoC reliability. A compile-time task mapping algorithm is proposed in [12] to balance the MTTF of NoC. However, at runtime the tasks are mapped on NoC-based MPSoC without considering the variation of runtime operating conditions. The reliability of NoC can also be improved through routing algorithms. Bhardwaj *et al.* proposed an aging-aware adaptive routing algorithm for NoC [6,7]. They introduced an aging model that defines stressed links and routers, in which the traffic of a router or link exceeds the upper limit called Traffic Threshold per Epoch (TTpE). However, the routing algorithm actually reduces the workloads of routers with high utilization, which may not exhibit the most aging effects. Different from their works, we directly apply reliability management to NoC, and propose a lifetime-aware routing algorithm to balance the lifetime distribution of NoC routers at runtime. The routing algorithm is based on the dynamic programming (DP) approach, which is proposed by Mak *et al.* [21]. The dynamic programming approach is proposed for adaptive routing, in which the shortest path problem is solved optimally. The dynamic programming based adaptive routing has already been applied in congestion avoidance [21], fault tolerance [35], thermal management [2], *etc.*

3   Lifetime Budget Definition

For lifetime-aware routing algorithm, the lifetime reliability of routers should be provided for the algorithm to update routing decisions. There are mainly two methods to estimate lifetime reliability:

(1) Reliability is estimated through operating conditions history [34]. Using existing mathematical failure models, aging is periodically computed. At runtime, the operating conditions are monitored and provided for lifetime estimation.

(2) Aging sensors are used to monitor the aging effects of transistors [18]. For example, NBTI sensors are exploited to monitor the variation of threshold voltage, as the NBTI causes an increase on the threshold voltage of PMOS transistors. However, besides NBTI, the wear-outs of transistors are also incurred by other failure mechanisms such as EM, which could not be monitored by sensors explicitly.

In fact, both methods can be used for our lifetime-aware routing algorithm because the lifetime-aware routing is independent of lifetime estimation. The primary objective of this chapter is on lifetime-aware routing for lifetime optimization. We adopt the first method for lifetime estimation, i.e., the lifetime of routers are estimated from temperature and workload stresses history. We also present a hardware implementation for lifetime estimation in Sect. 4.5.

For long term reliability management of routers, we only consider wear-out related faults. The failure rate, a metric for lifetime reliability, keeps almost constant if the operating conditions (e.g. constant current, temperature, frequency and voltage) keep unchanged. The mean time to failure (MTTF) is inverse of failure rate when the operating conditions are constant. The MTTF due to EM is based on Black's equation [1] as follows

$$MTTF \propto (J - J_{crit})^{-n} \exp\left(E_a/kT\right) \tag{1}$$

where J is the current density; J_{cris} is the critical current density; E_a is the activation energy; k is the Boltzmann's constant; T is temperature. n is a constant depend on interconnect metal used. However, this equation only assumes steady operating conditions, which is not realistic. The operating conditions (temperature, current density) are usually varying due to workload variation. Lu. et al. [19] derived MTTF under time-varying current density and temperature stresses as

$$T^f = \frac{A}{E\left[j(t)\left(\frac{exp(\frac{-Q}{kT(t)})}{kT(t)}\right)\right]} \tag{2}$$

where A is a constant related to the structure. $j(t)$ is current, and $T(t)$ is temperature. The varying failure rate, also called lifetime consumption rate, is denoted as $\lambda(t) = j(t)\left(\frac{exp(\frac{-Q}{kT(t)})}{kT(t)}\right)$. The MTTF is the inverse of failure rate expectation value. Equation 2 is based on the assumption of Electromigration (EM) failure mechanism. We only consider EM because EM is the primary aging factor for interconnection, and the reliability of both routers and links are closely related to interconnection.

Based on Eq. 2, we also derive an equation as an approximation relationship between $\lambda(t)$ and the routers workload. The current is $j(t) = \frac{CV_{dd}}{WH} \times f \times p$ [26], where p is switch activity. The voltage and frequency are assumed constant. In a router, switch activity is proportional to the incoming rate of a router because the incoming flits are assumed the only stimuli to the allocator. The failure rate can be represented as follows:

$$\lambda(t) \propto d(t) \left(\frac{exp(\frac{-Q}{kT(t)})}{kT(t)} \right) \tag{3}$$

where $d(t)$ is the flits incoming rate at time t. The flits incoming rate is the number of flits passing through the router per unit time. The incoming rate also stands for the workload of a router. It is assumed that the ports of the incoming flits are not considered. The equation provides an approximated relationship between the lifetime and routers workloads.

Another equation derived in [19] is $\int_0^{T^f} r(t)dt = C$, where C is a constant. In the equation, lifetime is modeled as a resource consumed over time. As suggested by [19], we define a lifetime budget for each router, denoted as

$$LB(t) = \int_0^t (\lambda_{nominal} - \lambda(t))dt \tag{4}$$

where $\lambda_{nominal}$ is derived from the specified expected lifetime, indicating the constant lifetime consumption rate under nominal conditions. $\lambda_{nominal}$ is the inverse of expected MTTF, i.e., $\lambda_{nominal} \cdot T^f = C$. If $LB(t) > 0$, the expected lifetime could satisfy the predefined constraint, and vice versa. The failure rate is related to operating conditions, i.e., temperature and workload, which are monitored periodically. Under discrete monitored conditions, the lifetime budget is represented as

$$LB(n) = \begin{cases} 0, & \text{if } n \text{ is } 0 \\ LB(n-1) + \lambda_{nominal} - \lambda(n), & \text{Otherwise} \end{cases} \tag{5}$$

where $LB(n)$ and $\lambda(n)$ are the lifetime budget and failure rate respectively at the n-th time interval. The lifetime budget indicates the maximum allowed failure rate for current the period. Therefore, the lifetime is modeled as a source of routers to be consumed over time. The router with higher workloads consumes the lifetime source at a faster speed.

From the perspective of packets, the selected path determines the workloads of the routers along the path. Therefore the routing algorithm, which determines the routing paths, plays an important role in the lifetime distribution of routers. In following sections, we propose a lifetime-aware routing algorithm to balance the lifetime distribution of routers.

4   Lifetime-Aware Adaptive Routing

Since MTTF or failure rate of a router is relevant to the flits incoming rate and temperature. We propose to balance the MTTF of routers through an adaptive routing algorithm. In this section, we first define a problem for lifetime reliability optimization and present the dynamic programming formulation for the problem. Then we propose an adaptive routing algorithm for lifetime reliability optimization. Table 1 summarizes all notations in this section.

Table 1. Notations

Symbols	Semantics
$\mathcal{V}$	A set of nodes in network $\mathcal{G}$
$\mathcal{A}$	A set of edges in network $\mathcal{G}$
LB_i	Lifetime budget of the router i
$C_{u,d}$	Cost of edge $u \to d$
$V(s,d)$	The optimal cost from s to d in LP form
$V^*(s,d)$	The optimal cost from s to d in DP form
$V^{(k)}(s,d)$	The expected cost for s after k steps
$P_{s,d}$	Available paths from s to d
r_i	The i-th router along a path from s to d
$\mu(d)$	The optimal routing direction to node d
$N(j)$	The neighbor node in the direction j

4.1 Problem Definition

To balance the lifetime distribution, the lifetime-aware adaptive routing aims to find a path with maximum lifetime budget from designated path sets for each packet. Therefore we formulate a longest path problem as follows. Given a directed graph $\mathcal{G} = (\mathcal{V}, \mathcal{A})$ with $n = |\mathcal{V}|$ nodes, $m = |\mathcal{A}|$ edges, and a cost associated with each edge $u \to v \in \mathcal{A}$, which is donated as $C_{u,v}$. Given two nodes $s, d \in \mathcal{V}$, $P_{s,d}$ is the set of minimal distance paths from s to d. The cost of a path $p = \langle s = v_0, ..., d = v_k \rangle \in P_{s,d}$, from s to d, is the sum of the costs of its constituent edges: $Cost(p) = \sum_{i=0}^{k-1} C_{i,i+1}$. We aim to find the path with the maximum cost of the path, denoted as $V(s,d)$. The problem can be formally formulated as a linear optimization problem. Let u be a neighbor node of s, and on the one of the minimal distance paths. We have a constraint $V(s,d) \geq V(s,u) + C_{u,d}$. We can obtain the following linear programming:

$$\text{maximize} \quad \sum_{\forall s \in \mathcal{V}} V(s,d)$$
$$\text{subject to} \quad V(s,d) \geq V(u,d) + C_{s,u} \qquad (6)$$
$$V(d,d) = 0$$

The above formation yields the optimal path from any nodes s to the destination node d, known as multiple-source single-destination longest path problem. With the nodes corresponding to the routers, the key idea of the adaptive routing is to use lifetime budget as the cost for the path, denoted as

$$C_{r_i, r_{i+1}} = LB_i \tag{7}$$

LB_i is the lifetime budget of the i-th router r_i. The total lifetime budgets along the path $p = \langle r_0 = s, ..., r_{k-1} = d \rangle$ is

$$C_{s,d} = \sum_{i=0}^{k-1} LB_i \tag{8}$$

Taking lifetime budget as the cost, the problem is to find a path with maximum lifetime budgets.

4.2   Dynamic Programming-Based Formulation

Background of Dynamic Programming. Dynamic programming (DP) is an optimization technique which was first introduced by Richard Bellman in the 1940s [5]. DP has been applied in a variety practical problems, in which the main complex problem can be broken into simpler subproblems. It provides a systematic procedure for determining the optimal combination of decisions which takes much less time than naive methods. In contrast to other optimization techniques, such as linear programming (LP), DP does not provide a standard mathematical formulation of the algorithm. Rather, DP is a general type of approach to problem solving, and it restates an optimization problem in recursive form, which is known as Bellman equation. The optimization or decision-making problems can be expressed in a recursive form as follows:

$$V_i(t) = \max_{\forall k} \{ R_{i,k}(t) + V_k(t) \}, \ \forall i \tag{9}$$

where $V_i(t)$ is the expected reward of the i-th state and $R_{i,k}(t)$ is the reward of transition from state i to state k.

DP Formulation. The problem to find a path with maximum cost can also be stated in the form of dynamic programming, which defines a recursive process in step k. To obtain the optimal cost from node s to d, the process requires the notion of cost-to-go function, which is expect cost from node s to d. Based on the Bellman equation, the expected cost is updated recursively until the optimality criteria is reached. The Bellman equation can be expressed as

$$V^{(k)}(s, d) = \max_{\forall u \in V} \left\{ V^{(k-1)}(u, d) + C_{s,u} \right\} \tag{10}$$

$V^{(k)}(s, d)$ is the cost from s to d at the k-th iteration. The cost $C_{s,u}$ is associated with lifetime budget. Initially, $u = d$ and $V^{(0)}(d, d) = 0$. Then Eq. 10 is solved recursively and the recursion is expanded from s to d. After k iterations, the optimal cost from s to d is $V^*(s, d)$, which is maximum among all minimal distance paths $P_{s,d}$. The optimal cost is represented as following equation:

$$V^*(s, d) = \max_{\{r_0=s,\ldots,r_{k-1}=d\}\in P_{s,d}} \left\{\sum_{i=0}^{k-1} LB_i\right\} \tag{11}$$

At each node s, the optimal decision that leads to the optimal path to d can be obtained from the argument of the maximum operator at the Bellman equation as follows:

$$\mu(d) = arg \max_{\forall j}\{V^*(N(j), d) + LB_s\} \tag{12}$$

where j is the optimal decision, which represents the optimal output port or output direction. $N(j)$ is the neighbor node in the direction j. LB_s is the lifetime budget of node s.

Compared with linear programming, the dynamic programming presents an opportunity for solving the problem using parallel architecture and can greatly improve the computation speed.

4.3   Lifetime-Aware Adaptive Routing Algorithm

We propose a dynamic programming-based lifetime-aware adaptive routing algorithm, which is outlined in Algorithm 1. This algorithm outputs the direction to be taken for current node s. First, according to the positions of local node and destination node, the available directions D_s are restricted to the minimal distance paths to destination (line 1). If the local node is the destination, the optimal cost is 0 and the routing direction is local port. Given an available direction $j \in D_s$, the expected cost is computed by adding up the local cost LB_s and the optimal cost from neighbor node $N(j)$ to d (lines 6–8). The maximum cost is obtained by taking the maximum value from all $V_j(s, d)$, which are the costs of the paths that local node s takes direction j (line 9). Finally, the optimal direction $\mu(d)$ is obtained from the argument of the maximum operator (line 10). The dynamic programming-based adaptive algorithm outputs an optimal direction for each router. In the algorithm, the loop is realized in dynamic programming network. The optimal value for local node is propagated to the all neighbor nodes through dynamic programming network. The computational-delay complexity can be reduced to linear.

In this chapter, the routers are assumed wormhole flow control without virtual channel. Deadlock can effectively be avoided by adopting one of the deadlock-free turn model. We adopt west-first turn model for deadlock avoidance [11].

4.4   Dynamic Programming Network

The dynamic programming network, introduced by Mak et al. [21], is composed of distributed computation units and links. Figure 2 presents an example of 3×3

Algorithm 1. Lifetime-Aware Adaptive Routing

Definitions s: local node;

  D_s: set of directions to minimal distance paths;

  $N(j)$: the neighbor node in the direction j;

  $V_j(s, d)$: the cost of the path taking direction j for s;

Input d: destination node;

  $V^*(N(j), d)$: the optimal cost from $N(j)$ to d;

  LB_s: lifetime budget of node s,

Output $\mu(d)$: the optimal routing direction to d;

  $V^*(s, d)$: the optimal cost from s to d.

1: Calculate available direction D_s according to positions of s and d

2: **if** $s = d$ **then**

3:    $V^*(s, d) = 0$

4:    $\mu(d) = LOCAL$

5: **else**

6:    **for** all directions $j \in D_s$ **do**

7:      $V_j(s, d) = V^*(N(j), d) + LB_s$

8:    **end for**

9:    $V^*(s, d) = \max_{\forall j} V_j(s, d)$

10:    $\mu(d) = arg \max_{\forall j} V_j(s, d)$ ▷ Update optimal routing directions

11: **end if**

---

dynamic programming network. The dynamic programming network is coupled with NoC. Each computation unit implements the DP unit equations e.g. longest path calculations, and propagates the numerical solution to neighbor units. In addition, routing tables are implemented in routers. Algorithm 1 presents the operations required for updating the routing directions using the DP unit. The routing table will be updated periodically by the DP unit. For each router, the temperature and flits incoming rate are also monitored periodically. Failure rate is computed through the lifetime budget computation unit, which is presented in Sect. 4.5. According to the computed failure rate and nominal failure rate, the lifetime budget is updated. The lifetime budget values also propagated to the DP units as the DP costs. The dynamic programming network quickly resolves the optimal solution and passes the control decisions to routers, then the routing tables are updated.

The DP network presents several features to NoC:

(1) The distributed units enable a scalable monitoring functionality for NoC. Each unit monitors local information and communicates with neighbor units, achieving a global optimization.
(2) The DP network can provide a real-time response without consuming data-flow network bandwidth due to the simplicity of the the computational unit.
(3) The DP network provides an effective solution to the optimal routing.

To converge to the optimal solution, the delay of DP network depends on the network topology. Mak *et al.* have concluded that the network convergence

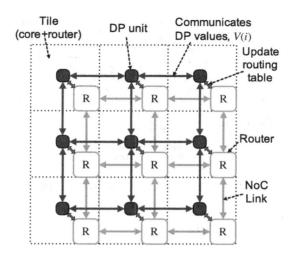

Fig. 2. An example of 3 × 3 dynamic programming network coupled with NoC

time is proportional to the network diameter, which is the longest path in the network [20].

4.5   Lifetime Budget Runtime Computation

The failure rate computation is an exponential function, not applicable for runtime computation. Similar to the methods proposed in [33], we use lookup tables that fit with Eq. 3 to pre-calculate failure rate. The runtime computation process is accelerated. To compute the lifetime budget at runtime, we design a hardware unit called lifetime budget computation unit (LBCU). The architecture of LBCU is presented in Fig. 3. The temperature related part $\left(\frac{exp(\frac{-Q}{kT(t)})}{kT(t)} \right)$ is pre-computed and kept in a lookup table. Each entry is corresponding to a temperature range. Another potential problem is that it may require much area to multiply with the incoming flit rate. Instead of computing the multiplication at the end of each time interval, we compute the failure rate per cycle. As shown in Fig. 3, E, S, W, N, L are from 5 ports of a router, indicating whether there is a flit in current cycle. The failure rate per cycle is computed by multiplying the lookup table result with the sum of the ports. Because the maximum number to be multiplied is 5, the multiplication is only achieved by shifting and addition in stead of a multiplier. A counter is used to judge if it reaches the end of the time interval. At the end of the time interval, the lifetime budget is attained through addition. Despite of a little accuracy loss, the lifetime budget computation is accelerated at runtime while only some basic logic units are used. The implementation of LBCU will be evaluated in terms of area in Sect. 5.7.

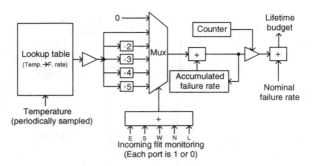

Fig. 3. Lifetime Budget Computation Unit

5   Experimental Results

5.1   Experimental Setup

Experiments are performed using Noxim simulator, which is an open source SystemC simulator for mesh-based NoC. In Noxim, the power of routers are modeled using ORION 2.0 NoC power simulator [16]. To model the temperature, we adopt HotSpot thermal model [15]. The thermal configuration is the default configuration of HotSpot. To be more accurate, we adopt the floorplan of Tilera64 processor [4] as the input of HotSpot. The frequency of NoC is configured 1 GHz. The simulation runs for 10^7 cycles. The time interval for temperature monitoring is 5000 clock cycles. And the routing tables and lifetime budgets are only updated at the end of each time interval. We employ Electromigration as the failure mechanism. The buffer depth is 10 flits and the packet size is 5 flits.

Table 2. Benchmarks

PARSEC	Streamcluster, swaptions, ferret, fluidanimate, blackscholes, freqmine, dedup, canneal, vips
SPLASH-2	Barnes, raytrace

In the experiments, we compare the lifetime-aware routing algorithm with XY routing, NoP routing and Oddeven routing, respectively. The NoP routing algorithm, a congestion-aware routing, is the west-first turn model with neighbors-on-path (NoP) selection scheme; the Oddeven routing is the oddeven turn model [10] with random selection scheme. Besides, the evaluations are also performed over a suite of benchmarks: 9 benchmarks in PARSEC [8] and 2 benchmarks in SPLASH-2 [32]. The benchmarks are listed in Table 2. These experiments are performed in an in-house developed simulator [30]. The configurations for the simulator are listed in Table 3.

Table 3. Simulator setup

Number of cores	64 (MIPS ISA 32 compatible)
L1 D cache	16 KB, 2-way, 32B line, 2 cycles, 2 ports, dual tags
L1 I cache	32 KB, 2-way, 64B line, 2 cycles
L2 cache (shared) MESI protocol	64 KB slice/node, 64B, 6 cycles, 2 ports
Main memory	2 GB
Data packet size	5 flits
Meta packet size	1 flit
NoC flit size	72-bit
NoC VC number	4
NoC buffer	5 × 10 flits

5.2 MTTF Distribution

As comparisons with the case study mentioned in Sect. 1, we evaluate the MTTF distribution of the lifetime-aware routing and NoP routing. The injection rate is also 0.005 flits/cycle; the NoC size is 8 × 8. Figure 4 presents the histogram of lifetime distribution. For the lifetime-aware routing, the MTTF distribution is more concentrated than others, namely, the MTTF is more evenly distributed.

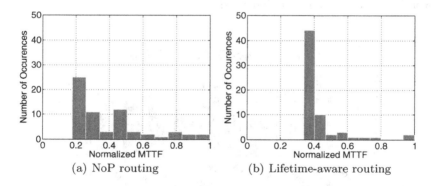

(a) NoP routing   (b) Lifetime-aware routing

Fig. 4. MTTF distribution of NoP routing and lifetime-aware routing

5.3 Minimal MTTF Evaluation

The minimal MTTF router is the router with the highest probability to wear out. Because the minimal MTTF is critical for the system lifetime, we evaluate the minimal MTTF of routers, expressed in $\min\{MTTF_i\}$. The evaluation is under synthetic traffic. The traffic pattern is set random and the injection rate is set 0.005 flits/cycle. The routing algorithms are also compared in different NoC size, 8 × 8, 10 × 10, 12 × 12. The results are shown in Table 4. In the

Table 4. Minimal MTTF comparisons under different routing algorithms (hours).

NoC size	XY	NoP	Oddeven	Lifetime	MTTF improvement (Lifetime vs.)		
					XY	NoP	Oddeven
8x8	577490	453085	435682	683209	18.3 %	50.8 %	56.9 %
10x10	321487	264756	253358	393711	22.4 %	48.7 %	55.4 %
12x12	173618	144960	133637	203117	16.9 %	40.1 %	52.0 %

table, the minimal MTTF value is evaluated. The evaluation metric is hour. It can be observed that the lifetime-aware routing has around 20 %, 45 %, 55 % minimal MTTF improvement than XY routing, NoP routing, Oddeven routing, respectively. Additionally, the minimal MTTF also decreases dramatically with NoC size, because the workloads of routers increase with the area of NoC. The MTTF improvement against XY routing is relatively smaller as the XY routing also brings relatively less traffic for the routers in the central region.

We also evaluate the minimal MTTF with real benchmarks. The experimental results are demonstrated in Fig. 5. Here all the minimal MTTF values are normalized to the values under lifetime-aware routing. The minimal MTTF under lifetime-aware routing is highest, which is consistent with previous results. In addition, the minimal MTTF under different benchmarks varies a lot because the workloads are inherently unbalanced.

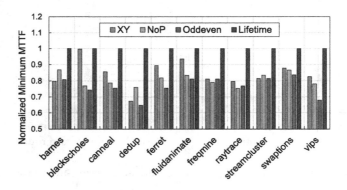

Fig. 5. Minimal MTTF evaluation with real benchmarks

5.4 NoC Overall MTTF Evaluation

We take NoC as a whole and evaluate the overall MTTF of NoC. This based on the assumption that NoC fails when a router fails. Therefore, the failure rate of NoC is the sum of all routers, denoted as $\lambda_{NoC} = \sum_{i=1}^{N} \lambda_i$. The MTTF of NoC is calculated according to Eq. 2. We evaluate the MTTF of NoC under real benchmarks with 4 different routing algorithms. The results are presented in Fig. 6. From the results, we found that the lifetime-aware routing leads to around 5 % NoC MTTF improvement due to its better lifetime distribution. This is because the overall workloads are almost the same for different routing algorithms, while the lifetime-aware routing algorithm also leads to better temperature distribution.

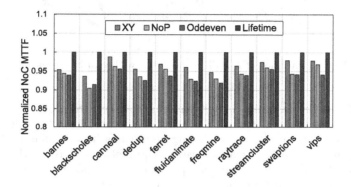

Fig. 6. NoC MTTF evaluation with real benchmarks

However, the overall MTTF cannot effectively reflect the reliability of routers. The unbalanced lifetime distribution would make some routers age much faster despite of the small differences of overall MTTF. An example is illustrated in [24], showing that overall MTTF metric is not adequate for overall reliability specification.

5.5   Variance of MTTF

Besides overall MTTF, we also use the MTTF variance metric to show that the lifetime-aware routing distributes the lifetime more evenly. The results are shown in Fig. 7. In the figure, the MTTF variance is normalized for comparisons. The lifetime-aware routing algorithm exhibits the less variance, showing that the lifetime distribution is more balanced.

5.6   Average Packets Delay Comparison

To evaluate the impacts on the global average delay, the lifetime-aware routing is also compared with the other three routing algorithms. The global average delay is evaluated with random traffic pattern. The buffer size is configured 10 flits. The comparisons are under flits injection rate from 0.01 to 0.17 flits/cycle. The experimental results are shown in Fig. 8. The delay is measured in cycles. It can be observed that the saturated flit injection rate of the lifetime-aware routing is

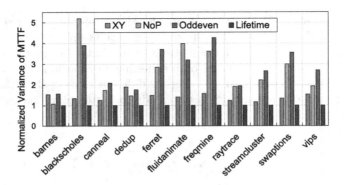

Fig. 7. Variance of MTTF comparison with real benchmarks

around 0.10 flits/cycle, which is 0.02 less than oddeven routing, 0.03 less than NoP routing, and 0.04 less than XY routing. Therefore, when the injection rate is less than 0.10 flits/cycle, these routing algorithms have similar performance in terms of average packet delay. However, the lifetime-aware routing achieves longer life while has smaller saturation point. It is concluded there is a trade-off between lifetime and performance (average packet delay).

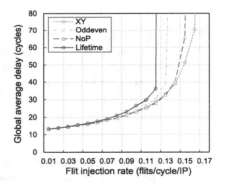

Fig. 8. Global average delay comparison

5.7 Hardware Evaluation

We implement lifetime budget computation unit (LBCU) with Verilog HDL and compare LBCU with router in terms of area. The lookup table of LBCU contains 64 entries to keep pre-computed values, which corresponds to different temperature ranges. The size of each entry is 32 bits. The registers for lifetime budget and failure rate value are 32 bits. The router is open-source and developed by Becker [3]. The frequency is 1 GHz. The router is 5-ports input-buffered with wormhole flow control. The buffer size is 4 flits; the flit size is 75 bits.

They are synthesized using Synopsys Design Compiler under 45 nm TSMC library. The areas of router and LBCU are 29810 μm^2 and 1529 μm^2 respectively. It can be concluded that LBCU leads to around 5.13 % increase in terms of area. In other words, LBCU can be integrated with NoC with low overhead. In addition, the cost of dynamic programming network is not evaluated in this work. The detail evaluation for dynamic programming network can refer to [21].

6   Conclusions and Future Work

In this chapter, we propose a dynamic programming-based lifetime-aware routing algorithm for NoC reliability management. First, we define a lifetime budget metric for each router. With this metric, a problem is defined to optimize the lifetime by routing packets along the path with maximum lifetime budgets. We propose a lifetime-aware routing algorithm using dynamic programming approach. Finally, the lifetime-aware routing algorithms are evaluated in synthetic traffic and real benchmarks. The experimental results show that the lifetime-aware routing can distribute the lifetime of routers more evenly. The lifetime-aware routing has around 20 %, 45 %, 55 % minimal MTTF improvement than XY routing, NoP routing, Oddeven routing, respectively.

In the future, we plan to optimize both the lifetime distribution of routers and the average packet latency. This is because we observe that the lifetime-aware routing algorithm lowers the performance in terms of average packet delay. A hybrid routing algorithm will probably be proposed taking consideration of both packet delay and lifetime of routers. Similar to [22], the lifetime is optimized in long-term scale while the performance is optimized in short-term scale. Thus the lifetime can be improved without having much impact the performance. Another possible future work is to exploit the traffic throttling [9] or DVFS in NoC to maintain the MTTF of NoC above an expected value. This is because the lifetime reliability depends on the voltage, frequency and switching activity. The problem can be defined as maximizing performance given fixed lifetime budget. This is similar to the power budgeting problem [29, 31] which maximizes performance under limited power budget. However, the lifetime budgeting is different as the aging process is in a long-term scale. Therefore, the strategies for lifetime budgeting is possibly quite different from power budgeting. In the future work, we will exploit novel strategies for lifetime budgeting problem.

Acknowledgments. This research program is supported by the Natural Science Foundation of China No. 61376024 and 61306024, Natural Science Foundation of Guangdong Province No. S2013040014366, and Basic Research Programme of Shenzhen No. JCYJ20140417113430642 and JCYJ20140901003939020.

References

1. Failure mechanisms and models for semiconductor devices. JEDEC Publication (2003)
2. Al-Dujaily, R., Mak, T., Lam, K.P., Xia, F., Yakovlev, A., Poon, C.S.: Dynamic on-chip thermal optimization for three-dimensional networks-on-chip. Comput. J. **56**(6), 756–770 (2013)
3. Becker, D.U.: Efficient microarchitecture for network-on-chip routers. In: Ph.D. thesis, Stanford University (2012)
4. Bell, S., Edwards, B., Amann, J., et al.: Tile64 - processor: a 64-core soc with mesh interconnect. In: Proceedings of IEEE International Solid-State Circuits Conference (ISSCC), pp. 88–598 (2008)
5. Bellman, R.: Dynamic Programming. Princeton University Press, Princeton (1957)
6. Bhardwaj, K., Chakraborty, K., Roy, S.: An milp-based aging-aware routing algorithm for NoCs. In: Proceedings of Design, Automation Test in Europe Conference Exhibition (DATE), pp. 326–331 (2012)
7. Bhardwaj, K., Chakraborty, K., Roy, S.: Towards graceful aging degradation in NoCs through an adaptive routing algorithm. In: Proceedings of 2012 49th ACM/EDAC/IEEE Design Automation Conference (DAC), pp. 382–391 (2012)
8. Bienia, C., Kumar, S., Singh, J.P., Li, K.: The parsec benchmark suite: characterization and architectural implications. In: Proceedings of the 17th International Conference on Parallel Architectures and Compilation Techniques (PCAT), pp. 72–81 (2008)
9. Chang, K., Ausavarungnirun, R., Fallin, C., Mutlu, O.: Hat: heterogeneous adaptive throttling for on-chip networks. In: Proceedings of IEEE 24th International Symposium on Computer Architecture and High Performance Computing (SBAC-PAD), pp. 9–18 (2012)
10. Chiu, G.M.: The odd-even turn model for adaptive routing. IEEE Trans. Parallel Distrib. Syst. **11**(7), 729–738 (2000)
11. Dally, W.J., Seitz, C.L.: Deadlock-free message routing in multiprocessor interconnection networks. IEEE Trans. Comput. **36**(5), 547–553 (1987)
12. Das, A., Kumar, A., Veeravalli, B.: Reliability-driven task mapping for lifetime extension of networks-on-chip based multiprocessor systems. In: Proceedings of Design, Automation Test in Europe Conference Exhibition (DATE), pp. 689–694 (2013)
13. Hanumaiah, V., Vrudhula, S.: Temperature-aware DVFS for hard real-time applications on multicore processors. IEEE Trans. Comput. **61**(10), 1484–1494 (2012)
14. Hartman, A.S., Thomas, D.E.: Lifetime improvement through runtime wear-based task mapping. In: Proceedings of the Eighth IEEE/ACM/IFIP International Conference on Hardware/Software Codesign and System Synthesis, pp. 13–22 (2012)
15. Huang, W., Ghosh, S., Velusamy, S., Sankaranarayanan, K., Skadron, K., Stan, M.: Hotspot: a compact thermal modeling methodology for early-stage VLSI design. IEEE Trans. Very Large Scale Integr. VLSI Syst. **14**(5), 501–513 (2006)
16. Kahng, A., Li, B., Peh, L.S., Samadi, K.: Orion 2.0: a power-area simulator for interconnection networks. IEEE Trans. Very Large Scale Integr. VLSI Syst. **20**(1), 191–196 (2012)
17. Kim, H., Vitkovskiy, A., Gratz, P.V., Soteriou, V.: Use it or lose it: wear-out and lifetime in future chip multiprocessors. In: Proceedings of the 46th Annual IEEE/ACM International Symposium on Microarchitecture (MICRO), pp. 136–147 (2013)

18. Kim, T.H., Persaud, R., Kim, C.: Silicon odometer: an on-chip reliability monitor for measuring frequency degradation of digital circuits. In: Proceedings of IEEE Symposium on VLSI Circuits, pp. 122–123 (2007)
19. Lu, Z., Huang, W., Stan, M., Skadron, K., Lach, J.: Interconnect lifetime prediction for reliability-aware systems. IEEE Trans. Very Large Scale Integr. VLSI Syst. 15(2), 159–172 (2007)
20. Mak, T., Cheung, P., Lam, K.P., Luk, W.: Adaptive routing in network-on-chips using a dynamic-programming network. IEEE Trans. Industr. Electron. 58(8), 3701–3716 (2011)
21. Mak, T., Cheung, P.Y., Luk, W., Lam, K.P.: A DP-network for optimal dynamic routing in network-on-chip. In: Proceedings of the 7th IEEE/ACM International Conference on Hardware/Software Codesign and System Synthesis (CODES+ISSS), pp. 119–128 (2009)
22. Mercati, P., Bartolini, A., Paterna, F., Rosing, T.S., Benini, L.: Workload and user experience-aware dynamic reliability management in multicore processors. In: Proceedings of the 50th Annual Design Automation Conference (DAC), pp. 1–6 (2013)
23. Mulas, F., Atienza, D., Acquaviva, A., Carta, S., Benini, L., De Micheli, G.: Thermal balancing policy for multiprocessor stream computing platforms. IEEE Trans. Comput. Aided Des. Integr. Circuits Syst. 28(12), 1870–1882 (2009)
24. Ramachandran, P., Adve, S., Bose, P., Rivers, J.: Metrics for architecture-level lifetime reliability analysis. In: Proceedings of IEEE International Symposium on Performance Analysis of Systems and Software, pp. 202–212 (2008)
25. Shi, B., Zhang, Y., Srivastava, A.: Dynamic thermal management under soft thermal constraints. IEEE Trans. Very Large Scale Integr. VLSI Syst. 21(11), 2045–2054 (2013)
26. Srinivasan, J., Adve, S.V., Bose, P., Rivers, J.A.: The case for lifetime reliability-aware microprocessors. In: Proceedings of the 31st Annual International Symposium on Computer Architecture (ISCA), pp. 276–285 (2004)
27. Srinivasan, J., Adve, S.V., Bose, P., Rivers, J.A.: The impact of technology scaling on lifetime reliability. In: Proceedings of 2004 International Conference on Dependable Systems and Networks, pp. 177–186 (2004)
28. Wang, L., Wang, X., Mak, T.: Dynamic programming-based lifetime aware adaptive routing algorithm for network-on-chip. In: Claesen, L., Sanz, M.T., Reis, R., Sarmiento-Reyes, A. (eds.) VLSI-SoC 2014. IFIP AICT, vol. 464, pp. 1–20. Springer, Heidelberg (2015)
29. Wang, X., Li, Z., Yang, M., Jiang, Y., Daneshtalab, M., Mak, T.: A low cost, high performance dynamic-programming-based adaptive power allocation scheme for many-core architectures in the dark silicon era. In: Proceedings of IEEE 11th Symposium on Embedded Systems for Real-time Multimedia (ESTIMedia), pp. 61–67 (2013)
30. Wang, X., Mak, T., Yang, M., Jiang, Y., Daneshtalab, M., Palesi, M.: On self-tuning networks-on-chip for dynamic network-flow dominance adaptation. In: Proceedings of 2013 Seventh IEEE/ACM International Symposium on Networks on Chip (NoCS), pp. 1–8 (2013)
31. Wang, X., Wang, T., Mak, T., Yang, M., Jiang, Y., Daneshtalab, M.: Fine-grained runtime power budgeting for networks-on-chip. In: Proceedings of 20th Asia and South Pacific Design Automation Conference (ASP-DAC), pp. 160–165 (2015)

32. Woo, S., Ohara, M., Torrie, E., Singh, J., Gupta, A.: The splash-2 programs: characterization and methodological considerations. In: Proceedings of the 22nd Annual International Symposium on Computer Architecture (ISCA), pp. 24–36 (1995)
33. Zhu, C., Gu, Z., Dick, R., Shang, L.: Reliable multiprocessor system-on-chip synthesis. In: Proceedings of the 5th IEEE/ACM/IFIP International Conference on Hardware/Software Codesign and System Synthesis (CODES+ISSS), pp. 239–244 (2007)
34. Zhuo, C., Sylvester, D., Blaauw, D.: Process variation and temperature-aware reliability management. In: Proceedings of Design, Automation Test in Europe Conference Exhibition (DATE), pp. 580–585 (2010)
35. Zong, W., Wang, X., Mak, T.: On multicast for dynamic and irregular on-chip networks using dynamic programming method. In: Proceedings of the 6th International Workshop on Network on Chip Architectures (NoCArc), pp. 17–22 (2013)

Efficient Utilization of Test Elevators
to Reduce Test Time in 3D-ICs

Sreenivaas S. Muthyala[✉] and Nur A. Touba

Computer Engineering Research Center,
The University of Texas, Austin, TX, USA
sreenivaas@utexas.edu, touba@ece.utexas.edu

Abstract. Three Dimensional Integrated Circuits are an important new paradigm in which different dies are stacked atop one another, and interconnected by Through Silicon Vias (TSVs). Testing 3D-ICs poses additional challenges because of the need to transfer data to the non-bottom layers and the limited number of TSVs available in the 3D-ICs for the data transfer. A novel test compression technique is proposed that introduces the ability to share tester data across layers using daisy-chained decompressors. This improves the encoding of test patterns substantially, thereby reducing the amount of test data required to be stored on the external tester. In addition, an inter-layer serialization technique is proposed, which further reduces the number of TSVs required, using simple hardware to serialize and deserialize the test data. Experimental results are presented demonstrating the efficiency of the technique proposed.

Keywords: 3D-IC · Testing · TSVs · Test compression · Serialization

1 Introduction

Three-dimensional Integrated Circuits (3D-ICs) are stacked devices with low latency interconnections between adjacent dies, resulting in reduced power consumption in interconnects and higher bandwidth for communication across layers [Hamdioui 11]. 3D-IC designs are suitable for fabricating chips containing heterogeneous components like analog, digital, mixed signal, flash, DRAM components, which is usually the case in System-on-Chip designs. The different layers in a 3D-IC are connected using through-silicon-vias (TSVs) which are vertical interconnects across layers. There are different ways of stacking the dies, wafer-to-wafer (W2W), die-to-wafer (D2W) or die-to-die (D2D), each having its own set of pros and cons, described in [Patti 06].

3D-IC testing is more challenging than 2D-IC testing, since the components of the system are distributed across different layers and, as mentioned earlier, can have non-digital components. In addition, the dies comprising the different layers can be synthesizable designs (soft cores), in which the design-for-test (DFT) architecture can be customized. The designs can also be layouts (hard cores) for which the DFT architecture is already fixed. It can also contain IP cores, in which it is possible to perform test pattern generation to obtain test patterns that are applied during test. Another challenge in 3D-IC testing is that the input tester channels from the automatic test equipment (ATE),

© IFIP International Federation for Information Processing 2015
L. Claesen et al. (Eds.): VLSI-SoC 2014, IFIP AICT 464, pp. 21–38, 2015.
DOI: 10.1007/978-3-319-25279-7_2

i.e. the external tester, is fed only to the bottom layer in the 3D-IC, and to transfer the test data to the non-bottom layers, TSVs are used, like how the functional data is transferred. These TSVs used for testing purposes are also called test elevators [Marinissen 10]. This further constrains testing, the number of tester channels required for the non-bottom layers should be accommodated within the available number of TSVs, which is a challenge in hierarchical designs with numerous cores. Apart from these, it is also necessary to test the TSVs, since they are prone to defects such as insufficiently filled TSVs, development of micro-voids in the copper filling, and cracking, which is a result of having different coefficient of thermal expansion [Marinissen 09].

There are several stages in testing 3D-ICs; pre-bond testing is performed on each die individually, to ensure defective dies are not used in stacking and then post-bond testing is performed on the final stack, to ensure the 3D-IC as a whole is not defective. In some cases, testing is also done on partial stacks. In order to do pre-bond testing on the non-bottom layers, it is necessary to add probe pads for test purposes. This is because the TSV tips as well as the microbumps are too small to be probed and are very sensitive to scrub marks [Marinissen 09]. These probe pads are a test overhead that take up a lot of space and limit the locations where TSVs can be placed, which puts constraints on the design and floorplan of a die.

One important way to reduce test time is by test compression [Touba 06]. The conventional way of implementing test compression in core-based schemes is for each core to have its own local decompressor. This allows compressed test data to be brought over the Test Access Mechanism (TAM) lines to each decompressor in each core. In a 3D-IC, if a decompressor is shared across multiple cores that are in different layers, larger TAMs would be required, greatly increasing the routing complexity. In addition, this will also increase the number of test elevators required to transfer the uncompressed test data to the non-bottom layers, which is not desirable.

The existing methods for dynamically adjusting the number of free variables sent to each decompressor have the drawback that they increase the amount of routing (i.e. TAM width) required between the tester channels and the core decompressors. This is less suited for 3D-ICs because routing between layers requires additional test elevators (i.e., extra TSVs). This paper proposes a new architecture and methodology for test compression in core-based designs, which is better suited for 3D-ICs. It can be used to either provide greater compression for the same number of test elevators or reduce the number of test elevators while maintaining the same compression com-pared to existing methods.

This paper proposes a simple, elegant and scalable test compression architecture that reduces the required number of tester channels by sharing tester data amongst the different layers, which in turn, can be accommodated by using very few test elevators. In addition, further reduction in the number of test elevators can be obtained by using "Inter-layer serialization", a simple technique to send data serially across layers. Preliminary results were presented in [Muthyala 14].

2   Related Work

Testing a core based design typically involves designing wrappers around the cores, providing a test access mechanism, which transfers test data from the pins of the tester to the cores, and developing a test schedule, which decides the sequence in which the cores are tested, the set of cores that are tested concurrently and so on. There are several techniques to design wrappers, TAMs and test schedules, see [Xu 05] for a survey.

In the 3D-IC paradigm, an early work addressing the testability issues of 3D-ICs uses the concept of "scan island" for pre-bond testing [Lewis 09], which uses IEEE standards 1500 and 1149.1 to design wrappers for pre-bond testing. [Wu 07] proposes different optimization strategies for the number of scan chains and the length of TSV based interconnects for 3D-ICs. Heuristic methods for designing core wrappers is proposed in [Noia 09], however it does not involve the reuse of die level TAMs [Noia 10]. [Jiang 09] proposes using heuristics to reduce weighted test cost, while taking into account constraints on the widths of test pins for both pre-bond and post-bond testing. However, the above methods involve die-level optimization of TAMs. [Jiang 09] addresses TAM optimization for post bond testing by placing a constraint on the number of extra probe pads for pre-bond testing when compared to the post bond testing. [Lo 10] proposes reusing the test wrappers of individual cores embedded in the 3D-IC, for test optimization. Recently, the optimization procedures for minimizing test time under a constraint on the number of test elevators has been proposed in [Wu 08, Noia 10]. A feature of 3D-IC testing is that the number of probe pads on the non-bottom layers (which are added for test purposes, as explained in Sect. 1) is very limited, which results in limited bandwidth available from the tester for pre-bond testing. [Jiang 12] proposes having separate TAMs for pre-bond testing and post-bond testing. [Lee 13] uses a single TAM with a bandwidth adapter to manage bandwidth for pre-bond and post-bond testing. However, all the above works target test time reduction by optimization of test architectures.

Some recent work has looked at ways to improve encoding efficiency by dynamically adjusting the number of free variables sent to the decompressor in each core on a per test cube basis to try to better match the number of free variables sent to the decompressor with the number of care bits. This can be done by dynamically allocating the number of tester channels used to feed each decompressor [Janicki 12] or by selectively loading decompressors in each clock cycle [Kinsman 10, Muthyala 14]. [Larsson 08] presents selective encoding of test data for testing SOCs using codewords to represent the care bit profile of the test cubes. The conventional approach is to have independent decompressors for each core such that each of them has their own set of free variables so that the linear equations for each decompressor can be solved independently. This helps to reduce computational complexity. The drawback is that the unused free variables are wasted when the decompressor is reset between test cubes. This happens in all of the existing methods except [Muthyala 13], which allows limited sharing of free variables between decompressors during a few cycles in such a way that the linear equations are mostly independent and can be solved with only a small increase in computational complexity.

In conventional testing, the scan shift frequency is typically much slower than the functional clock frequency and the maximum ATE (automatic test equipment) clock frequency, due to power dissipation limitations as well as the fact that the test clock may not be buffered and optimized for high speed operation. In [Khoche 02], the ATE shifts in test data n times faster than the scan shift. An n-bit serial-to-parallel converter is used to take in serial data at the fast ATE shift rate and convert it to n-bits in parallel at the slower scan shift frequency. This allows a single ATE channel to fill n scan chains in parallel. This idea was combined with a test compression scheme in [Wang 05], where faster ATE channels are sent to a time division demultiplexing (TDDM) circuit which feeds the inputs of a VirtualScan decompressor [Wang 04], and the compacted output response is fed through a time division multiplexing (TDM) circuit to go to the ATE.

This paper proposes using a similar concept for test elevators when transferring test data from one layer to another layer in a 3D stack. The idea is to use a serializer in the layer sending the test data that accepts data in parallel at the scan shift frequency, and generates a serial output at the functional clock frequency which is sent over the test elevator to a deserializer on the receiving layer which converts the serial data coming in at the functional clock frequency into parallel outputs at the scan shift frequency. This approach is described in detail in Sect. 5.

3   Sequential Linear Decompression

Sequential linear decompressors are a major class of decompressors used for test compression, and are inherently attractive while encoding test cubes, i.e. test vectors with unassigned inputs represented as don't cares. The compressed test data, which is stored on the external tester (Automatic Test Equipment, ATE), is obtained using a two-step procedure as follows:

1. The test patterns applied to the scan cells are obtained from automatic test pattern generation (ATPG).
2. Since the decompressor architecture is known, the test patterns can be encoded to determine the compressed tester data.

Figure 1 shows an example of how the tester data is obtained by encoding using a 4-bit linear feedback shift register (LFSR) as the decompressor. To encode the test patterns, the tester data coming from the external tester are considered *free variables* and the dependence of scan cells on these free variables is obtained using symbolic simulation, which gives the linear equations for the free variable dependence of each scan cell. These equations are solved for each test pattern (Z in Fig. 2) by assigning values to the free variables, making them *pivots* (free variables that are not assigned any value are called *non-pivots*). These values of free variables (both pivots and non-pivots) constitute the tester data is stored on the tester to obtain the test pattern in the scan cells.

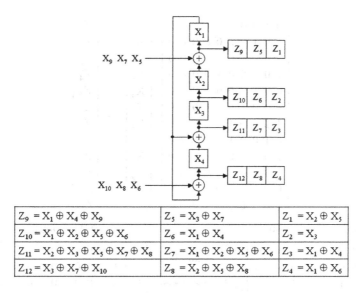

$Z_9 = X_1 \oplus X_4 \oplus X_9$	$Z_5 = X_3 \oplus X_7$	$Z_1 = X_2 \oplus X_5$
$Z_{10} = X_1 \oplus X_2 \oplus X_5 \oplus X_6$	$Z_6 = X_1 \oplus X_4$	$Z_2 = X_3$
$Z_{11} = X_2 \oplus X_3 \oplus X_5 \oplus X_7 \oplus X_8$	$Z_7 = X_1 \oplus X_2 \oplus X_5 \oplus X_6$	$Z_3 = X_1 \oplus X_4$
$Z_{12} = X_3 \oplus X_7 \oplus X_{10}$	$Z_8 = X_2 \oplus X_5 \oplus X_8$	$Z_4 = X_1 \oplus X_6$

Fig. 1. Example of symbolic simulation of sequential linear decompressor

More details about this procedure can be found in [Könemann 91, Krishna 01, Wang 06], which is used in Mentor Graphics' TestKompress tool [Rajski 04]. An important thing to notice is that the LFSR that is fed by the free variables is reset to zero after decompressing each test cube, to keep the complexity of solving equations within manageable limits. This means that the *non-pivot* free variables, which are not required to have any value to solve the equations, are not used and simply thrown away. This source of inefficiency in compression has been dealt with in several previous works.

The amount of compression achieved with sequential linear decompressors depends on the *encoding efficiency,* defined as the ratio of the number of free variables (bits stored on the tester) versus the number of care bits in the test data. The encoding efficiency achieved using the conventional approach of having fixed size TAMs feeding multiple independent core decompressors is limited by the fact that the TAM bandwidth to each core decompressor needs to be large enough to bring enough free variables to encode the worst-case test cube with the largest number of care bits. To maximize encoding efficiency, a special ATPG procedure is used to generate test cubes in a way that limits the number of care bits in each test cube. This typically comes at the cost of more test cubes being generated. Moreover, there can still be a considerable amount of variance in the number of care bits per test cube (profiles for industrial circuits showing how the percentage of care bits varies can be found in [Janicki 12]). The inherent drawback of the conventional approach is that the number of free variables brought in for decompressing each test cube is fixed by the worst-case test cube with the most care bits, and so, many free variables are wasted for test cubes with fewer care bits.

$$
\begin{pmatrix}
0 & 1 & 0 & 0 & 1 & 0 & 0 & 0 & 0 & 0 \\
0 & 0 & 1 & 0 & 0 & 0 & 0 & 0 & 0 & 0 \\
1 & 0 & 0 & 1 & 0 & 0 & 0 & 0 & 0 & 0 \\
1 & 0 & 0 & 0 & 0 & 1 & 0 & 0 & 0 & 0 \\
0 & 0 & 1 & 0 & 0 & 0 & 1 & 0 & 0 & 0 \\
1 & 0 & 0 & 1 & 0 & 0 & 0 & 0 & 0 & 0 \\
1 & 1 & 0 & 0 & 1 & 1 & 0 & 0 & 0 & 0 \\
0 & 1 & 0 & 0 & 1 & 0 & 0 & 1 & 0 & 0 \\
1 & 0 & 0 & 1 & 0 & 0 & 0 & 0 & 1 & 0 \\
1 & 1 & 0 & 0 & 1 & 1 & 0 & 0 & 0 & 0 \\
0 & 1 & 1 & 0 & 1 & 0 & 1 & 1 & 0 & 0 \\
0 & 0 & 1 & 0 & 0 & 0 & 1 & 0 & 0 & 1
\end{pmatrix}
\begin{pmatrix}
X_1 \\ X_2 \\ X_3 \\ X_4 \\ X_5 \\ X_6 \\ X_7 \\ X_8 \\ X_9 \\ X_{10}
\end{pmatrix}
=
\begin{pmatrix}
Z_1 \\ Z_2 \\ Z_3 \\ Z_4 \\ Z_5 \\ Z_6 \\ Z_7 \\ Z_8 \\ Z_9 \\ Z_{10} \\ Z_{11} \\ Z_{12}
\end{pmatrix}
$$

$Z = 1\text{--}011\text{----}0\text{-}$ $\qquad\qquad\qquad\qquad$ $X = 0111000001$

$$
\left[
\begin{array}{cccccccccc|c}
0 & 1 & 0 & 0 & 1 & 0 & 0 & 0 & 0 & 0 & 1 \\
1 & 0 & 0 & 0 & 0 & 1 & 0 & 0 & 0 & 0 & 0 \\
0 & 0 & 1 & 0 & 0 & 0 & 1 & 0 & 0 & 0 & 1 \\
1 & 0 & 0 & 1 & 0 & 0 & 0 & 0 & 0 & 0 & 1 \\
1 & 1 & 0 & 0 & 1 & 1 & 0 & 0 & 0 & 0 & 0
\end{array}
\right]
\xrightarrow[\text{Elimination}]{\text{Gaussian}}
\left[
\begin{array}{cccccccccc|c}
1 & 0 & 0 & 0 & 0 & 1 & 0 & 0 & 0 & 0 & 0 \\
0 & 1 & 0 & 0 & 0 & 0 & 1 & 0 & 0 & 0 & 1 \\
0 & 0 & 1 & 0 & 0 & 0 & 1 & 0 & 0 & 0 & 1 \\
0 & 0 & 0 & 1 & 0 & 1 & 0 & 0 & 0 & 0 & 1 \\
0 & 0 & 0 & 0 & 1 & 0 & 1 & 0 & 0 & 0 & 0
\end{array}
\right]
$$

$\qquad\qquad\qquad\qquad\qquad\qquad\qquad$ Pivots $\qquad$ Non-Pivots

Fig. 2. Gaussian elimination to obtain tester data for example in Fig. 1

Several improvements to the encoding procedure for sequential linear decompressors have been proposed, including reusing unused free variables [Muthyala 12]. In addition, a test scheduling procedure for hierarchical SoC based designs was proposed in [Muthyala 13], which enables free variable reuse.

To implement test compression in a core-based 3D-IC, it is necessary to design Test Access Mechanisms (TAMs) for each core. The IEEE 1500 standard, which was introduced to address the challenges in SoC testing, would be a very suitable solution for 3D-IC testing. In addition, the provision of a test wrapper, which standardizes the test interface, further tilts the scales towards the IEEE 1500 standard for 3D-IC testing, since the same interface can be used for pre-bond and post-bond testing. However, the implementation of a test wrapper should also consider the fact that the number of test elevators used for testing should be minimized. There are several ways to design the connection between the test wrappers of each core, one of them, similar to the one shown in Fig. 3, is used in the test architecture proposed in this paper.

However, it is not necessary to design wrappers in the way shown in Fig. 3; several other ways of designing core wrappers are possible, any design can be selected based on the need. Another application for wrappers is for bypassing cores that cannot be tested in tandem with other cores. For instance, if analog cores are present, the test wrapper for the analog core can be bypassed. These wrappers can be designed using the IEEE 1500 standard for testing SoCs, since the logic between the wrappers, namely the TSVs, are also required to be tested.

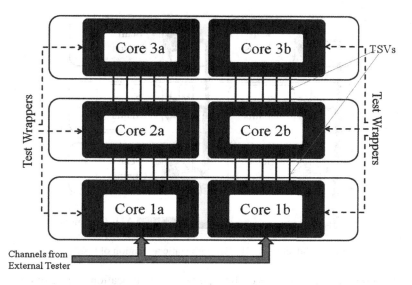

Fig. 3. Test architecture for a 3D-IC with wrappers for each core

4 Proposed Architecture

The conventional approach for test compression in a core-based 3D-IC design, with each layer having several cores operating independently of other cores, is shown in Fig. 4. In this architecture, which uses static allocation of tester channels, the input test data bandwidth from the Automatic Test Equipment (ATE) is distributed to core decompressors using Test Access Mechanisms (TAMs) according to the free variable demand of each core. This distribution is done in a way to minimize the total time required to test the entire 3D-IC with no additional control information. However, the distribution of the tester channels among the decompressors is static and cannot be changed for every test cube. In addition, the tester channels allocated to each core should be large enough in number to ensure sufficient free variables are provided in symbolic simulation to encode the test cube that requires the largest number of free variables (in other words, the most difficult to encode test cube). However, there is a disadvantage if the decompressor is encoding a test cube that requires fewer free variables. Since the tester channels feed the same number of free variables for encoding all the test cubes, many free variables are wasted while encoding "easier-to-encode" test cubes, which results in increase in tester storage, as even the free variables not assigned any value (non-pivots) have to be stored on the tester. This extra tester storage, which is not used, is necessary to support the test architecture implemented in the 3D-IC.

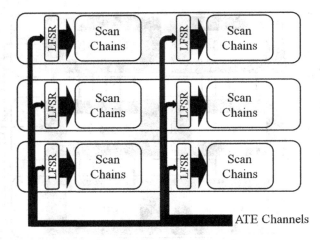

Fig. 4. Test architecture of 3D-ICs with static allocation of tester channels

To overcome this disadvantage, the tester channel allocation can be dynamic (i.e. changed for every test cube); however, to do so it is necessary to route the entire ATE bandwidth to all the layers, and control the number of channels allocated by providing additional control signals, which need more test elevators compared to static channel allocation. This presents a significant advantage that, because the number of channels allocated while decompressing every test cube can be changed, the number of wasted free variables from the tester can be reduced. In the context of 3D-ICs, the number of tester channels to each core also translates into the number of TSVs or test elevators required. Thus, dynamic allocation of tester channels requires lot more test elevators than static allocation, which may not be feasible for designs with large number of cores, as the number of TSVs available is limited.

The proposed architecture is shown in Fig. 5; with the decompressors of the cores daisy-chained together. This architecture uses the same number of test elevators as the static channel allocation, while providing an advantage almost equivalent to the dynamic channel allocation. In the architecture shown in Fig. 5, the decompressors of the cores are daisy-chained together, with a tapering bandwidth between successive higher layers of the 3D-IC. In other words, the number of channels between the highest layer and the middle layer is less than the number of channels between the bottom layer and the middle layer, which in turn is less than the input bandwidth to the decompressors in the bottom layer, i.e. total bandwidth from the ATE. Using this architecture, some free variables from the decompressor in the bottom layer is sent to the decompressor in the middle layer and so on. This provides some flexibility in encoding the test cubes. Free variables unused while encoding a core in a layer are available to encode other cores in the layers above with which they are shared, hence reducing free variable wastage and improving encoding efficiency.

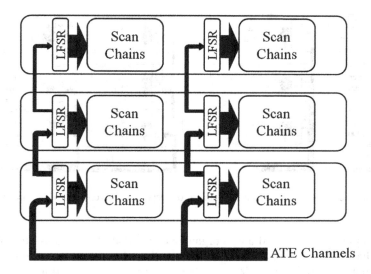

Fig. 5. Proposed architecture with daisy-chained decompressors

The rationale behind such bandwidth allocation is that the bandwidth feeding each layer should be sufficient to supply enough free variables to encode the test cubes for the core in that layer and the test cubes for the layers above, as the decompressor in each layer is fed via taps from the decompressor of the layer below. Hence, the bandwidth supplied to the bottom layer should be big enough to supply free variables to encode test cubes of the cores in the bottom layer as well as cores in the middle layer and the top layer. Similarly, the bandwidth supplied to the middle layer should be big enough to supply free variables to encode test cubes of the cores in the middle layer and the top layer. In other words, the number of free variables supplied to decompressor in each layer decreases as we move from the bottom layer to the top layer. Hence, a tapering bandwidth is used, as shown in Fig. 5, proportional to the number of free variables required to be supplied to the decompressor in each layer. An example comparing the bandwidth allocation for the two architectures is shown in Fig. 6. It should be noted that the number of test elevators required to implement both the architectures is the same.

The proposed architecture provides flexibility in utilization of free variables; any free variable coming from the tester can be used in any of the layers, provided it is distributed across all the layers.

Consider the decompressor in the top layer is encoding an easy-to-encode test cube with few specified bits, which needs less than average free variables, while the test cube being encoded in the middle layer is hard-to-encode with a larger number of specified bits, needing more free variables than average. In the proposed architecture, the free variables which are not required in the top layer can be used in the middle layer in help encode the hard-to-encode test cube. This reduces the number of free variables required to encode the entire test set for the 3D-IC, without additional hardware and control, with the same number of TSVs as used in the conventional architecture shown in Fig. 4. However, to accomplish this, the test cubes for

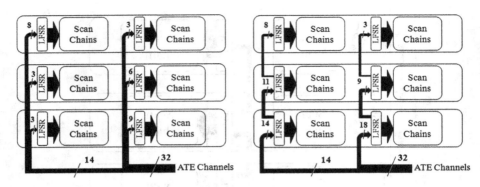

Fig. 6. Example for comparing channel allocation between conventional (left) and proposed architectures (right).

the cores should be reordered and reorganized such that all the cores are not being tested by hard-to-encode test cubes at the same time. In other words, the number of free variables required to encode test cubes that are decompressed together should be reduced as much as possible. This reduces the tester storage and thereby, the test time. This reordering can be accomplished heuristically by a test scheduling algorithm similar to the one explained in [Muthyala 13], with a few modifications to suit the 3D-IC testing paradigm. However, additional control data is not required, unlike [Muthyala 13], unless a subset of cores from those daisy-chained together have to be selected.

To illustrate the encoding advantage of the proposed approach, consider a small example in which a 3D-IC has three layers with each layer having one core. Let the set of test cubes for the cores have care-bit profiles as shown in Table 1. Consider each care bit in a test cube needs one free variable to encode, as a first order approximation. To

Table 1. Example - care bit profile of test cubes for the three cores of the example 3D-IC

Test cube	# Care bits in test cube		
	Core 1	Core 2	Core 3
1	13	11	12
2	12	11	10
3	10	10	9
4	9	7	8
5	8	6	7
6	7	5	5
7	7	5	4
8	6	4	3

encode the entire 3D-IC using the conventional architecture shown in Fig. 1, core 1 would need a minimum of 13 free variables per test cube, core 2 would need 11 free variables and core 3 would need 12 free variables per test cube. Since there are 8 test cubes for each core, a total of $(13 + 11 + 12) \times 8 = 288$ free variables are required to encode the 3D-IC.

Consider the same 3D-IC, now using the proposed architecture. In this case, encoding is done in groups of three test cubes, with one test cube from each core. Optimizing the test cubes in the group for minimizing the total number of care bits in the group, the test cubes are grouped as shown in Table 2.

Table 2. Care bit profile of test cube groups for encoding using proposed architecture

Test cube group	# Care bits in test cube			Total care bits in test cube group
	Core 1	Core 2	Core 3	
1	13	4	7	24
2	12	5	8	25
3	10	5	12	27
4	9	6	10	25
5	8	7	9	24
6	7	10	5	22
7	7	11	3	21
8	6	11	4	21

By encoding in groups according the above table, the maximum number of care bits in any group is 27, and hence, to encode the entire set of eight test cube groups, $27 \times 8 = 216$ free variables are required using the proposed architecture, which is less than the number of free variables required to encode using the conventional architecture shown in Fig. 4. Thus, it is seen that the proposed architecture gives better compression and hence reduces the tester storage requirements and test time.

The drawback in the proposed architecture is that the linear equations for scan cells driven by daisy-chained decompressors cannot be solved independently. In order to make sure the shared free variables are used in only one of the decompressors, the equations for all the scan cells fed by the connected decompressors have to be solved concurrently. Consider one test cube from each layer being encoded. The total number of free variables brought in from the tester has to be sufficiently large enough to encode all three test cubes. Hence, creating pivots for care bits in all the three test cubes involves a lot of computation. The total number of XOR operations required to create pivots is $9n^3$ as compared to $3n^3$ XOR operations required to encode using the conventional approach, where n is the number of free variables. Hence, this method is reasonable when the additional computation is a reasonable price to pay for the test time reduction achieved.

5   Optimizing Number of Test Elevators by Inter-layer Serialization of Test Data

In this section, an implementation is proposed using a serializer-deserializer structure to further reduce the number of test elevators required to implement the proposed architecture. The scan shift frequency is usually lower than the functional frequency, since the scan clock tree is generally not buffered up for high speeds. Another reason is that during scan shift, a large percentage of flip-flops toggle, and hence a large amount of power is drawn from the power grid of the chip. This causes a voltage drop in the power lines. To avoid these problems, scan shifting is generally considerably slower than functional frequency.

By using the proposed implementation, the difference between the slower scan shift frequency and the faster functional frequency can be exploited to further reduce the number of test elevators. The idea is to use a serializer at the layer sending test data to serialize the test data from the decompressor taps. The test elevators are driven in the sending layer by this serial test data. At the receiving layer, the data from the test elevators are restored in parallel and sent to the decompressor in the same format as sent by the LFSR in the sending layer (Fig. 7). This is possible because the test elevators are optimized for the functional frequency. However, even if the transfer of data cannot be done at the functional frequency, it can be done at a frequency higher than the scan shift rate, as long as it is a multiple of the scan shift frequency.

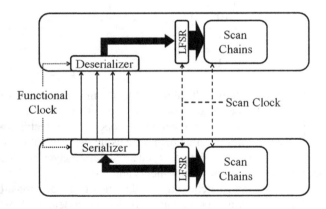

Fig. 7. Proposed implementation of inter-layer serialization of test data

If the test elevators can be operated at n times the scan shift frequency, then instead of having m test elevators to transfer data across layers, $\lceil m/n \rceil$ test elevators are required. On the other hand, it is also possible to have the same number of test elevators and increase the effective bandwidth by n times, i.e. $m \times n$ bits of data can be shifted in one shift cycle using m test elevators implementing inter-layer serialization, as compared to m bits of data shifted in one shift cycle using m test elevators without serialization. Hence, depending on the constraints on the number of test elevators, this architecture can be used at an advantage to either increase the effective bandwidth or reduce the number of test elevators required in the design.

Consider a serializer driven by m taps from the LFSR in the sending layer. Let the functional clock be n times faster than the scan clock. Therefore, as explained previously, the number of test elevators required would be m/n. Let the number of test elevators required be represented as t, which, here, is equal to m/n. Inter-layer serialization would require an $m \times t$ serializer in the sending layer driving the test elevators between the layers and a $t \times m$ deserializer driving the LFSR in the receiving layer. The simplest way of implementing an $m \times t$ serializer in the sending layer is by using a $m{:}t$ multiplexer controlled by a modulo m counter driven by the faster functional clock (Fig. 8).

This ensures that the test data coming in at scan shift frequency from the LFSR is coupled to the test elevators at the faster functional clock frequency. Similarly, the deserializer can be implemented as an m bit shift register driven by the faster functional clock, whereas the data in the shift register is sampled at the slower scan clock rate (Fig. 9).

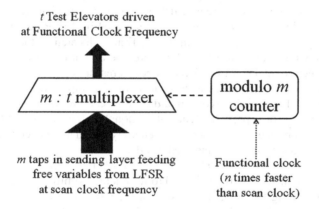

Fig. 8. Serializer implementation for functional clock operating n times faster than scan clock, where number of test elevators, $t = m/n$

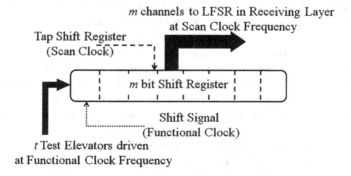

Fig. 9. Deserializer implementation for functional clock operating n times faster than scan clock, where number of test elevators, $t = m/n$

Alternatively, if the LFSRs can be operated at the functional frequency, or at any other faster frequency, the need for additional serializer and deserializer can be avoided. The LFSRs can just transfer the data at the faster frequency, while the scan chains shift in data at the scan frequency. However, this needs the time domains of the different cores to be synchronized or the frequency has to be reduced in such a way that the receiving LFSR can sample the data from the test elevators without any loss in data or introducing metastability concerns.

As discussed above, inter-layer serialization has a small area overhead; hence, it can be used in cases where the advantage of using it outweighs the additional cost of implementing the required architecture in the design.

6 Experimental Results

Experiments were conducted on six different 3D-IC designs and the results are presented in this section. These 3D-ICs have three layers, with each layer having one core. Three different test compression architectures were experimented using these test chips. In the first test architecture (*arch1*), each core has a 64-bit LFSR, acting as a decompressor. The input tester channels from the ATE are allocated to the decompressors statically as shown in Fig. 4. In this architecture, the output cone of the each decompressor is confined to the layer in which the decompressor is present, i.e. test elevators are required to transfer the compressed test data to the decompressors in the non-bottom layers. However, all scan cells driven by a decompressor are localized to the layer in which the decompressor is present. Hence, it is enough to have sufficient test elevators to transfer the compressed test data, which is generally less in number compared to using test elevators to transfer the uncompressed test data.

In the second architecture (*arch2*), the 64-bit LFSRs that were local to each layer in *arch1*, are interconnected and reconfigured to form a big primitive LFSR with number of flip-flops in this big LFSR being the sum of the number of flip-flops in the *arch1* LFSRs in all the three layers. It should be noted that the LFSR in *arch2* is distributed across the three layers, i.e. sections of LFSR are present in each of the three layers and these sections are interconnected using test elevators in such a way that a primitive LFSR is formed and this 192-bit LFSR drives scan chains in all three layers of 3D-IC. In this case also, the scan chains are confined within the layer, i.e. test elevators are required to transfer compressed test data to the sections of LFSR in the non-bottom layers. In addition, test elevators are also required to interconnect the sections of LFSR that are in different layers. Hence, more test elevators are required in *arch2* compared to *arch1*. Using this architecture, the equations for the scan cells of the three layers are solved together and since the pivots for the test cubes are created in common, the free variables are used more efficiently and results in better compression and increased encoding efficiency.

The third architecture (*arch3*) is the proposed architecture using daisy-chained decompressors shown in Fig. 5. In this case, the decompressors used are similar to the ones used in *arch1*, a local 64-bit LFSR in each core acting as a decompressor for the core, with all the decompressors daisy-chained together. The tester channels are allocated to the decompressors as described in Sect. 4. This method combines the advantages of *arch1* and *arch2* at the cost of increased computational complexity of encoding the test cubes together. By using this architecture, some of the free variables are distributed to the decompressors in the other layers and the encoding of the test cubes of the three layers are done together, thereby the free variables are used more efficiently and results in better compression and increase in encoding efficiency similar to *arch2*. However, in this method, test elevators are required only to transfer the compressed test data to the non-bottom layers, similar to *arch1*, while providing an encoding advantage similar to arch2. In addition, reconfiguration of the local 64-bit LFSRs into a big LFSR for post bond testing of the 3D-IC is also not necessary when using *arch3*.

Experiments were run on six different designs of 3D-ICs, each containing three layers. The test cubes used provided 100 % coverage of detectable faults. Static encoding was used to encode the test cubes. The compressed test data, i.e. tester storage required for the three architectures explained above and the number of test elevators (TSVs) required to implement the test architecture is presented in Table 3. As shown in Table 3, there is reduction in the amount of tester data while using *arch2* when compared to *arch1*.

Table 3. Comparison of tester data for the three architectures

	Test vectors	Scan cells	Local independent decompressors (*arch1*)		Global decompressor (*arch2*)		Proposed daisy-chained decompressors (*arch3*)		Percentage reduction in tester data
			Tester data (# of bits)	TSVs	Tester data (# of bits)	TSVs	Tester data (# of bits)	TSVs	
A	838	2578	8272	13	6016	21	6016	13	27.27 %
B	606	6747	18245	15	11070	21	11070	15	39.33 %
C	686	5662	9512	13	6560	21	6560	13	31.03 %
D	751	8724	13314	15	9193	21	9193	15	30.95 %
E	803	9432	13583	15	10144	21	10144	15	25.32 %
F	807	10538	17538	15	12046	21	12046	15	31.31 %

As explained earlier, similar benefit is obtained by using *arch3* as well. This is because both *arch2* and *arch3* provide flexible use of free variables across layers and the free variables that are not used in encoding test cube of one layer can be used to encode test cubes of other layers. In addition, by using daisy-chained decompressors (*arch3*), the number of test elevators required is less compared to *arch2*, since the decompressors are local to each layer.

7   Conclusion and Future Work

The proposed daisy-chain test architecture for 3D-ICs implements a free-variable sharing technique, which allows test patterns to be encoded more efficiently thereby reducing the amount of tester data that needs to be stored on the tester. Given the larger transistor count of 3D-ICs, reducing tester data is of a great importance. In addition, this architecture can use inter-layer serialization, where the number of test elevators required is reduced even further, by utilizing the faster functional frequency to transfer test data across layers. Experimental results are presented comparing the tester storage requirements of the conventional architecture and the proposed architecture, and it is shown that the proposed daisy-chain architecture presents a significant reduction in the amount of tester storage required, for the same set of test patterns.

This work opens up avenues of possible future work. The method proposed is an aggressive way of minimizing the number of test elevators at the cost of additional computation in the linear equation solver. One direction for reducing the amount of computation would be to develop intelligent partitioning methods for which cores are tested together that reduce the total amount of free variable sharing, but still retain most of the encoding flexibility where it is most needed. Another direction for further research would be to consider ways to reduce power dissipation during decompression by using the added encoding flexibility to reduce transitions in the decompressed scan vectors.

References

[Hamdioui 11]   Hamdioui, S., Taouil, M.: Yield improvement and test cost optimization for 3D stacked ICs. In: Proceedings of Asian Test Symposium (ATS), pp. 480–485 (2011)

[Janicki 12]   Janicki, J., Kassab, M., Mrugalski, G., Mukherjee, N., Rajski, J., Tyszer, J.: EDT bandwidth management in SoC designs. IEEE Trans. Comput. Aided Des. Integr. Circuits Syst. 31(12), 1894–1907 (2012)

[Khoche 02]   Khoche, A., Volkerink, E., Rivoir, J., Mitra, S.: Test vector compression using EDA-ATE synergies. In: Proceedings of VLSI Test Symposium, pp. 97–102 (2002)

[Kinsman 10]   Kinsman, A.B., Nicolici, N.: Time-multiplexed compressed test of SOC designs. IEEE Trans. Very Large Scale Integr. (VLSI) Syst. 18(8), 1159–1172 (2010)

[Könemann 91]   Könemann, B.: LFSR-coded test patterns for scan designs. In: Proceedings of European Test Conference, pp. 237–242 (1991)

[Könemann 01]   Könemann, B., Barnhart, C., Keller, B., Snethen, T., Farnsworth, O., Wheater, D.: A SmartBIST variant with guaranteed encoding. In: Proceedings of Asian Test Symposium, pp. 325–330 (2001)

[Krishna 01]   Krishna, C.V., Touba, N.A.: Test vector encoding using partial LFSR reseeding. In: Proceedings of International Test Conference, pp. 885–893 (2001)

[Jiang 09]   Jiang, L., Xu, Q., Chakrabarty, K., Mak, T.M.: Layout-driven test-architecture design and optimization for 3D SoCs under pre-bond test-pin-count constraint. In: Proceedings of IEEE International Conference on Computer-Aided Design, pp. 191–196 (2009)

[Jiang 12]   Jiang, L., Xu, Q., Chakrabarty, K., Mak, T.M.: Integrated test-architecture optimization and thermal-aware test scheduling for 3-D SoCs under pre-bond test-pin-count constraint. IEEE Trans. Very Large Scale Integr. (VLSI) Syst. 20(9), 1621–1633 (2012)

[Larsson 08]   Larsson, A., Larsson, E., Chakrabarty, K., Eles, P., Peng, Z.: Test architecture optimization and test scheduling for SOCs with core-level expansion of compressed test patterns. In: Proceedings of Design, Automation and Test in Europe, pp. 188–193 (2008)

[Lee 13] Lee, Y.-W., Touba, N.A.: Unified 3D test architecture for variable test data bandwidth across pre-bond, partial stack, and post-bond test. In: Proceedings of Defect and Fault Tolerance Symposium, pp. 184–189 (2013)

[Lo 10] Lewis, D.L., Lee, H.-H.S.: Testing circuit-partitioned 3D IC designs. In: Proceedings of IEEE Computer Society Annual Symposium on VLSI (ISVLSI), pp. 139–144, May 2009

[Lewis 09] Lo, C.-Y., Hsing, Y.-T., Denq, L.-M., Wu, C.-W.: SOC test architecture and method for 3-D ICs. IEEE Trans. Comput. Aided Des. Integr. Circuits Syst. 29(10), 1645–1649 (2010)

[Marinissen 09] Marinissen, E.J., Zorian, Y.: Testing 3D chips containing through-silicon vias. In: Proceedings of International Test Conference, pp. 1–6 (2009)

[Muthyala 10] Marinissen, E.J., Verbree, J., Konijnenburg, M.: A structured and scalable test access architecture for TSV-based 3D stacked ICs. In: Proceedings of VLSI Test Symposium (2010)

[Muthyala 12] Muthyala, S.S., Touba, N.A.: Improving test compression by retaining non-pivot free variables in sequential linear decompressors. In: Proceedings of International Test Conference, Paper 9.1 (2012)

[Muthyala 13] Muthyala, S.S., Touba, N.A.: SOC test compression scheme using sequential linear decompressors with retained free variables. In: Proceedings of VLSI Test Symposium (2013)

[Muthyala 14] Muthyala, S.S., Touba, N.A.: Reducing test time for 3D-ICs by improved utilization of test elevators. In: Proceedings of International Conference on Very Large Scale Integration (VLSI-SoC) (2014)

[Noia 09] Noia, B., Chakrabarty, K.: Test-wrapper optimization for embedded cores in TSV-based three-dimensional SOCs. In: International Conference on Computer Design, pp. 70–77 (2009)

[Noia 10] Noia, B., Goel, S.K., Chakrabarty, K., Marinissen, E.J., Verbree, J.: Test-architecture optimization for TSV-based 3D stacked ICs. IEEE Trans. Comput. Aided Design Integr. Circuits Syst. 30(11), 1705–1718 (2011)

[Patti 06] Patti, R.S.: Three dimensional integrated circuits and the future of system-on-chip designs. Proc. IEEE 94(6), 1214–1224 (2006)

[Rajski 04] Rajski, J., Tyszer, J., Kassab, M., Mukherjee, N.: Embedded deterministic test. IEEE Trans. Comput. Aided Des. 23(5), 1306–1320 (2004)

[Touba 06] Touba, N.A.: Survey of test vector compression techniques. IEEE Des. Test Mag. 23(4), 294–303 (2006)

[Wang 04] Wang, L.-T., Wen, X., Furukawa, H., Hsu, F.-S., Lin, S.-H., Tsai, S.-W., Abdel-Hafez, K.S., Wu, S.: VirtualScan: a new compressed scan technology for test cost reduction. In: Proceedings of International Test Conference, pp. 916–925 (2004)

[Wang 05] Wang, L.-T., Abdel-Hafez, K.S., Wen, X., Sheu, B., Wu, S., Lin, S.-H., Chang, M.-T.: UltraScan: using time-division demultiplexing/multiplexing (TDDM/TDM) with VirtualScan for test cost reduction. In: Proceedings of International Test Conference, pp. 946–953 (2005)

[Wang 06] Wang, L.-T., Wu, C.-W., Wen, X.: VLSI Test Principles and Architectures: Design for Testability. Morgan Kaufmann, Amsterdam (2006)

[Wu 07] Wu, X., Falkenstern, P., Xie, Y.: Scan chain design for three-dimensional integrated circuits (3D ICs). In: Proceedings of International Conference on Computer Design (ICCD), pp. 212–218, October 2008

[Wu 08] Wu, X., Chen, Y., Chakrabarty, K., Xie, Y.: Test-access mechanism optimization for core-based three-dimensional SOCs. In: Proceedings of International Conference on Computer Design, pp. 212–218 (2008)

[Xu 05] Xu, Q., Nicolici, N.: Resource-constrained system-on-a-chip test: a survey. IEE Proc. Comput. Digital Tech. **152**(1), 67–81 (2005)

Design and Optimization of Multiple-Mesh Clock Network

Jinwook Jung$^{(\boxtimes)}$, Dongsoo Lee, and Youngsoo Shin

Korea Advanced Institute of Science and Technology, 291 Daehak-ro,
Yuseong-gu, Daejeon 305-701, Korea
jinwookjung@kaist.ac.kr

Abstract. A clock mesh, in which clock signals are shorted at mesh grid, is less susceptible to on-chip process variation, and so it has widely been studied recently for a clock network of smaller skew. A practical design may require more than one mesh primarily because of hierarchical clock gating architecture; a single mesh, however, can also support the same architecture after some hierarchies are removed but at the cost of gating efficiency. We experimentally compare multiple- and single-mesh using a few test circuits, and show that the former consumes smaller clock power (16.3 %) but exhibits larger clock skew (10.2 ps) and longer clock wirelength (21.7 %). We continue to study how multiple meshes should be floorplanned on the layout, specifically whether or not we allow the overlaps among meshes. The choice is translated into different physical design strategy, and causes different amount of clock skew, critical path delay, clock wirelength, and clock power consumption, which we experimentally evaluate. We give at last the comparison of clock skew variation for each mesh implementation and clock tree, and show that floorplanning of multiple meshes helps to reduce the variation of clock skew.

Keywords: Clock distribution · Clock mesh · Multiple-mesh clock network

1 Introduction

Big industrial designs such as SoCs and processors are often embedded with multiple levels of clock gating to efficiently reduce the power consumption of clock distribution network [1–3]. Some clock gating is inserted by automatic CAD tools, e.g. by compiling load-enable registers into normal registers driven by clock gating cells (CGCs); designers may also insert clock gating in manual fashion, especially at module- or system-level, based on the knowledge of the usage scenario of a design [4].

If the clock network of such a design is to be constructed using clock meshes to achieve lower clock skew, multiple meshes may be inserted as shown in Fig. 1. This is a natural choice in terms of power consumption because each mesh can be gated whenever the block it spans is not actively switching. Furthermore, it is

© IFIP International Federation for Information Processing 2015
L. Claesen et al. (Eds.): VLSI-SoC 2014, IFIP AICT 464, pp. 39–57, 2015.
DOI: 10.1007/978-3-319-25279-7_3

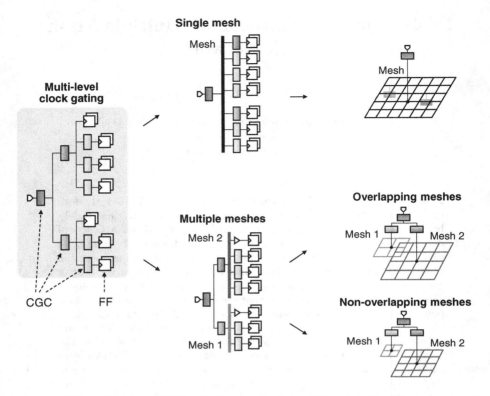

Fig. 1. Design of mesh clock network for multi-level clock gating.

well known that mesh consumes more power than standard clock tree network [5] due to more wire capacitance and excessive short-circuit current; a study indicates that 33.4 % more power is consumed in comparison with the standard clock tree [6], so it helps to gate mesh whenever it is possible. A single big mesh, however, may be inserted instead after some clock gating hierarchies are removed, which is also illustrated in Fig. 1. This choice is not efficient in terms of power consumption, but it has the benefits of shorter design time because of its simpler structure, as well as shorter clock wires and more importantly smaller clock skew. In this paper, we quantitatively explore the two styles of mesh implementation, using some test circuits in 28-nm technology, which is the first contribution.

When multiple meshes are employed, it is important to decide how to floorplan them. If overlaps between meshes are allowed, physical design can be done in flat. No overlap, on the other hand, implies hierarchical physical design. The two styles will have different impact on clock power, clock wirelength, clock skew, and timing closure, which we want to quantitatively assess; this constitutes the second contribution of the paper.

The remainder of this paper is organized as follows. The basic mesh network structure and the steps to synthesize it are reviewed in Sect. 2; clock gating

in multiple levels of hierarchy is also described. In Sect. 3, we address the procedures to design single- and multiple-mesh clock networks in the context of
multi-level clock gating, and use some test circuits to experimentally assess the
two implementation styles. Section 5 discusses the floorplan of multiple meshes
and provides experimental evaluation. Section 6 gives the comparison of the three
mesh implementations with the standard clock tree, and evaluates clock skew
variation. Several related works are reviewed in Sect. 7, and we finally conclude
the paper in Sect. 8.

2   Preliminaries

2.1   Clock Mesh Structure and Its Synthesis

Figure 2 illustrates a structure of mesh clock network that we are concerned with
in this paper. It consists of three main components: a premesh tree, a mesh grid,
and a postmesh tree. Clock sinks are connected to the mesh through postmesh
buffers and stub wires. A premesh tree can be a balanced H-tree or standard
clock tree, and connects the mesh to the clock source. Leaf-stage buffers in the
premesh tree will be called mesh drivers.

Figure 3 illustrates the overall synthesis flow of a mesh clock network; we
synthesize a mesh clock network in a bottom-up manner. Clock sinks are first
grouped together based on their locations; maximum fanout of postmesh buffers,
which are inserted and sized properly once the groups are formed, determines the
group size. A mesh grid is constructed and connected to the postmesh buffers
through stub wires; a grid structure is designated by the numbers of vertical
and horizontal wires. It is determined in a way that minimum length of wires
are used for mesh grid and stub wires. The pitch of grid wires that gives the

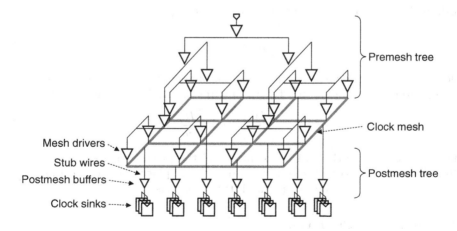

Fig. 2. Mesh clock network.

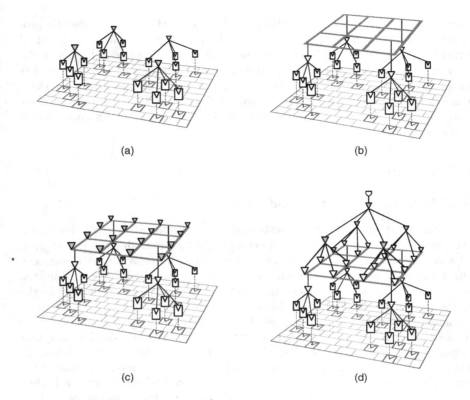

(a)

(b)

(c)

(d)

Fig. 3. Mesh clock network synthesis: (a) postmesh buffer insertion, (b) mesh grid construction, (c) mesh driver insertion, and (d) premesh tree synthesis.

mesh of the minimum wire length is calculated as [7]:

$$p = \sqrt{\frac{12}{\rho}}, \tag{1}$$

where ρ denotes the density of the postmesh buffers in the placement area. Then we can determine the number of vertical wires m and horizontal wires n:

$$m = \left\lceil \frac{W}{p} \right\rceil, \; n = \left\lceil \frac{H}{p} \right\rceil, \tag{2}$$

where W and H are the width and height of the placement area, respectively. After the mesh grid construction, mesh drivers are placed at each grid location; they then serve as the sinks of premesh tree synthesis.

2.2   Multi-level Clock Gating

Clock gating is a standard technique to reduce clock power. It is often applied in multiple levels, particularly in big industrial designs [1–4]. This is illustrated

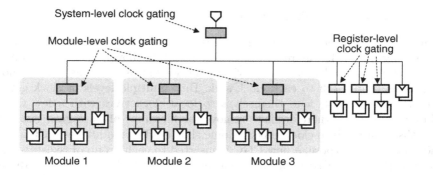

Fig. 4. Clock gating in multiple levels.

in Fig. 4. Register-level clock gating is mostly realized through automatic CAD tools, e.g. by replacing load-enable registers with clock gating cells (CGCs) and normal registers, and by employing XOR self-gating [8].

In addition, designers may explicitly instantiate CGCs at module level or system level (right after the clock source) according to the usage scenario of a chip. This type of clock gating gives the capability to turn off the clock signal of specific modules or entire systems, and shuts down a large portion of clock distribution network.

3   Mesh Clock Networks for Multi-level Clock Gating

A design of multiple level clock gating encounters the choice of mesh implementation styles as shown in Fig. 4. Specifically, a single big mesh may be inserted at system level (or at each clock domain) or more than one small meshes may be inserted with each mesh assigned to a module or to a group of registers. The two styles incur different clock power consumption, as well as different clock skew, wirelength, and design time, which we want to explore in this section.

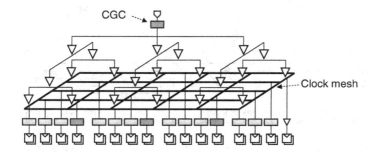

Fig. 5. Single mesh implementation of multi-level clock gating.

3.1   Single-Mesh Implementation

In this implementation, a single big mesh is inserted right after the system level clock gating of Fig. 4. The resulting clock network is shown in Fig. 5. To retain the advantage of smaller clock skew of mesh network, it is desirable to have short clock paths from mesh to each clock sink. But, multiple levels of clock gating after mesh (see Fig. 4) lend themselves to local clock trees with a few CGCs and buffers. The key therefore is to remove the hierarchy of clock gating so that the paths from mesh to clock sinks become shorter. The module-level CGCs are removed for this purpose; a new CGC is inserted to each group of registers that have directly been gated by a module-level CGC; a CGC that has been driven by module-level CGC is now gated by its original gating logic and the logic that has gated module-level CGC.

It is well known that mesh consumes more power than clock tree due to more wire capacitance and short-circuit current [5,7]. It is thus important to gate mesh as often as possible. A single big mesh, however, is gated less frequently, thus has disadvantage in power consumption. Balancing postmesh trees should be easier, which yields smaller skew. Test circuits will be used to assess these factors, as well as wirelength and design time.

The maximum fanout of newly inserted CGCs, which serve as postmesh buffers, may be increased to reduce the additional capacitance of mesh wires; from Eqs. 1 and 2, reducing the number of postmesh buffers results in fewer mesh grid segments. Therefore we can consider using a small number of postmesh buffers to cut down the power consumption of clock meshes. However, it leads us to choose postmesh trees containing multiple levels of buffers which incur additional clock skew, since the maximum transition constraint of clock signal may be violated without a buffered tree structure. We will see how the maximum fanout of newly inserted CGCs affects clock skew and power consumption of the single-mesh implementation later in this section.

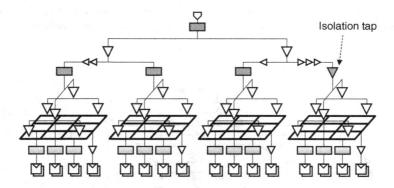

Fig. 6. Multiple mesh implementation of multi-level clock gating.

3.2   Multiple-Mesh Implementation

Another implementation of mesh is shown in Fig. 6. This time, a mesh is assigned to each module as well as to registers that have not belonged to any modules, which we call top-level registers. The initial clock network shown in Fig. 4 may be very unbalanced; in particular, the path from the clock source to top-level registers tends to be shorter. This is alleviated by inserting isolation taps, which have comparable delays to CGCs. If there are some modules without module-level clock gating, their clock sinks are also isolated by the isolation taps. Mesh drivers are inserted at each grid of meshes; they are then considered as sinks of premesh tree synthesis.

Since each mesh is gated at module-level, it can be gated more frequently, and leads to smaller power consumption. Clock skew can arise between different meshes as well as between different clock sinks under the same mesh; so skew is very likely to be larger than that in a single mesh implementation. Design complexity and wires will also increase.

3.3   Assessment

The design flow of mesh network synthesis for single- and multiple-mesh implementation has been implemented in Tcl, which runs on commercial placement and route tool; it is illustrated in Fig. 7. To determine the number of mesh wires in each implementation, we used Eq. 2 A few test circuits have been chosen from OpenCores [9]; the RTL description of each circuit has been modified to insert module- and system-level clock gating. A library of 28 nm industrial technology has been used to compile each circuit and to obtain a netlist. The last column of Table 1 corresponds to the number of meshes when clock is implemented as multiple meshes; the numbers of gates and flip-flops are also shown. Clock skew and power consumption have been measured using SPICE after parasitics are extracted from layout.

Table 1. Test circuits

Circuits	# Gates	# FFs	# Meshes
ac97	3225	1067	4
mc	6211	1069	3
usbf	7647	1736	3
pci	11142	3206	4
sdc	11815	3760	5
spi	13964	4656	2
des3	63217	8811	4
fft64	71263	15996	4

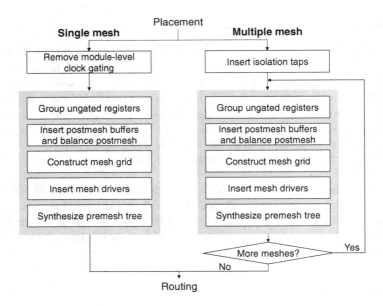

Fig. 7. Design flow of mesh network synthesis.

Comparison of Single- and Multiple-mesh Implementations. Single- and multiple-mesh implementations are compared in Table 2. Multiple meshes consume on average of 16.3 % smaller power than single mesh. This has been expected because small multiple meshes are gated more often than a single big mesh; meshes are gated 78 % of time in multiple meshes (on average of meshes, and on average of circuits), while a single mesh is gated 49 % of time. Relatively small difference in power, considering the big difference in mesh gating probability, is due to more clock wires in multiple-mesh implementation as indicated in columns 5–7. Figure 8 depicts how respective mesh grids of single- and multiple-mesh networks are constructed in circuit ac97. Multiple meshes are placed as overlapped each other due to irregular module boundaries, causing the sum of mesh wires to be increased by 21.7 % compared to single mesh on average of the circuits.

Clock skew is compared in the last three columns. It clearly shows the advantage of the single-mesh implementation of which clock skew is 10.2 ps smaller than that of the multiple meshes on average, which also has been expected. Postmesh buffers are close to a mesh grid in the single-mesh while the stub wires of the multiple-mesh implementations becomes longer (see Fig. 8(b)), which introduce additional clock skew due to the stub wire delay. Also, different meshes themselves contribute to clock skew in the multiple-mesh implementation due to the different latenciy from the clock source to each mesh (see Fig. 6).

Figure 9 compares the time elapsed for clock network synthesis. Multiple-mesh implementation takes 35.4 % more time than single-mesh, on average. This is mainly due to the fact that designing mesh grid and postmesh trees has to be

Table 2. Comparison of single- and multiple-mesh implementation

Circuits	Clock power (mW)			Clock wirelength (mm)			Clock skew (ps)		
	Single	Multiple	Diff. (%)	Single	Multiple	Diff. (%)	Single	Multiple	Diff. (ps)
ac97	0.52	0.43	17.1	5.5	6.6	-20.0	13.5	26.6	-13.1
mc	0.18	0.15	18.2	4.8	6.3	-31.7	13.4	20.9	-7.5
usbf	0.89	0.85	10.0	7.6	10.0	-31.8	11.8	27.0	-15.2
pci	0.50	0.45	11.8	13.9	17.8	-28.7	13.4	26.1	-12.7
sdc	0.45	0.32	28.2	14.3	17.6	-23.6	14.0	23.3	-9.3
spi	0.84	0.62	26.1	18.3	20.2	-10.8	12.5	19.6	-7.0
des3	2.95	2.55	13.6	38.2	45.5	-19.4	14.0	24.5	-10.5
fft64	1.74	1.55	10.9	62.6	67.7	-8.0	19.8	26.0	-6.2
Average			16.3			-21.7			-10.2

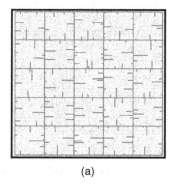
(a)

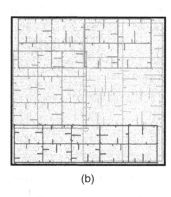
(b)

Fig. 8. Layouts of (a) single- and (b) multiple-mesh implementations for circuit ac97.

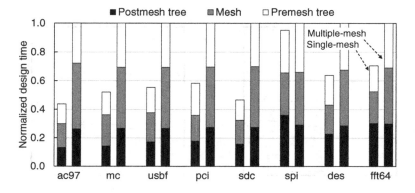

Fig. 9. Comparison of design time.

iterated in the multiple-mesh implementation. A circuit spi is an exception. It contains only two meshes in its multiple-mesh implementation; more times are spent in the postmesh tree synthesis of single-mesh implementation due to the large number of clock sinks (in consideration of circuit size).

Impact of Using Fewer Postmesh Buffers. We took the circuit ac97 and implemented two more single-mesh clock networks with two and four times bigger maximum fanouts of newly inserted CGCs, respectively, to see how reducing postmesh buffers affects clock skew and power consumption of the single-mesh implementation. The respective postmesh trees are now synthesized as 2-level and 3-level clock trees. The measured clock power, wirelength, and clock skew are summarized in Table 3 along with the results of single- and multiple-mesh implementations of the previous section.

Table 3. Experimental results for various postmesh trees of ac97

Scheme	Clock power (mW)	Clock wirelength (mm)	Clock skew (ps)
Single	0.52	5.5	13.5
w/ 2-level postmesh	0.47	5.3	33.1
w/ 3-level postmesh	0.43	5.0	51.3
Multiple	0.43	6.6	30.6

Figure 10 shows the clock mesh layouts. The number of grid segments are reduced due to the increased fanout of mesh grid; the clock wirelengths of the single-mesh network with 2- and 3-level postmesh trees are decreased by 3.3 % and 8.7 % compared to the original single-mesh implementation. It results in lower power consumption; the power consumption of the single-mesh implementation with 3-level postmesh is now close to the multiple-mesh implementation

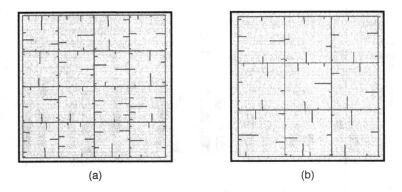

(a)   (b)

Fig. 10. Layouts of single-mesh networks of different postmesh structures.

(see column 2 of Table 3). As the depth of postmesh trees becomes deeper, however, clock skew is increased; it is now even larger than the multiple-mesh implementation, and the benefit of using single-mesh implementation in terms of clock skew diminishes. Therefore, it is better to choose the multiple-mesh implementation over the single-mesh network with deeper-levels of postmesh trees for lower power consumption.

4   Choosing Mesh Implementation Style

Assessments in Sect. 3.3 indicate that a single big mesh has advantages over a multiple-mesh network in terms of clock skew. On the other hand, the multiple-mesh implementation shows reduced power consumption due to the capability of shutting down a large portion of clock network; a low-power design may take multiple-mesh as the design strategy of choice.

Although our evaluation results show that all the test circuits taken for the assessments consume lower power in the multiple-mesh implementation, they also result in longer clock wirelengths. This fact implies the excessive metal resources may cause power overhead when gating probabilities of CGCs in a design are small. Here, let us briefly address the impact of gating probabilities in power consumptions. We took the circuit ac97 and generated SPICE netlist of single- and multiple mesh clock networks with parasitics extracted. To see how gating probabilities affect the power consumption, we controlled the enable signals arbitrarily and estimated power consumptions of different gating scenarios.

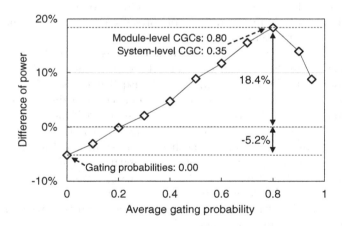

Fig. 11. Difference in power consumption between two mesh implementations for ac97 with respect to gating probabilities.

Figure 11 plots the difference of power consumption between two design options with respect to different gating probabilities; the difference is calculated by subtracting the power of single-mesh from that of multiple-mesh. If a circuit does not gate at all, a single big mesh consumes lower power due to shorter wire-length. As the gating probabilities become larger, multiple mesh implementation begins to have smaller power consumption. The difference of power consumption has the maximum at average gating probability of 0.8. As the gating probabilities are still more increased, the power advantage of multiple-mesh implementation begins to shrink; this is because system-level clock gating also has large gating probability in that case.

4.1   Switching Capacitance Estimation

The mesh implementation of choice depends on the gating probabilities in a design. It may raise the question of how we know which mesh network has a benefit of power consumption. If there is a method of estimating switching capacitance of two strategies, we can select the mesh network of lower power before mesh construction; power is proportional to switching capacitance as is well known.

Let ΔC be the difference of the total capacitances in single- and multiple-mesh implementations. The following equation then allows us to select the suitable design strategy of mesh network before actual mesh construction:

$$\Delta C = k \left(\alpha_s C_m - \sum_{\forall m_i} \alpha_i C_m^i \right), \tag{3}$$

where k is an empirical constant, α_s and α_i are the switching activities of system- and module-level clock gatings, C_m is the capacitance of a single big mesh, m_i is the ith mesh in multiple-mesh, and C_m^i denotes the capacitance of the ith mesh of multiple-mesh implementation.

The structure of a mesh and the area it spans can be known just after the placement stage. So we can calculate the capacitance involved in a mesh from Eq. 2 and capacitance per unit length. Eq. 3 expresses the difference in switching capacitance of mesh clock network between the single- and multiple-mesh implementations. To consider premesh tree capacitance, we multiply an empirical constant k (e.g., 1.75 for H-tree); the wirelength of premesh tree is almost proportional to the size of mesh grid, as shown in Fig. 12. Functional simulation at earlier design stage provides the gating probability. If α_is are relatively small, ΔC can be negative; the high gating probabilities will yield the positive value of ΔC. Therefore, we can evaluate the equation Eq. 3 and predict which implementation will have smaller power consumption without actually constructing the two mesh clock networks.

We will not take up this matter further in this paper since our assessments in Sect. 3.3 show that gating probability is relatively high, and multiple-mesh is always better in terms of power consumption for the test circuits. Nevertheless, if the functional simulation at earlier design phase indicates that the design has smaller value of gating probability, designers may consider the adoption of single-mesh for lower power.

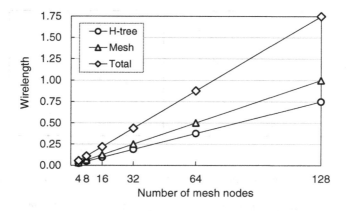

Fig. 12. Estimation of k value for H-tree premesh.

5   Floorplanning of Multiple Meshes

It has been shown in Sect. 3 that multiple mesh implementation has advantage in clock power even though it incurs longer clock wirelength and larger clock skew. In this section, we want to explore how multiple meshes can be floorplanned. Specifically, we may or may not allow the overlaps between meshes[1] as shown in Fig. 13. Note that the overlap does not cause the use of additional metal wires as illustrated in Fig. 14.

The choice of mesh floorplanning has significant implication in physical design process. Figure 13(a) allows flat placement and routing, thus more flexibility in achieving timing closure even though more wires will be used for mesh grid; Fig. 13(b) on the other hand assumes hierarchical physical design which is associated with more design steps and less design flexibility, but with less usage of wires for mesh grid. We want to experimentally assess the two choices in terms of clock power, clock wirelength, clock skew, and critical path delay.

5.1   Assessment

When overlap is allowed, placement is performed in flat. The region is identified from the location of flip-flops that belong to the same mesh, and mesh grid is constructed accordingly. The remaining steps of mesh network synthesis follow those of Sect. 3.2. For meshes without overlap, floorplanning is performed manually by referring to the relative locations of meshes with overlap (i.e. obtain Fig. 13(b) from 13(a)). We then assign a bounding box to all flip-flops and combinational gates that belong to the same mesh. Automatic placement is then performed with a set of bounding boxes as placement constraints, which is followed by mesh network synthesis.

---

[1] We wanted to compare single- and multiple-mesh implementation using the same placement, so overlap was allowed in Sect. 3.

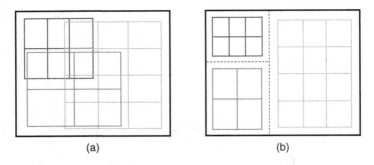

Fig. 13. Floorplanning of multiple meshes: (a) with overlap and (b) without overlap.

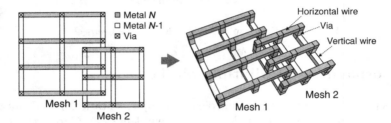

Fig. 14. Three-dimensional illustration of overlapped clock meshes.

The two mesh floorplanning methods are compared in Table 4. Floorplanning without overlap yields smaller clock power (5.2 % on average), which is mainly due to shorter clock wirelength (15.9 % on average). A circuit usbf is an exception, i.e. clock power is not very different even with large difference in clock wirelength. Its meshes are not gated very often (28 % of time); it consists of one big mesh and two small meshes, so large number of buffers are inserted to balance clock arrival time to three meshes, much more when overlap is not allowed.

Table 4. Comparison of overlapping and non-overlapping meshes

Circuits	Clock power (mW)			Clock wirelength (mm)			Clock skew (ps)		
	Overlap	No overlap	Diff (%)	Overlap	No overlap	Diff. (%)	Overlap	No overlap	Diff. (ps)
ac97	0.43	0.43	1.1	6.6	5.8	11.1	26.6	18.3	8.3
mc	0.15	0.13	12.0	6.3	4.8	24.0	20.9	20.1	0.7
usbf	0.85	0.83	2.4	10.0	7.6	23.4	27.0	25.5	1.5
pci	0.45	0.39	12.8	17.8	14.0	21.4	26.1	20.0	6.1
sdc	0.32	0.31	3.5	17.6	14.9	15.8	23.3	20.6	2.7
spi	0.62	0.60	4.1	20.2	18.1	10.5	19.6	13.4	6.2
des3	2.55	2.50	1.8	45.5	38.1	16.2	24.5	16.3	8.2
fft64	1.55	1.48	4.2	67.7	64.1	5.3	26.0	21.6	4.4
Average			5.2			15.9			4.8

Table 5. Critical path delays of multiple mesh designs

Circuits	Overlap (ns)	No overlap (ns)	Diff. (ns)
ac97	1.70	1.72	-0.01
mc	3.18	3.21	-0.03
usbf	2.12	2.30	-0.18
pci	2.59	2.70	-0.11
sdc	2.67	2.77	-0.10
spi	2.70	2.82	-0.11
des3	2.43	2.46	-0.03
fft64	3.84	4.07	-0.23
Average			-0.10

Clock skew becomes smaller when overlap is not allowed; it is reduced by 4.8 ps average. Meshes are smaller in this case (see Fig. 13), so mesh grid pitch also becomes smaller; the longest stub wire, which affects the skew, becomes shorter as a result.

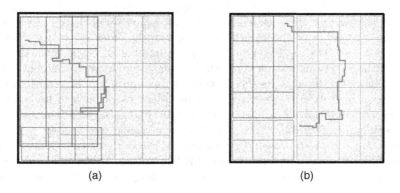

(a)   (b)

Fig. 15. Critical paths in usbf: (a) meshes with overlap and (b) meshes without overlap.

We have also measured the critical path delay, which are reported in Table 5. It is clearly shorter when overlap is allowed (0.10 ns), because placement is performed in flat with greater flexibility in meeting circuit timing. Figure 15 illustrates how critical paths are identified in two mesh floorplans of the circuit usbf.

6   Comparison with Clock Tree

In this section, we compare the three mesh implementation styles, that we have covered, with the standard clock tree. We implemented a clock tree in each test

Table 6. Experimental results of clock trees

Circuits	Clock power (mW)	Clock wirelength (mm)	Clock skew (ps)
ac97	0.37	4.5	32.2
mc	0.13	4.2	39.9
usbf	0.74	7.1	52.6
pci	0.34	12.4	53.6
sdc	0.31	12.2	58.3
spi	0.57	15.6	54.4
des	2.33	31.9	69.6
fft64	1.22	54.8	69.2

circuit for this purpose using the commercial placement and route tool. Clock power, wirelength, and clock skew of the clock trees are reported in Table 6.

Figure 16(a) shows the clock skew of each clock network (normalized to the clock of the clock tree). Compared to clock tree, a 39.7 ps reduction of clock skew is achieved by adopting the single-mesh implementation. Two multiple meshes also significantly improve clock skew; 29.5 ps and 34.3 ps reductions are observed in multiple meshes with and without overlap, respectively. Note that the benefit of reducing clock skew by clock mesh grows as the number of clock sinks becomes larger; the divergence of clock paths increases, so the clock skew of a clock tree tends to increase. On the other hand, a large number of clock sinks share the clock path in a mesh clock network. Delay balancing between different meshes should be done for different meshes in the multiple-mesh implementation, but it is easier than in the clock tree since there are a few clock path to be balanced.

Power consumptions are also compared in Fig. 16(b) (normalized to the single-mesh implementation). As is well known, clock trees shows less power consumption than mesh networks; it needs 29 % less power than a single mesh on average. Multiple meshes can reduce this large power overhead of clock mesh; floorplanned multiple meshes consume only 8 % larger power than clock tree.

6.1 Clock Skew Variation

We generated the SPICE netlists of the three mesh implementations and a clock tree from the circuit ac97 with parasitics extracted, and conducted Monte Carlo simulation of 1,000 samples to evaluate clock skew variation. We obtained the arrival times of all clock sinks, and calculated the global clock skew by subtracting the minimum arrival time from the maximum arrival time.

Figure 17 shows the histogram of the clock skew for each clock network. Single-mesh network and clock tree show the smallest and the largest clock skew variations, respectively. Multiple-mesh implementation with mesh overlap is affected on-chip variation more than multiple meshes without overlap. It is due to its longer latency; a mesh network of overlapped multiple meshes has

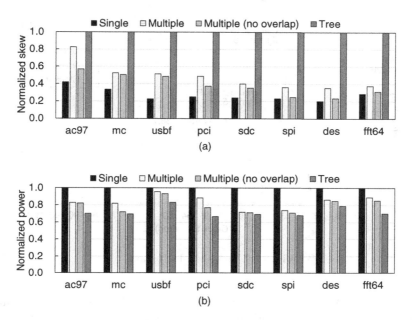

Fig. 16. (a) Normalized clock skew and (b) clock power.

longer wirelength and thereby more wire capacitance, so it shows larger clock latency than floorplaned meshes. Floorplanning the multiple meshes reduces the clock wirelength, so it can reduce the clock skew variation.

7   Related Work

There have been various studies concerning mesh clock network, particularly on the reduction of its excessive power consumption. A representative method is to reduce the wire usage of a mesh clock network thereby the wire capacitance. Such approach can be divided into two big categories; one is the reduction of unnecessary mesh grid segments [10], and another approach is the shortening the stub wires by moving clock sinks or grid wires [11,12]. Short circuit current is also an important source of power consumption in mesh clock network, so several researches have proposed dedicated mesh driver to cut off the short circuit current [7].

However, there are few studies on mesh network design considering the clock gating although it is a pervasive technique to reduce clocking power. Lu et al. proposed a mesh clock network with several gated local trees [13]. They grouped FFs in the same grid after the mesh grid construction, and extracted gating function from the FF group. However, there is the limit to extract gating functions from only the adjacent FFs in the same grid box. Also, their methodology is impractical since in most cases the clock gating structure is defined before the

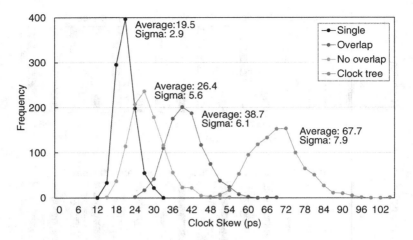

Fig. 17. Clock skew histogram.

placement stage. Wilke and Reis [14] compared clock skew and power consumption of a multiple-mesh network with a single-mesh network. They concluded that although the former has greater power consumption and larger clock skew, clock gating can be adopted to reduce power consumption, in that the multiple meshes becomes more power efficient solution. But they did not use the actual clock gated circuits for their assessments, and the multi-level clock gating structure covered in our study was not also considered.

In [15], which is the preliminary version of this paper, Jung et al. in the first time consider practical multi-level clock gating structure in the design of the single-mesh and multiple-mesh network. They presented the comparison of the two mesh networks, and showed that the multiple-mesh network consumes lower power while the single-mesh has the advantages in clock skew and design complexity. It is also presented that the floorplanning of multiple meshes can be used to reduce the power consumption of multiple meshes at the cost of critical path delay.

8   Conclusion

The clock network of a design with hierarchical clock gating can be implemented by a set of meshes. If some hierarchies are removed, however, it also can be implemented by a single big mesh. We have shown that multiple-mesh implementation has advantage in clock power (16.2 % smaller power on average of test circuits); but single mesh consumes shorter clock wires, yields smaller clock skew, and takes less time to design.

Multiple meshes can be floorplanned with some overlaps if placement is performed in flat, or they can be floorplanned without overlap if hierarchical physical design is assumed. The experiments have shown that the mesh floorplan with overlap yields smaller clock power owing to shorter clock wires, smaller clock skew, and more variation tolerance, but timing closure is easier if overlap are not allowed.

References

1. Shin, Y., Shin, K., Kenkare, P., Kashyap, R., Lee, H.J., Seo, D., Millar, B., Kwon, Y., Iyengar, R., Kim, M.S., Chowdhury, A., Bae, S.I., Hong, I., Jeong, W., Lindner, A., Cho, U., Hawkins, K., Son, J.C., Hwang, S.H.: 28nm high-k metal-gate heterogeneous quad-core CPUs for high-performance and energy-efficient mobile application processor. In: Proceedings of International Solid-State Circuits Conference, pp. 154–155, February 2013
2. Singh, T., Bell, J., Southard, S.: Jaguar: a next-generation low-power x86–64 core. In: Proceedings of International Solid-State Circuits Conference, pp. 52–53, February 2013
3. Xu, K., Choy, C.S.: Low-power H.264/AVC baseline decoder for portable applications. In: Proceedings of International Symposium on Low Power Electronics and Design, pp. 256–261, August 2007
4. Guthaus, M.R., Wilke, G., Reis, R.: Revisiting automated physical synthesis of high-performance clock networks. ACM Trans. Design Autom. Electron. Syst. **18**(2), 31:1–31:27 (2013)
5. Chinnery, D.: High performance and low power design techniques for ASIC and custom in nanometer technologies. In: Proceeding of International Symposium on Physical Design, pp. 25–32, March 2013
6. Cyclos: Clock design for SoCs with lower power and better specs. http://www.cyclos-semi.com
7. Shim, S., Mo, M., Kim, S., Shin, Y.: Analysis and minimization of short-circuit current in mesh clock network. In: Proceedings of International Conference on Computer Design, pp. 459–462, October 2013
8. Ezroni, J.: Advanced dynamic power reduction techniques: XOR self-gating. White paper, April 2011
9. OpenCores. http://www.opencores.org
10. Rajaram, A., Pan, D.Z.: MeshWorks: a comprehensive framework for optimized clock mesh network synthesis. IEEE Trans. Comput. Aided Des. Integr. Circuits Syst. **29**(12), 1945–1958 (2010)
11. Lu, J., Mao, X., Taskin, B.: Integrated clock mesh synthesis with incremental register placement. IEEE Trans. Comput. Aided Des. Integr. Circuits Syst. **31**(2), 217–227 (2012)
12. Guthaus, M.R., Wilke, G., Reis, R.: Non-uniform clock mesh optimization with linear programming buffer insertion. In: Proceedings of Design Automation Conference, pp. 74–79 (2010)
13. Lu, J., Mao, X., Taskin, B.: Clock mesh synthesis with gated local trees and activity driven register clustering. In: Proceedings of International Conference on Computer-Aided Design, pp. 691–697, April 2012
14. Wilke, G.R.: Design and analysis of "tree+local meshes" clock architecture. In: Proceedings of International Symposium on Quality Electronic Design, pp. 165–170, March 2007
15. Jung, J., Lee, D., Shin, Y.: Design and optimization of multiple-mesh clock network. In: Proceedings of International Conference on VLSI and System-on-Chip, pp. 171–176, October 2014

Energy-Efficient Partitioning of Hybrid Caches in Multi-core Architecture

Dongwoo Lee and Kiyoung Choi[✉]

Department of Electrical and Computer Engineering,
Seoul National University, Seoul, Republic of Korea
dongwoolee@dal.snu.ac.kr, kchoi@snu.ac.kr

Abstract. This chapter presents a technique for reducing energy consumed by hybrid caches that have both SRAM and STT-RAM (Spin-Transfer Torque RAM) in multi-core architecture. It is based on dynamic way partitioning of the SRAM cache as well as the STT-RAM cache. Each core is allocated with a specific number of ways consisting of SRAM ways and STT-RAM ways. Then a cache miss fills the corresponding block in the SRAM or STT-RAM region based on an existing technique called read-write aware region-based hybrid cache architecture. Thus, when a store operation from a core causes an L2 cache miss (store miss), the block is assigned to the SRAM cache. When a load operation from a core causes an L2 cache miss (load miss) and thus causes a block fill, the block is assigned to the STT-RAM cache. However, if all the allocated ways are already placed in the SRAM, then the block fill is done into the SRAM regardless of store or load miss. The partitioning decision is updated periodically. We further improve our technique by adopting the so called *allocation switching technique* to avoid too much unbalanced use of SRAM or STT-RAM. Simulation results show that the proposed technique improves the performance of the multi-core architecture and significantly reduces energy consumption in the hybrid caches compared to the state-of-the-art migration-based hybrid cache management.

Keywords: Spin-Transfer Torque RAM (STT-RAM) · Hybrid caches · Cache partitioning

1 Introduction

Non-volatile memories such as Spin-Transfer Torque RAM (STT-RAM) have been researched as alternatives to SRAMs due to their low static power consumption and high density. Among such memories, STT-RAM has a relatively high endurance compared to other memories and thus it is regarded as the best candidate for substituting SRAM used in last-level shared caches in modern chip multi-processors [2].

However, STT-RAM has asymmetric characteristics of read and write. Writing into STT-RAM consumes significantly larger energy and takes more time than reading. Such characteristics can significantly increase energy consumption

© IFIP International Federation for Information Processing 2015
L. Claesen et al. (Eds.): VLSI-SoC 2014, IFIP AICT 464, pp. 58–74, 2015.
DOI: 10.1007/978-3-319-25279-7_4

and degrade performance of the system if the program running on the processor cores need frequent writes into the shared cache. To mitigate the adverse effect of the characteristics of STT-RAM, many methods are proposed [1, 3, 7, 9, 17, 18] on hybrid caches, where a small SRAM cache is combined with a large STT-RAM cache. In the hybrid caches, a block that is expected to be written frequently is placed in the SRAM cache, which has much lower write overhead compared to STT-RAM. So, in the hybrid cache approaches, where to place a block between SRAM and STT-RAM is one of the most important issues in reducing energy consumption and enhancing performance.

Figure 1 shows that block fill on a read miss is one major source of write operations into a cache. So reducing the number of block fills is another method of lowering dynamic energy consumption of hybrid caches. A cache partitioning technique is developed to increase the performance of chip multi-processors by dynamically partitioning ways of the cache such that the number of misses is minimized and consequently the number of block fills is reduced. So the application of cache partitioning has great potential of reducing the dynamic energy consumption of the hybrid caches. However, conventional cache way partitioning techniques cannot be applied to hybrid caches directly, because ways in the hybrid caches are separated into SRAM and STT-SRAM and thus ways assigned to a core as a result of partitioning also should be divided into SRAM and STT-RAM. Properly dividing the ways of a partition into the two caches and placing a block into a more efficient cache are new challenging issues when applying a partitioning technique to hybrid caches.

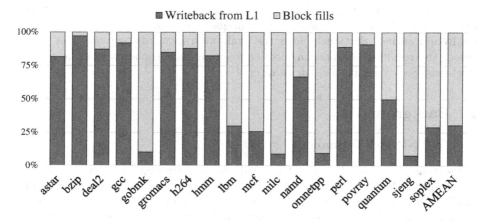

Fig. 1. Breakdown of write-inducing events in the L2 cache.

This chapter proposes a technique that adopts the cache partitioning scheme in a hybrid cache for reducing the energy consumption. We assume that the hybrid cache is a last-level shared cache in multi-core architecture. A conventional partitioning technique called utility-based partitioning is used to determine the sizes of the partitions, one for each core, such that the number of misses is minimized. To incorporate the technique into hybrid caches, the replacement policy should be redesigned. When a store operation of a core causes a miss in the shared cache, the corresponding new block is placed in SRAM. If all the allocated ways in the SRAM are already in use, a victim is selected among them. In the case of a load miss, the block is placed in STT-RAM if there is an unused way among those allocated to the core. If all the allocated ways in the STT-RAM are full, a victim block is selected. However, if all the ways allocated to the core have already been assigned to SRAM, a victim is selected among these blocks in SRAM. So, within a partition, the ratio between SRAM ways and STT-RAM ways can be adjusted and the ratio can be adjusted differently for different sets. Simulation results show that our techniques improve the performance of a quad-core system by 4.9 %, reduce the energy consumption of hybrid caches by 10.0 %, and decrease the DRAM energy by 5.9 % compared to the state-of-the-art migration based hybrid cache management technique.

In the above scheme, it is possible that cache accesses are concentrated to either SRAM or STT-RAM so that the partitioning decision does not fully apply to hybrid caches. We resolve this situation by switching an allocation policy of load and store miss with small constant probability. Thus, within the small constant probability, the block allocation on a load miss is done as if it were a store miss and vice versa. This switching technique, which we call allocation switching technique, further improves the performance of a multi-core system by 1.8 % (6.7 % in total), and reduces the energy consumption by 6.6 % (16.6 % in total), and DRAM energy by 1.6 % (7.5 % in total).

This chapter is organized as follows. Section 2 explains the background of STT-RAM technology, hybrid caches, and partitioning techniques. Section 3 describes the details of our proposed technique that exploits partitioning scheme for hybrid caches. Section 4 shows the evaluation methodology and Sect. 5 discusses the results of evaluation. Section 6 summarizes the survey of the related work and Sect. 7 concludes this chapter.

2 Background

2.1 STT-RAM Technology

Spin-Transfer Torque RAM (STT-RAM) is an emerging memory technology, which uses a Magnetic Tunnel Junction (MTJ) as an information carrier. The MTJ consists of two ferromagnetic layers and one tunnel barrier between them as shown in Fig. 2. The reference layer has a fixed direction of magnetic flow and the free layer can change its magnetic direction when a spin-polarized current flows through the MTJ with intensity above a threshold. If the directions of the two layers are in parallel, the MTJ has resistance lower than that of anti-parallel case. Thus, by measuring the voltage difference across the MTJ with a small current flow, the state of MTJ can be detected. Because of its non-volatility, STT-RAM has a very low leakage current. For read operations, it requires energy and latency comparable to SRAM, but in case of write operations, it consumes much higher energy and takes much longer than SRAM. Other noticeable properties of STT-RAM are its high endurance compared to other non-volatile memories such as Phase Change RAM (PRAM) or Resistive RAM (ReRAM) and its high density compared to SRAM.

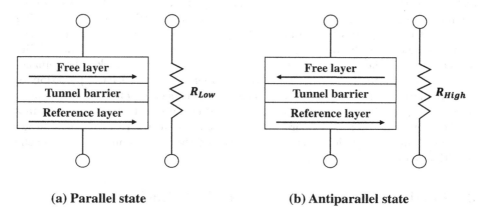

(a) Parallel state   (b) Antiparallel state

Fig. 2. Magnetic tunnel junction of STT-RAM.

2.2   Hybrid Approach for Last-Level Caches

Unlike other emerging non-volatile memories targeting off-chip storage, STT-RAM is expected to replace SRAM used for current last-level caches (LLCs) in chip multi-processors mainly due to its fast read latency close to that of SRAM and high endurance. But its high overhead of write operation obstructs the use of pure STT-RAM LLCs. To mitigate the shortcoming, there have been researches on hybrid caches that combine a small sized SRAM cache with a large sized STT-RAM cache, which lowers the write overhead of STT-RAM significantly. These two different caches are usually combined by a region-based manner. The two memories are placed at a same level of cache hierarchy and share tags of the caches. Ways are divided into the SRAM and the STT-RAM region and consequently, block placement becomes an important issue. It will be more efficient to place blocks that will be frequently written in SRAM and place others in STT-RAM.

One of the state-of-the-art techniques is the read-write aware hybrid cache architecture [17], in which a block fill caused by a store miss is made to a write-efficient SRAM region and a block fill caused by a load miss is made to a read-efficient STT-RAM region based on the assumption that a block filled by a store miss is prone to frequent write and a block filled by a load miss is prone to frequent read. If there are consecutive hits on a block in a way opposite to the initial assumption, the block is migrated to the other region.

2.3   Cache Partitioning Technique

The utility-based cache partitioning technique is proposed to improve the performance of chip multiprocessors by minimizing the number of misses on a shared cache [12]. It has the same number of Utility-MONitors (UMONs) and CPU cores. A UMON consists of an Auxiliary Tag Directory (ATD) and counters for measuring the number of hits for each position of LRU stack by observing the access of sampled sets in a cache. The algorithm periodically calculates the partition size of each core to maximize the number of hits in the cache. Bits are added to cache tags to identify the core that owns the block. The replacement policy gradually adjusts the size (number of ways) of each partition to the calculated size. The partitioning technique is especially efficient when cache insensitive (e.g., low hit rate) applications and cache sensitive ones are running at the same time on a multi-core processor. It tends to restrict the cache usage of the low hit-rate applications, while increasing the performance of other cache sensitive ones.

3   Partitioning Technique for Hybrid Caches

This section explains the details of our technique proposed in [6], which exploits the partitioning technique to reduce the energy consumption of hybrid caches in a multi-core processor. It also describes the extended work on the allocation switching technique to mitigate too much concentration on SRAM or STT-RAM.

3.1   Motivation

Read access of the last-level shared cache comes from a load or store miss of the upper level cache. In the case of store miss, a block written into the upper level cache becomes dirty, and so it eventually causes a write-back to the shared cache. Write access of the last-level cache can be classified into a write-back from the upper-level cache and a block-fill on a read miss. A read-write aware hybrid cache [17] utilizes the property of read access. If a read miss on the shared cache is caused by a store miss of the upper level cache (store miss), the new block is placed in SRAM so that a write-back to that block occurs in the write-efficient region. In case of a read miss caused by a load miss of the upper level cache (load miss), the block is placed in STT-RAM where read operations are efficient. If the decision is wrong, migration from one cache to the other occurs to remedy the situation. However, this technique does not consider the block-fill caused by a read miss in the shared cache and a write-back to a block (in the shared cache) that was originally loaded by a load miss of the upper level cache.

We propose a technique for hybrid caches that handles these cases by exploiting the advantage of a dynamic cache partitioning technique. The dynamic partitioning scheme adjusts the sizes of partitions such that the total number of misses in the shared cache is minimized. Thus it helps reduce the number of block-fills caused by read misses. In case that the number of SRAM ways used by a core is already greater than[1] or equal to that allocated to the core, a new block loaded into the LLC due to a miss is placed in the SRAM even if the miss is a load miss. The rationale is that utilizing the already allocated SRAM ways helps reducing energy and latency since subsequent write-backs to the block can be done in SRAM.

3.2   Architecture

Figure 3 shows a structure to implement our technique. Basically, it combines a cache partitioning architecture with hybrid caches. For a dynamic cache partitioning technique, it has a set of UMONs that sample cache accesses to designated sets of the cache and count the number of hits on each position of an LRU stack. It periodically calculates the partition size of the cache for each of the multiple cores such that the total number of misses in the cache is minimized. It is done by using the values of hit counters collected by the UMONs during the previous period. In the cache tags, bits are added per block to identify the core that owns the block.

The last-level shared cache consists of SRAM and STT-RAM. Thus the data array is a hybrid of the two memories, but the tags are made of SRAM only. Ways of a set are divided unevenly; SRAM contains a smaller number of ways and STT-RAM covers the rest. When a new block needs to be placed in hybrid caches, the result of the partitioning technique is used to decide the type of caches for allocation and select a victim block in the resulting type of cache as explained in the following section.

For simplicity, we assume that an independent application runs on each core in a multi-core architecture, so a UMON is attached to each core. However, the technique can also be applied in a per-application manner. In that case, the UMONs are required as many times as the number of applications running on the architecture.

3.3   Replacement Policy

To maximize the effect of applying a partitioning technique to hybrid caches, where to insert a new block should be carefully decided. If a core performs a store operation and eventually causes a miss in the shared cache, SRAM in the shared cache is selected as a location to place a new block because the block allocated in the upper level cache will become dirty, and thus there will be a write-back into the LLC. The victim selection policy within the SRAM is changed from the traditional LRU policy to a more complicated one that involves partitioning decision.

Let us define several notations as follows.

---

[1] Since we perform dynamic partitioning, the number of cache ways allocated to a core can be reduced after repartitioning. Thus $N_S(i, j)$ can temporarily exceed $N_{UT}(i)$ set by the new partitioning. The excess ways can be claimed later by other cores and thus $N_S(i, j)$ will be reduced to the new value of $N_{UT}(i)$.

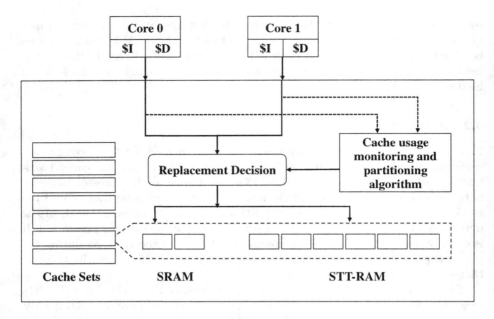

Fig. 3. Structure of hybrid cache partitioning.

- $N_S(i, j)$: the number of SRAM blocks currently in use by core i in set j.
- $N_M(i, j)$: the number of STT-RAM blocks currently in use by core i in set j.
- $N_{UT}(i)$: the total number of ways allocated to core i by the partitioning.
- $N_{UM}(i, j) = N_{UT}(i) - N_S(i, j)$: the maximum number of ways that can be allocated to core i in set j of STT-RAM.

If $N_S(i, j) \geq N_{UT}(i)$, then the LRU among these blocks is chosen as a victim. If $N_S(i, j) < N_{UT}(i)$, the LRU among all blocks in SRAM is selected as a victim. This modification is to better utilize SRAM ways which is relatively smaller than STT-RAM ways.

If a miss in the shared cache is caused by a load miss in the upper level cache, the new block can be placed either in SRAM or in STT-RAM. If $N_S(i, j) \geq N_{UT}(i)$, the LRU among them is chosen as a victim. This decision procedure is exactly the same as that of the store miss case. It allows using already allocated SRAM ways and avoids unnecessary overhead of allocating a new way in STT-RAM. And by placing the block into the SRAM, the block-fill due to the read miss is done in the write-efficient region, reducing the dynamic energy of caches without performance degradation of multi-core processors.

If $N_S(i, j) < N_{UT}(i)$, the new block is placed in STT-RAM. The total number of blocks in a set of both caches is maintained not to exceed $N_{UT}(i)$, and thus $N_M(i, j)$ is maintained not to exceed $N_{UM}(i, j)$. Therefore, $N_M(i, j)$ is adjusted dynamically according to the change of $N_S(i, j)$ and/or $N_T(i)$. For example, if $N_M(i, j)$ becomes larger than $N_{UM}(i, j)$ due to a new partitioning, the LRU among the STT-RAM blocks owned by core i is selected to be replaced by a new block of another core. If $N_M(i, j) < N_{UM}(i, j)$, the LRU of blocks owned by other cores is chosen as a victim. Contrary to the utility-based partitioning, our approach allows a zero value for $N_{UM}(i, j)$, and thus we allow to select the LRU of blocks allocated by other cores in the STT-RAM is chosen as a victim when there is no existing block in the STT-RAM owned by the core that requests the new block.

In this replacement policy, new blocks introduced by store misses can be placed only in SRAM, but new blocks introduced by load misses can be placed either in SRAM or in STT-RAM so that the utilization of the SRAM region can be maintained relatively high. The ratio between $N_S(i, j)$ and $N_M(i, j)$ can be adjusted freely under the constraint given by $N_S(i, j) + N_M(i, j) \leq N_{UT}(i)$, which results in a decrease of the total misses in hybrid caches.

3.4   Allocation Switching Technique

In the above replacement policy, it is possible that too many block-fills are guided into either SRAM or STT-RAM, in which case, the partitioning decision cannot be properly applied to hybrid caches. For example, if there is an application that has a large number of load misses and no store miss, then a cache block of this application cannot be allocated to the SRAM. Similarly, if there is an application that has plenty of store misses and rare load misses, then a cache block of this application cannot be allocated to STT-RAM. If such applications are cache-size sensitive, then the partitioning decision of the applications cannot be applied to hybrid caches properly.

To resolve this situation, we devise an allocation switching technique where a block allocation on a load miss is done as if there were a store miss and vice versa within a small constant probability. By applying this switching technique, the concentration on either SRAM or STT-RAM can be relaxed.

The allocation switching technique works as follows. Consider the case where most of the misses occurring during the execution of an application are load misses. Then the application will put most of its blocks in the STT-RAM region even if some extra ways allocated to the application (or core) are in SRAM, making the STT-RAM crowded. It may not be able to move the extra ways in the SRAM to the STT-RAM side since other cores are already taking the STT-RAM space. In that case, it will be beneficial to place new blocks into the extra SRAM ways. Thus, sometimes on a load miss, placing the corresponding block into the SRAM region instead of the STT-RAM region helps alleviating the congestion in the STT-RAM region.

We set the probability of such allocation switching to a small constant value obtained empirically. But there is still room for further research on adjusting the probability value dynamically to achieve even higher performance because the characteristics of applications are very different.

4 Evaluation Methodology

This section describes the experimental setup and methodology used to evaluate our hybrid cache partitioning technique.

4.1 Simulator

We evaluate our cache partitioning technique using a cycle accurate simulator MARSSx86 [11]. For off-chip memory model, we use DRAMSim2 simulator [13], which is integrated into MARSSx86. The details of our system configuration are listed in Table 1. The system has a 3.0 GHz, quad-core out-of-order processor based on x86 ISA. The cache hierarchy is configured with 32 KB, 4-way set-associative L1 instruction/data caches and 4 MB, 16-way set-associative L2 shared caches. We implement the shared L2 hybrid cache with a bank contention model. The L2 cache is a 16-way set associative cache consisting of 4 ways of SRAM and 12 ways of STT-RAM with asymmetric read/write latency. The off-chip DRAM is configured as a DDR3-1333 in which CL, tRCD, tRP timings are 10, 10, and 10, respectively.

The parameters of the hybrid cache model are calculated using NVSim [4] and CACTI 6.0 [10] under 45 nm technology. A tag of 16-way 4 MB SRAM is borrowed for hybrid caches. 4-way 1 MB SRAM and 4-way 1 MB STT-RAM is configured for the data array. By combining one SRAM bank and three banks of STT-RAM, 16-way 4-bank data array is designed for the hybrid cache. Table 2 lists the energy consumption of the L2 cache.

Table 1. System configuration

Parameters	Configuration
Processor	3.0 GHz, 4-core CMP, 4-wide, out-of-order, 128-entry ROB, 48-entry
L1 Caches	I-cache: 32 kB, 64B lines, 4-way, 2-cycle latency
	D-cache: 32 kB, 64B lines, 4-way, 2-cycle latency
L2 Cache	Unified, 4 MB, 64B lines, 16-way (4-way SRAM and 12-way STT-RAM), 10 cycle latency for SRAM, 10 cycle (read) and 38 cycle (write) latency for STT-RAM
DRAM	DDR3-1333 (10-10-10), 1 channel, 8 banks, 32-entry queue, open-page policy, FR-FCFS policy

4.2 Workloads

We use SPEC 2006 [5] with reference input as workloads for the evaluation. For more precise analysis, the simulation method is changed from the work in [6] where 10 billion instructions were fast-forwarded per core to skip the initialization phase of code and multi-core workloads were mixed with high and low-MPKI

Table 2. Energy Consumption of the L2 Cache

	Read Energy	Write Energy	Static Power
SRAM Region	0.217 nJ	0.217 nJ	14.682 mW
STT-RAM Region	0.097 nJ	0.670 nJ	3.438 mW

applications. In the simulation of this chapter, we annotate a synchronization point in the program source code after some initialization code part. As a result, a multi-core simulation always starts at the same points of benchmarks in the MARSSx86 simulator. Because of this modification, the simulation region of a benchmark can be different from that in [6].

Workloads have also been selected differently; in this chapter, cache sensitivity of benchmarks is considered. We analyze the cache sensitivity of benchmarks by simulating benchmarks on a 16-way 4 MB L2 cache and on a 2-way 512 kB L2 cache. If the number of L2 misses per kilo instructions (MPKI) of a benchmark on the 16-way 4 MB L2 cache is greater by more than 10 % compared to that on the 2-way 512 kB L2 cache, then we classify this benchmark as cache-sensitive. Otherwise, we classify it as cache-insensitive. The benchmarks are listed in Table 3.

Table 3. Benchmark analysis of SPEC CPU2006

	L2 MPKI		-Diff (%)	Type
Benchmark	512 kB	4 MB		
quantum	24.7	24.7	0.0	Insensitive
milc	24.3	24.3	0.1	
sjeng	56.2	56.1	0.1	
gobmk	11.9	11.6	3.0	
lbm	35.2	33.5	4.8	
namd	0.8	0.8	7.0	
soplex	31.9	27.2	14.9	Sensitive
mcf	78.8	66.3	15.9	
h264	0.3	0.1	65.6	
gromacs	2.1	0.5	73.3	
hmm	2.5	0.5	78.7	
deal2	0.3	0.1	80.3	
perl	0.5	0.1	80.8	
astar	15.8	2.3	85.5	
povray	1.2	0.2	85.8	
gcc	1.6	0.2	87.5	
bzip	4.7	0.1	97.4	
omnetpp	102.3	2.6	97.5	

Now we randomly assemble 20 quad-core workloads considering cache sensitivity. Workloads are categorized into five groups, four workloads in each group. For each quad-core workload, we mix four benchmarks. There is no cache-insensitive benchmark in the workloads in group1, one in each workload in group2, two in group3, three in group4, and group5 has only cache-insensitive benchmarks. Workloads are listed in Table 4.

After 5 million cycles cache warm up, 2 billion instructions are simulated for multi-programmed workloads on quad-core processors. For the partitioning technique, we use a 5 million cycle period for monitoring and partitioning decisions as was done in [12]. We use a 2 % probability value for an allocation switching technique which is obtained empirically (the performance is not sensitive to the value around 2 %).

Table 4. Workloads from SPEC CPU2006

	Set	Workloads			
group1	1	soplex	perl	gcc	omnetpp
	2	soplex	povray	bzip	hmm
	3	gcc	h264	hmm	soplex
	4	perl	povray	h264	hmm
group2	5	bzip	omnetpp	hmm	quantum
	6	omnetpp	gromacs	soplex	gobmk
	7	soplex	mcf	gromacs	quantum
	8	milc	monetpp	h264	deal2
group3	9	omnetpp	quantum	soplex	sjeng
	10	omnetpp	h264	namd	quantum
	11	sjeng	milc	deal2	bzip
	12	quantum	sjeng	gromacs	bzip
group4	13	milc	omnetpp	sjeng	quantum
	14	omnetpp	quantum	sjeng	gobmk
	15	quantum	milc	lbm	omnetpp
	16	soplex	quantum	milc	gobmk
group5	17	milc	namd	gobmk	lbm
	18	lbm	milc	sjeng	gobmk
	19	quantum	sjeng	gobmk	milc
	20	sjeng	quantum	gobmk	lbm

5   Results

This section discusses the results of simulation. We compared our techniques with and without the allocation switching technique to the state-of-the-art migration-based hybrid cache management technique, called read-write aware hybrid cache architecture (RWHCA) [17].

5.1   Performance

A weighted speedup is used as a performance metric, which is the sum of per-application speedups in IPC compared to the baseline (RWHCA running a single application is used as the baseline). Figure 4 shows the weighted speedups normalized to those of RWHCA (the weighted speedups of RWHCA are also obtained by using the same baseline). The left bar in each workload set represents the speedup of the proposed approach without the switching technique and the right bar represents that with the switching technique.

In the hybrid caches partitioning technique without switching, the performance improvement is 4.9 % in geometric mean over the total of 20 workloads. For the workloads in group3, where two cache-sensitive and two cache-insensitive benchmarks are mixed, the performance improvement is 8.7 % on average; the useless preemption of cache ways by cache-insensitive benchmarks can degrade the performance of the cache-sensitive applications, and thus the partitioning technique can be very effective in this group. In the case of group5 where four cache-insensitive benchmarks are mixed, the partitioning scheme can improve cache utilization by assigning an optimal number of ways to each application, but the improvement is not as significant as group3.

The hybrid caches partitioning technique with allocation switching improves the performance by 6.7 % in geometric mean over the total of 20 workloads. Some workloads show drastic performance improvement such as set1 and set10. These improvements come from some benchmarks that have little store access. So the SRAM is underutilized in these workloads. If both SRAM and STT-RAM caches are fully utilized, then an allocation switching scheme can harm the performance improvement of cache partitioning as shown in set5, but its degradation is not significant.

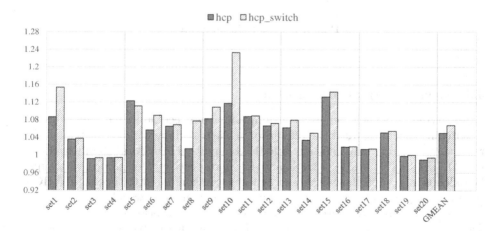

Fig. 4. Normalized weighted speedup.

5.2   Miss Rates

Figure 5 reports the difference in L2 miss rates between the RWHCA and our techniques with and without allocation switching. Left bars are the results of the proposed technique without allocation switching, and right bars are the results with switching. The former case reduces the miss rate by 4.8 % on average for the 20 workloads. The miss rate increases for set3, but the difference is ignorable. Among the five groups, group3 shows the highest reduction of miss rates (9.2 % on average), which is similar to the trend of performance.

In the technique with switching, the miss rate reduction is 6.7 % on average compared to the reference technique, which is 1.8 % more reduction compared to the technique without switching. The miss rate is reduced by 13.3 % for group2 compared to the reference technique.

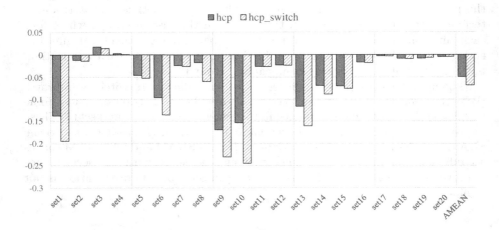

Fig. 5. Difference in miss rates.

5.3   Cache Energy Consumption

Figure 6 compares the L2 energy consumption of our techniques with and without a switching scheme against the reference. In the technique without switching, the reduction of energy consumption is 10.0 % on average for a total 20 of workloads and 11.7 %, 10.4 %, 11.0 %, 12.0 %, and 4.4 %, respectively, for group1 to group5. Workloads in group5 show little energy reduction compared to those of RWHCA because the partitioning technique is not efficient in these workloads.

The technique with switching reduces energy consumption by 16.6 % on average over the total of 20 workloads, which corresponds to 6.6 % more reduction compared to the technique without switching. All groups except group5 show more reduction of energy consumption. Compared to the reference technique, energy reductions by groups are 12.1 %, 22.3 %, 22.9 %, 20.7 %, and 3.2 %.

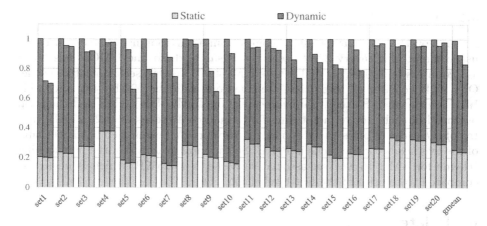

Fig. 6. Energy consumption of RWHCA (left), our architecture without allocation switching (middle), and our architecture with allocation switching (right).

5.4 DRAM Energy Consumption

Figure 7 shows the DRAM energy consumption during the simulation. The results of our techniques with and without the switching scheme are normalized to that of RWHCA. In the technique without switching, the decrease of energy consumption is 5.9 % on average for the 20 workloads. Group3 shows the highest energy saving of 9.6 % on average and group5 shows the lowest of 3.4 %.

The technique with allocation switching decreases DRAM energy consumption by 7.5 % on average over the 20 workloads, which corresponds to 1.6 % more reduction compared to the technique without the switching scheme.

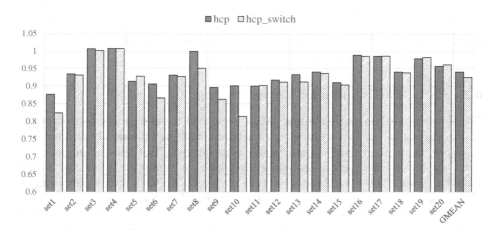

Fig. 7. Normalized energy consumption of DRAM.

5.5   Area Overhead

An area overhead of our technique comes from a partitioning scheme. For cache usage monitoring, every 32nd cache set is sampled, so one UMON has 16 of 4 B counters and an ATD of 128 sets for a 4 MB 16-way set-associative cache. One ATD consists of 16 entries, each has one valid bit, 24-bit tag and 4-bit LRU information. So the total overhead of one UMON is 7.3 KB and the total overhead of cache usage monitoring for a quad-core processor is 29.25 KB. In a tag of the cache, 2-bit is added to identify the core that owns each block, the sum of the overheads for the cache is 16 KB. So the total overhead of the partitioning scheme for 4 MB 16-way set-associative cache is 45.25 KB, which is negligible compared to the size of the last-level cache.

6   Related Work

6.1   Reducing Write Overhead of STT-RAM

A write intensity predictor [1] is proposed to find a write intensive block and allocate the block to SRAM. This approach achieves high energy reduction of hybrid caches, but does not consider cache partitioning, and thus it may increase miss rates of the cache in some workloads, worsening the DRAM energy efficiency. Obstruction-aware cache management technique (OAP) [16] increases the efficiency of a last-level STT-RAM cache by bypassing some application that has no merits of using the last-level cache. The technique collects information on latency, number of accesses, and miss rates of the applications in a period and exploits the data for the detection of bypassing applications. But the target of this technique is a pure STT-RAM cache, so it can not be applied directly to hybrid caches.

A lot of researches [3,8,9,14,17,18] utilize a migration technique for adapting block placements, but in our proposed partitioning technique, a conventional migration scheme [17] can reduce the energy efficiency of hybrid caches by breaking the partitioning decision.

6.2   Cache Partitioning for Energy Saving

Cooperative partitioning technique [15] is proposed to save energy consumption of a shared cache. In this technique, a partition is aligned physically and unused ways are disabled to reduce static power consumption. But this technique does not consider hybrid caches, and thus the block placement problem should be solved to apply this technique to hybrid caches. Writeback-aware partitioning [19] assumes an off-chip memory of phase change RAM (PRAM) and reduces the number of write operations in PRAM by dynamic partitioning of a shared cache to decrease the energy consumption of the write-inefficient memory.

7   Conclusion

We address the potential of the dynamic cache partitioning technique for reducing energy consumption of hybrid caches. We propose an energy-efficient partitioning technique for hybrid caches in which the number of blocks installed by a core is adaptively balanced between SRAM and STT-RAM while satisfying a partitioning decision. If a miss is caused by a store miss in the upper-level cache, the corresponding block is placed in SRAM. If the miss is originated from a load miss in the upper-level cache, a new block can be placed in either SRAM or STT-RAM according to the number of blocks installed by the core in SRAM. In addition, we apply the allocation switching technique to avoid too much unbalanced use of SRAM or STT-RAM. The simulation results show that our partitioning technique improves the performance of the multi-core system by 6.7 % on average, saves the energy consumption of the hybrid cache by 16.6 %, and reduces the DRAM energy by 7.5 % compared to the state-of-the-art migration-based hybrid cache management technique.

Acknowledgment. This work was supported by the National Research Foundation of Korea (NRF) grants funded by the Korean government (MEST) (No. 2012R1A2A2A06047297).

References

1. Ahn, J., Yoo, S., Choi, K.: Write intensity prediction for energy-efficient nonvolatile caches. In: Proceedings of the 2013 International Symposium on Low Power Electronics and Design, ISLPED 2013, pp. 223–228. IEEE Press, Piscataway (2013)
2. Apalkov, D., Khvalkovskiy, A., Watts, S., Nikitin, V., Tang, X., Lottis, D., Moon, K., Luo, X., Chen, E., Ong, A., Driskill-Smith, A., Krounbi, M.: Spin-transfer torque magnetic random access memory (stt-mram). J. Emerg. Technol. Comput. Syst. **9**(2), 13:1–13:35 (2013)
3. Chen, Y.T., Cong, J., Huang, H., Liu, C., Prabhakar, R., Reinman, G.: Static and dynamic co-optimizations for blocks mapping in hybrid caches. In: Proceedings of the 2012 ACM/IEEE International Symposium on Low Power Electronics and Design, ISLPED 2012, pp. 237–242. ACM, New York (2012)
4. Dong, X., Xu, C., Xie, Y., Jouppi, N.: Nvsim: a circuit-level performance, energy, and area model for emerging nonvolatile memory. IEEE Trans. Comput. Aided Des. Integr. Circuits Syst. **31**(7), 994–1007 (2012)
5. Henning, J.L.: Spec cpu2006 benchmark descriptions. SIGARCH Comput. Archit. News **34**(4), 1–17 (2006)
6. Lee, D., Choi, K.: Energy-efficient partitioning of hybrid caches in multi-core architecture. In: 2014 22nd International Conference on Very Large Scale Integration (VLSI-SoC), pp. 37–42, October 2014
7. Li, J., Xue, C., Xu, Y.: STT-RAM based energy-efficiency hybrid cache for cmps. In: 2011 IEEE/IFIP 19th International Conference on VLSI and System-on-Chip (VLSI-SoC), pp. 31–36, October 2011

8. Li, Q., Li, J., Shi, L., Xue, C.J., He, Y.: Mac: Migration-aware compilation for stt-ram based hybrid cache in embedded systems. In: Proceedings of the 2012 ACM/IEEE International Symposium on Low Power Electronics and Design, ISLPED 2012, pp. 351–356. ACM, New York (2012)
9. Li, Y., Chen, Y., Jones, A.K.: A software approach for combating asymmetries of non-volatile memories. In: Proceedings of the 2012 ACM/IEEE International Symposium on Low Power Electronics and Design, pp. 191–196. ISLPED 2012. ACM, New York (2012)
10. Muralimanohar, N., Balasubramonian, R., Jouppi, N.P.: Cacti 6.0: A tool to model large caches. HP Laboratories (2009)
11. Patel, A., Afram, F., Chen, S., Ghose, K.: Marss: A full system simulator for multicore x86 cpus. In: 2011 48th ACM/EDAC/IEEE Design Automation Conference (DAC), pp. 1050–1055, June 2011
12. Qureshi, M., Patt, Y.: Utility-based cache partitioning: A low-overhead, high-performance, runtime mechanism to partition shared caches. In: 2006 MICRO-39. 39th Annual IEEE/ACM International Symposium on Microarchitecture, pp. 423–432, December 2006
13. Rosenfeld, P., Cooper-Balis, E., Jacob, B.: Dramsim2: a cycle accurate memory system simulator. Comput. Archit. Lett. **10**(1), 16–19 (2011)
14. Sun, G., Dong, X., Xie, Y., Li, J., Chen, Y.: A novel architecture of the 3D stacked mram l2 cache for cmps. In: 2009 HPCA 2009 IEEE 15th International Symposium on High Performance Computer Architecture, pp. 239–249, February 2009
15. Sundararajan, K., Porpodas, V., Jones, T., Topham, N., Franke, B.: Cooperative partitioning: energy-efficient cache partitioning for high-performance cmps. In: 2012 IEEE 18th International Symposium on High Performance Computer Architecture (HPCA), pp. 1–12, February 2012
16. Wang, J., Dong, X., Xie, Y.: Oap: An obstruction-aware cache management policy for stt-ram last-level caches. In: 2013 Design, Automation Test in Europe Conference Exhibition (DATE), pp. 847–852, March 2013
17. Wu, X., Li, J., Zhang, L., Speight, E., Xie, Y.: Power and performance of read-write aware hybrid caches with non-volatile memories. In: 2009 DATE 2009 Design, Automation Test in Europe Conference Exhibition, pp. 737–742, April 2009
18. Wu, X., Li, J., Zhang, L., Speight, E., Rajamony, R., Xie, Y.: Hybrid cache architecture with disparate memory technologies. In: Proceedings of the 36th Annual International Symposium on Computer Architecture, ISCA 2009, pp. 34–45. ACM, New York (2009)
19. Zhou, M., Du, Y., Childers, B., Melhem, R., Mossé, D.: Writeback-aware partitioning and replacement for last-level caches in phase change main memory systems. ACM Trans. Archit. Code Optim. **8**(4), 53:1–53:21 (2012)

Interval Arithmetic and Self Similarity Based Subthreshold Leakage Optimization in RTL Datapaths

Shilpa Pendyala and Srinivas Katkoori$^{(\boxtimes)}$

Department of Computer Science and Engineering,
University of South Florida, 4202 East Fowler Avenue, ENB 118,
Tampa, FL 33620, USA
{spendya2,katkoori}@mail.usf.edu

Abstract. We propose top-down and bottom-up interval propagation techniques for identifying low leakage input vectors at primary inputs of an RTL datapath. Empirically, we observed self-similarity in the leakage distribution of adder/multiplier modules i.e., leakage distribution at the sub-space level is similar to that at the entire input space. We exploit this property to quickly search low leakage vectors. The proposed module library leakage characterization is scalable and is demonstrated on adders/multipliers. Given an RTL datapath, interval propagation is carried out with the low leakage intervals of the module instances with primary inputs. The reduced interval set is further processed with simulated annealing, to arrive at the best low leakage vector set at the primary inputs. Experimental results for various DSP filters simulated in 16 nm CMOS technology with top-down and bottom-up approaches yield leakage savings of 93.6 % and 89.2 % respectively with no area, timing, or control overheads.

Keywords: Sub-threshold leakage optimization · Minimum leakage input vector · Interval arithmetic · Self similarity · RTL datapath optimization

1 Introduction and Motivation

Excessive subthreshold leakage power consumption is a serious concern in deep-submicron technology nodes [1]. Input vector control technique is widely used for subthreshold leakage optimization due to its low latency overhead. However, determination of *minimum leakage vector* (MLV) for large circuits is a difficult problem by itself as it requires excessive simulation time [2]. An MLV is an input vector that puts the circuit in lowest leakage state possible i.e., it is an *optimal* vector. We refer to sub-optimal MLVs as *low leakage vectors* (LLVs) that put the circuit with leakage *close* to the optimal leakage.

For a given datapath, applying MLV to each RTL module incurs significant area and control overhead. The additional area stems from input multiplexers

© IFIP International Federation for Information Processing 2015
L. Claesen et al. (Eds.): VLSI-SoC 2014, IFIP AICT 464, pp. 75–94, 2015.
DOI: 10.1007/978-3-319-25279-7_5

needed to apply the minimum leakage vector. Control overhead is incurred from the select lines of these multiplexers. As data values propagate through RTL modules, we have proposed [3] to identify a set of input vectors such that they not only put the module instances at primary inputs (PIs) into low leakage, but also result in low leakage input vectors at internal module instances. In [4] (conference version of this chapter), we leverage self-similarity of module-level leakage distributions. In this book chapter, we further extend the idea by experimenting with bottom up interval propagation. We experimented with five DSP filters and obtained average leakage savings of 93 % with top down approach and 89.2 % with bottom up approach. In both cases, we did not require any internal control points for any design, thus the proposed approaches incur no overhead in terms of area, control, or delay.

The overall optimization flow is as follows: First, we characterize the module library to gather low leakage vector intervals with two-phase Monte-Carlo simulation. Next, we propagate interval sets of module instances at primary inputs through the datapath. We have two choices: top-down or bottom-up. In top-down interval sets at PIs are propagated to primary outputs (POs) and in case of bottom-up, interval sets at POs are propagated back to PIs. The interval propagation yields a reduced set of low leakage intervals at the PIs. A simulated annealing algorithm is devised to find the best input vector set from the reduced interval set. Next, we briefly describe the self-similarity based scalable module leakage characterization for bit-sliced adder/multipliers.

As the search space grows exponentially with the module bit-width, finding low leakage vectors by exhaustive simulation is infeasible. In order to make the problem tractable, we exploit the self-similarity property of leakage distribution of a given functional unit. Briefly, given a stochastic distribution, it is said to be self-similar [5,6], if any arbitrary sub-distribution (built by choosing contiguous samples) is similar to the original distribution. Hurst parameter is a commonly used metric to determine self-similarity of a distribution. For two module types, adder and multiplier, we empirically observe that their leakage distributions are self-similar. Given a confidence level (α) and an error tolerance (β), Halter and Najm [7] derived a formula to determine the minimum number of random vectors needed to find a LLV that is no worse than β % of vectors with α % confidence, provided the leakage distribution is normal. While the goal of any MLV heuristic is to find one vector, our goal is to find as many LLVs as possible so that we can expand them into LLV data intervals. For adder and multiplier, we also empirically observe that their leakage distributions are normal. This normal leakage distribution along with self-similarity of a module enables us to partition the input space into small sub-spaces and then randomly sample each subspace with fixed number of vectors.

The chapter organization as follows: Section 2 presents background, related work, and terminology. Section 3 describes the module library characterization. Section 4 presents the proposed top-down and bottom-up interval propagation approaches followed by simulated annealing. Section 5 reports experimental results. Finally, Section 6 draws conclusions.

2   Background, Related Work, and Terminology

We first review input vector control techniques from the literature. We then provide a brief overview of fractal theory and self-similarity. Lastly, we present an overview of interval arithmetic.

2.1   Input Vector Control Techniques

As the leakage depends only on the current input vector, during the idle mode, we can apply the minimum leakage vector (MLV). Thus, MLV needs to be determined *a priori* and incorporated into the circuit. This technique is known as the Input Vector Control (IVC). For an n-input module, as the input space grows exponentially (2^n), MLV determination heuristics have been proposed [2,8]. For an IVC technique, the area penalty occurs due to additional hardware needed to incorporate MLV into the circuit. Delay penalty is incurred if this additional hardware is in the critical path of the circuit.

To the best of our knowledge, all the proposed IVC techniques are at the logic level. Abdollahi, Fallah, and Pedram [2] propose gate-level leakage reduction with two techniques. The first technique is an input vector control wherein SAT based formulation is employed to find the minimum leakage vector. The second technique involves adding nMOS and pMOS transistors to the gate in order to increase the controllability of the internal signals. The additional transistors increase the stacking effect leading to leakage current reduction. The authors report over 70 % leakage reduction with up to 15 % delay penalty. Gao and Hayes [9] present integer linear programming (ILP) and mixed integer linear programming (MILP) approaches, wherein MILP performs better than ILP and is thirteen times faster. Average leakage current is about 25 % larger than minimum leakage current. IVC technique does not work effectively for circuits with large logic depth. Yuan and Qu [8] have proposed a technique to replace the gates of worst leakage state with other gates in active mode. A divide-and-conquer approach is presented that integrates gate replacement, an optimal MLV searching algorithm for tree circuits, and a genetic algorithm to connect the tree circuits. Compared with the leakage achieved by optimal MLV in small circuits, the gate replacement heuristic and the divide-and-conquer approach can reduce on average 13 % and 17 % leakage, respectively.

2.2   Fractals and Self Similarity

Fractals are shapes made of parts similar to the whole [5]. Property of scaling is exhibited by fractals, which means the degree of irregularity in them tends to be identical at all scales [5,6]. Many examples of fractal behaviors are observed in nature. Figure 1 shows a romanesco broccoli in which we can observe the self similar property of its shape. In VLSI structures, H-tree based clock signal network, employed for zero-skew, exhibits fractal behavior (Fig. 2).

The main classifications of fractals are time or space, self-similar or self-affine, and deterministic or stochastic. Space fractals are structures exhibiting the fractal property in the space domain. While time fractals are those exhibiting in time domain. Self-similar fractals have symmetry over entire scale, which is identical to recursion, i.e., a pattern inside another pattern. The details spread across finer and finer scales with certain constant measurements. Hurst parameter ($0 < H < 1$), is a measure of the correlation or long range dependence in the data which leads to the fractal behavior of the data set [10]. A random process has H value equal to 0.5. If H is less than 0.5 then the process exhibits anti-persistence. If H value is between 0.5 and 1, then the process has long term persistence [5]. A stochastic process can be said to exhibit fractal behavior [11] if the H value is between 0.5 and 1. Methods to estimate Hurst parameter are described in [10]. In this work, we employed the R/S plot method.

Fig. 1. Romanesco broccoli - an example of self-similar behavior occurring in nature. Photo credit [12].

Self similarity has been leveraged in estimation and optimization problems in diverse fields. We give three examples. Premarathne *et al.* [14] employ self-similarity to detect anamalous events in network traffic by showing that traffic's self-similarity property is temporarily disturbed in the event of an attack. Radjassamy and Carothers [10] proposed a vector compaction technique to generate a compact vector set representative of original vector set such that it mimics power-determining behavior of the latter. Such vector compaction can speed up power estimation of circuits. Qian and Rasheed [15] proposed Hurst parameter based financial market analysis wherein series with high H are predicted more accurately than those with H close to 0.5. For more examples, interested reader is referred to [16].

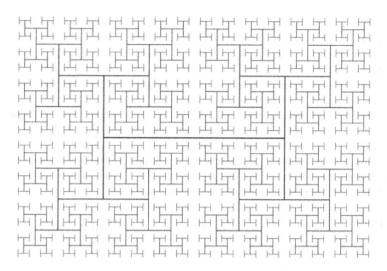

Fig. 2. H tree - an example of a VLSI structure exhibiting self-similar behavior. Photo credit [13].

2.3 Interval Arithmetic

Interval arithmetic (IA) [17] is concerned with arithmetic operations such as addition and subtraction on intervals. The intervals can be either discrete or continuous. IA has been extensively applied in error bound analysis arising in numerical analysis.

In this work, we are concerned with integer arithmetic therefore we restrict our discussion to integer intervals. An interval $I = [a, b]$ represents all integers $a \leq i \leq b$. Further, the above interval is a *closed* interval as it includes both extremal values. We can have an *open* interval, such as $I = (a, b)$ where $a < i < b$. The *width* of an interval is the difference between the extremal values $|b - a|$. If the interval width is zero, then the interval is referred to as a *degenerate* interval (for example $[1, 1]$). We can represent a given integer, say a, as a degenerate interval $[a, a]$.

Given two intervals $U = [a, b]$ and $V = [c, d]$, the following equations hold:

$$U + V = [a + c, b + d] \tag{1}$$

$$U - V = [a - d, b - c] \tag{2}$$

$$U * V = [min(a * c, a * d, b * c, b * d), max(a * c, a * d, b * c, b * d)] \tag{3}$$

$$U \div V = [min(a \div c, a \div d, b \div c, b \div d), max(a \div c, a \div d, b \div c, b \div d)] \tag{4}$$

2.4 Notation and Problem Formulation

- A DFG, $G(V, E)$, is a directed graph such that $v_i \in V$ represents an operation and $e = (v_i, v_j) \in E$ represents a data transfer from operation v_i to v_j.

- A low leakage interval set, $\mathcal{L}(t, w)$, is the set of all low leakage intervals of a given module of type t and w.
- A low leakage output interval set, $\mathcal{LO}(t, w)$, is the set of corresponding outputs of all low leakage input intervals of a given module of type t and w.
- $\mathcal{P}(V, t, w)$ is the leakage power function which calculates the total leakage of the filter.
- *Problem Formulation:* Given the following inputs: (1) a data flow graph $G(V, E)$; (2) set of low leakage interval sets, $\bigcup_{t,w} \mathcal{L}(t, w)$, and (3) $\bigcup_{t,w} \mathcal{LO}(t, w)$, for all distinct operations of type t and width w, we need to identify best low leakage vector on primary inputs and a set of control points $\mathcal{C}$ such that the objective functions, $\sum_{v_i \in V} \mathcal{P}(V, \mathcal{T}(v_i), \mathcal{W}(v_i))$ and $\mathcal{C}$, are minimized, where $\mathcal{C}$ is the set of control points.

3   Self Similarity Based Monte Carlo Characterization for Low Leakage Intervals

In this Section, we first study the leakage profiles of adder and multiplier modules. Then we introduce a Monte Carlo leakage characterization technique based on self-similarity to extract low leakage interval set of a functional unit.

3.1   Leakage Profile and Scope for Optimization

Figure 3 shows the leakage current distribution of an 8 bit ripple carry adder based on simulation with all possible (exhaustive) vectors and 1000 vectors. Similarly, Fig. 4 shows the leakage current distributions of an 8 bit parallel multiplier for exhaustive and 1000 vectors respectively. The data has been generated by Synopsys Nanosim simulations of the CMOS layouts in 16 nm technology node with PTM spice models [18–20]. Similar normal leakage distribution plots were obtained for 16 bit adder and 16 bit multiplier with 1000 random vectors as shown in Figs. 5 and 6 respectively. We observed that even with increased bit width, the leakage distribution is normal for both adder and multiplier. Several prior works in literature for eg., [21,22] report similar nomal power distributions. Based on this empirical evidence, we assume that the leakage distribution of adder and multiplier modules with any bit width is normal.

Consider the exhaustive simulation of 8 bit adder and multiplier. The leakage current ranges are [0.084 μA, 4.3 μA] and [1.4 μA, 56 μA] respectively. Thus, the approximate max-to-min leakage current ratio for 8b adder and 8b multiplier are 51 and 40 respectively. For 10 % tolerance (ε=0.1), the number of distinct LLVs for the adder is 119. Thus, the percentage of input space that puts the adder in a low-leakage state is $(119/(2^8 \times 2^8)) \times 100 = 0.18\,\%$. These vectors can be merged into 80 low leakage intervals. Similarly, for multiplier, number of low leakage vectors is 490 and the size of the interval set is 329. The percentage of input space that puts the multiplier in a low-leakage state for ε=0.1, is $(490/(2^8 \times 2^8)) \times 100 = 0.74\,\%$. Based on these numbers, we can see only a small percentage of input space can result in significant leakage reduction. Our next challenge is to locate all these low leakage intervals in the entire input space.

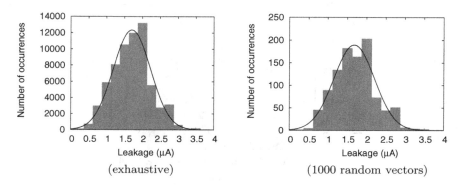

Fig. 3. Leakage current distribution for 8 bit adder.

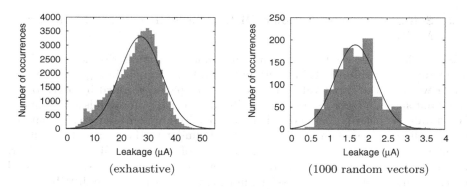

Fig. 4. Leakage current distribution for 8 bit parallel multiplier.

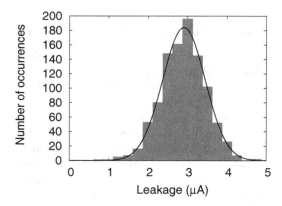

Fig. 5. Leakage current distribution for 16 bit adder (1000 random vectors).

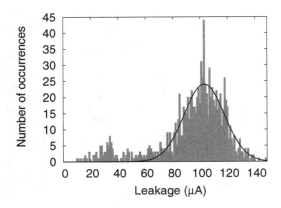

Fig. 6. Leakage current distribution for 16 bit parallel multiplier (1000 random vectors).

3.2 Self Similarity of Leakage Distributions in n Bit Adders and Multipliers

We empirically observed that the sub-threshold leakage distributions of adders and multipliers exhibit self similarity property. For example, in Fig. 7 for an 8 bit adder we show the Hurst values for various sub spaces obtained by partitioning the input space in three different ways. Recall that a distribution is self similar if Hurst value is between 0.5 and 1. For each partitioning scheme, we see that the leakage distribution of each sub space is self similar to the parent distribution. Similar results have been obtained in the case of 8 bit multiplier, 16 bit adder, and 16 bit multiplier. Due to limited space, we do not include these plots. Based on these empirical results, we assume in general that the leakage distribution of a n bit adder or multiplier is self-similar. The concept of self similarity enables us to develop a *scalable* methodology to identify low leakage intervals for a given module.

3.3 Monte Carlo Based Low Leakage Interval Search

We propose a two-stage Monte Carlo (MC) approach to deal with large input space. Typically, an MC based approach has four steps: (a) input space determination; (b) input sampling based on a probability distribution; (c) computation of property of interest; and (d) result aggregation.

Given a confidence level (α) and error tolerance (β) and assuming a normal leakage distribution, Halter and Najm [7] derived a formula (Eq. 5) to determine the minimum number of random vectors needed to guarantee with ($100 \times \alpha$) % confidence that the number of vectors with leakage lower than the lowest leakage found is ($100 \times \beta$) %. For example, if α=0.99 and β=0.01, then 460 random vectors are sufficient to give us 99 % confidence that only 1 % of vectors will have better leakage than the observed.

$$n = \log_e(1 - \alpha)/\log_e(1 - \beta) \tag{5}$$

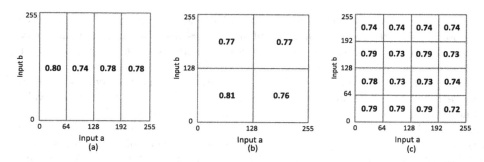

Fig. 7. Eight bit adder - Measured H values of leakage distributions at sub-space level with: (a) vertical partitioning into 4 sub-spaces; (b) horizontal and vertical partitioning into four sub-spaces; and (c) sixteen sub-spaces. Note that in each partition H value satisfies the self-similarity condition ($0.5 < H < 1$).

In Sects. 3.1 and 3.2 we empirically observed that the leakage distributions of n bit adders/multipliers are normal and self-similar. Consequently, we can now partition a module instance's input space into sub-spaces and then sample each sub-space with a fixed number of vectors as determined by Eq. 5 for user specified confidence and error tolerance levels.

Given the SPICE-level model of an n bit module instance, we perform two successive MC runs. The property of interest is the leakage power.

Stage I - Coarse grained MC run: The input space under consideration is the entire space, i.e., 2^{2n} input vectors, which is partitioned into equal sized sub-spaces (as illustrated in Fig. 7). Let us assume $\alpha=0.99$ and $\beta=0.01$. Then, we uniformly sample each sub-space to identify 460 random vectors and then simulate with the vectors. For result aggregation in this stage, from each sub-space, we collect 5 % of the vectors that yield low leakage for further consideration in Stage II.

Stage II - Fine grained MC run: From the leakage profiles of the functional units, we also observed that low leakage values are clustered. Hence, the sampling in this stage is biased in the neighborhood of low leakage vectors identified in previous stage. The result aggregation involves merging input vectors to create set of low leakage intervals.

Run Time Complexity. We would like to estimate the run time complexity of the characterization for a module of size n.

Stage I: The total run time of Stage I is $S \times K \times T(n)$, where S is the number of sub-spaces resulting from partitioning the entire input space, K is the minimum number of vectors required for user-given confidence (α) and error tolerance (β) levels, and $T(n)$ is the simulation time for one vector. Note that K is a constant for fixed α and β values. The user can keep the number of sub-spaces fixed i.e., S is a constant. $T(n)$ is proportional to the gate complexity. In case of ripple carry adder, $T(n) = O(n)$ as gate complexity grows linearly with bit width, while for parallel multiplier, $T(n) = O(n^2)$. Therefore, the complexity of Stage I is $O(n)$ and $O(n^2)$ for adder and multiplier respectively. If the user chooses to linearly scale the number of sub-spaces with the module complexity (i.e., $S = O(n)$), then the run time complexity increases to $O(n^2)$ and $O(n^3)$ for adder and multiplier respectively.

Stage II: We perform two steps: (1) local search around the vectors found in Stage I; and (2) then merge the low leakage vectors into low leakage intervals. The run-time complexity of first step is same as that of stage I, as we sample fixed number of vectors in the neighborhood of each vector from Stage I. The worst-case run time complexity of step 2 is same as that of a two-key sorting algorithm, $O(n\log n)$, since, we sort all input vectors and then merge immediate neighbors into intervals. Therefore, the complexity of Stage II in case of an adder is $O(n) + O(n\log n) = O(n\log n)$, while for multiplier it is $O(n^2) + O(n\log n) = O(n^2)$.

Since the two stages are performed sequentially, the overall runtime complexity of MC based leakage interval characterization procedure is $O(n\log n)$ and $O(n^2)$ for n bit adder and multiplier respectively.

4   Proposed Approach

For low leakage interval propagation, we propose two variants: *top down* and *bottom up* approaches. The motivation to propose the two variants is to compare the amount of leakage savings possible by starting at PIs and at POs.

- In top down approach, we carry out the propagation in two iterations. In first iteration, we start with a raw set of low leakage intervals at PIs and propagate them to the POs i.e., forward propagation. The raw low leakage intervals at PIs are obtained through characterization presented in detail in Sect. 3. In second iteration, these output intervals are propagated backwards reducing the input interval set at each intermediate node and thus ending up with a sparser set of low leakage intervals at PIs. This sparser interval set is further processed with simulated annealing to identify the best LLV.
- In bottom up approach, we start with raw set of low leakage output intervals at POs and propagate them all the way to the PIs where we end up with a minimized interval set. This minimized set is again processed with simulated annealing to arrive at the best LLV.

We present two motivating examples illustrating top down and bottom up approaches.

4.1   Motivating Examples

Example 1: Top Down Approach. In Fig. 8, we show an example DFG with two adders (A1, A2) and one multiplier (M1). Let us say the low leakage vector sets are: $\mathcal{L}(+, 8) = \{([2, 4], [6, 8]), ([8, 12], [8, 12]), ([14, 20], [14, 24])\}$ and $\mathcal{L}(*, 8) = \{([3, 4], [5, 6]), ([9, 10], [5, 6]), ([13, 24], [5, 6])\}$.

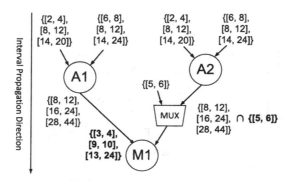

Fig. 8. Example 1: Top down approach - forward propagation of interval sets.

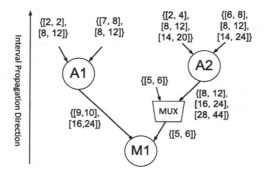

Fig. 9. Example 1: Top down approach - backward propagation of interval sets.

We start applying low leakage vector interval sets for A1 and A2 i.e., $\{[2, 4],$ $[8, 12], [14, 20]\}$ on the first input and $\{[6, 8], [8, 12], [14, 24]\}$ on the second input. Using Eq. (1) of interval arithmetic, we compute A1's and A2's output range to be $\{[8, 12], [16, 24], [28, 44]\}$. As we want to apply low leakage vector to M1, we need to reduce the interval sets generated by A1 and A2 to those identified as LLVs for M1. Thus, the interval set of M1 for input 1 is $\{[8, 12], [16, 24], [28, 44]\} \cap \{[3, 4], [9, 10], [13, 24]\} = \{[9, 10], [16, 24]\}$ and for input 2 is $\{[8, 12], [16, 24], [28, 44]\} \cap \{[5, 6]\} = \varnothing$. In Fig. 8, for sake of clarity, we show the intervals corresponding to multiplier in bold font, while those for adders in regular font. At the second input of M1 as we obtained an empty set, we will introduce a *control point* to put M1 in low leakage mode. The control point consists of a multiplexer that can be used to force a low leakage vector in idle state. Generally speaking, if the interval intersection results in an empty set, we will insert a control point and start with an entire low leakage vector set from that point.

To determine the LLV at PIs, a backward propagation of minimized interval sets is implemented. Figure 9 illustrates this step for this example. The intervals available at input 1 of M1 are fed as outputs to A1 and these intervals are

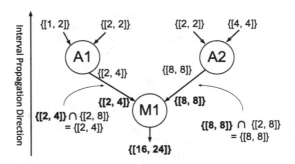

Fig. 10. Example 2: Bottom up approach - backward propagation of output intervals.

propagated to the inputs of A1. This gives a minimized interval set on which simulated annealing algorithm is applied to find the best LLV.

Example 2: Bottom Up Approach. Now consider the same DFG for bottom up approach, however with output low leakage vector sets: $\mathcal{L}(+, 8) = \{[2, 8]\}$ and $\mathcal{L}(*, 8) = \{[16, 24]\}$. For a given output low leakage set $\{[16, 24]\}$ to M1, the corresponding input leakage set is $\{([2, 4], [8, 8])\}$. Similarly, for an adder's output set $\{[2, 4]\}$, input sets are $\{([1, 2], [2, 2])\}$ and $\{[8, 8]\}$, the corresponding input sets are $\{([2, 2], [4, 4])\}$. We apply output low leakage vector interval sets on primary outputs (Fig. 10).

We start applying output low leakage vector set for M1 i.e., $\{[16, 24]\}$ at output. It propagates corresponding input vectors $\{[2, 4]\}$ to input 1 and $\{[8, 8]\}$ to input 2 and M1 is set to low leakage mode. The input intervals at M1 are intersected with $\mathcal{L}(+, 8)$ and $\mathcal{L}(*, 8)$. For the resulting output intervals $\{[2, 4]\}$ and $\{[8, 8]\}$ the corresponding input intervals of A1 and A2 are $\{([1, 2], [2, 2])\}$ and $\{([2, 2], [4, 4])\}$, respectively. The best LLV is found by processing the reduced set with simulated annealing algorithm described in Sect. 4.2.

4.2   Low Leakage Vector Determination

Figure 11 shows the pseudo-code of the proposed heuristic for low leakage vector determination. It accepts an input DFG (directed acyclic graph) and low leakage vector sets for distinct types and operations obtained from the characterization procedure as described in Sect. 3. Breadth First Search is used to cover all the nodes of the graph. Flag is used to determine the direction of propagation (top down or bottom up).

First, the graph is topologically sorted (line 5) to yield a sorted list L. A set $\mathcal{C}$ that collects the control points, is initialized (line 6). The for loop in lines 8–27 visits each node in the order specified by L. If a node is a PI node (i.e., both inputs to the node are primary), then the intervals on both inputs are intialized to the appropriate low leakage vector sets (line 13). Both inputs are added to the set $\mathcal{C}$ (line 14). On line 16, we call a function *Interval_Propagate()* that accepts an ordered interval pair and the operation type of the node (i.e., $\mathcal{T}(v_i)$).

1 **Algorithm** find_LLV
2 Inputs: (a) Graph G(V,E); (b) Low Leakage Vector Sets;
        (c) Flag $\in$ {TopDown, BottomUp}
3 Outputs: *output_llv* and Control Points
4 **begin**
5    $L \leftarrow$ Topological_Sort(G) /* L is a sorted list */
6    $C \leftarrow \emptyset$ /* internal control points */
7   **if**($Flag ==$ TopDown) **then**
8   **foreach** $v_i \in L$ **do**
9   Let a and b denote input edges of v_i
10   c the output edge of v_i
11   **if** v_i is a PI node
12   **then**
13         $I_{a,b} \leftarrow \mathcal{L}(\mathcal{T}(v_i), \mathcal{W}(v_i))$
14         $C \leftarrow C \cup \{a, b\}$
15   **end if**
16      $I_c \leftarrow Interval\_Propagate(I_{a,b}, \mathcal{T}(v_i))$
17   Let v_j be the successor of v_i
18   Let d be the second input of v_j
19   /* check for interval intersection */
20   *contains* $\leftarrow$ FALSE
21      $Interval\_Intersection(I_c, \mathcal{L}(\mathcal{T}(v_j), \mathcal{W}(v_j))$
22   **if**(**not** *contains*) **then**
23   /* insert a new control point */
24         $I_{c,d} \leftarrow \mathcal{L}(\mathcal{T}(v_j), \mathcal{W}(v_j))$
25         $C \leftarrow C \cup \{c, d\}$
26   **end if**
27   **end for**
28   reduced LLV set $\leftarrow Back\_Propagate$ ($\mathcal{LO}reduced(\mathcal{T}(v_j), \mathcal{W}(v_j))$)
29   **else**
30   reduced LLV set $\leftarrow Back\_Propagate$ ($\mathcal{LO}(\mathcal{T}(v_j), \mathcal{W}(v_j))$)
31   **end if**
32   *output_llv* $\leftarrow Simulated\_Annealing\_Leakage$ (reduced LLV set)
33 **end Algorithm**

Fig. 11. Algorithm to determine low leakage vector.

Interval_Propagate() implements the interval arithmetic equations as mentioned in Sect. 2.3 and returns an appropriate output interval I_c. In line 21, we invoke *Interval_Intersection()* that checks if the computed interval is contained in low leakage vector set of the successor v_j. If the check succeeds, then we move onto to the next node in the list. If the check fails, then a new control point is inserted by resetting the inputs of node v_j to its low leakage vector set (lines 22–26) and adding the inputs of v_j to control point set. On line 28, *Back_Propagate()* further reduces interval set at primary outputs, $\mathcal{LO}reduced(t, w)$, by performing similar propagation in backward direction to primary inputs as shown in Fig. 12. *Back_Propagate()* function (line 30) performs backward propagation on the complete low leakage output interval set, $\mathcal{LO}(t, w)$, to obtain reduced interval set

```
 1 Algorithm Back_Propagate
 2 Inputs: (a) Graph G(V,E); (b) Low Leakage Output Vector Set
 3 Outputs: reduced LLV set and Control Points
 4 begin
 5    foreach v_i ∈ L do
 6      Let a and b denote input edges of v_i
 7      c the output edge of v_i
 8       if v_i is a PO node
 9       then
10          I_c ← LO(T(v_i), W(v_i))
11          C ← C ∪ {c}
12       end if
13       I_{a,b} ← Interval_Propagate(I_c, T(v_i))
14       Let v_j be the predecessor of v_i
15       Let a be the output of v_j
16       /* check for interval intersection */
17       contains ← FALSE
18       Interval_Intersection(I_a, LO(T(v_j), W(v_j)))
19       if(not contains) then
20          /* insert a new control point */
21          I_a ← L(T(v_j), W(v_j))
22          C ← C ∪ {a}
23       end if
24    end for
25 end Algorithm
```

Fig. 12. Interval back propagation algorithm.

at primary inputs. The algorithm is similar to *find_LLV()*, therefore we do not elaborate in detail.

On line 32 of *find_LLV()*, we invoke *Simulated_Annealing_Leakage()* (Fig. 13) to find the best LLV from the reduced LLV set. The initial temperature value *Temp* is set to 100 and cooling coefficient γ to 0.99 on lines 5 and 6 respectively. The number of iterations at each temperature is equal to (500 x *Temp*) (line 11). An LLV is initially chosen at random (line 7) from the reduced interval set. In each iteration, a new LLV is chosen (line 12) from the neighborhood of the current LLV. The neighborhood window size is equal to the current temperature (*Temp*). *Est_Leakage()* function (line 26) calculates the leakage of the DFG for any given input vector. *output_llv* is the best LLV found by the algorithm.

In the *find_LLV()* algorithm, we assume only one successor for each node. This assumption is made to simplify the presentation of the algorithm. It is straightforward to extend the algorithm to multiple successors.

Run Time Complexity. In the first step of *find_LLV()*, topological sort has a time complexity of $O(|V| + |E|)$. The maximum number of edges in a DAG is $(|V|)(|V| - 1)/2$. Hence the time complexity of topological sort is $O(|V|^2)$. The for loop (lines 8–27) runs $|V|$ times. If the node is PI, initial interval set is initialized at the node. This initialization takes a constant time. We also have the

```
1 Algorithm Simulated_Annealing_Leakage
2 Inputs: (a) Reduced low leakage vector sets
3 Output: Best low leakage vector output_llv
4 begin
5    Temp ← 100
6    γ ← 0.99
7    best_llv ← random(reduced LLV set)
8    curr_llv ← best_llv
9    best_leak ← leakage(curr_llv)
10 while Temp > 0 do
11    foreach iteration in 1 to 500×Temp do
12       curr_llv ← curr_llv + random(reduced LLV set in Temp window)
13       curr_leak ← leakage(curr_llv)
14       if curr_leak <best_leak or random(0,1) ≤ e^{-(best_leak-curr_leak)/Temp}
15       then
16          if curr_leak <best_leak
17          then
18             output_llv ← curr_llv
19          end if
20          best_llv ← curr_llv
21          best_leak ← leakage(curr_llv)
22       end if
23    end for
24    Temp ← Temp × γ
25 end while
26 best_leak ← Est_Leakage(output_llv)
27 end Algorithm
```

Fig. 13. Simulated annealing algorithm to find the best LLV.

Interval_Propagate() and *Interval_Intersection()* which take time proportional to I^2, where I is the number of low leakage intervals. The number of intervals I is a constant obtained from characterization as described in Subsect. 3.3. *Back_Propagate()* function on lines 28 and 31 has the same complexity as that of the code on lines 8–27. Finally, simulated annealing algorithm takes a constant time based on the quality of solution desired. Hence, the run time complexity of the algorithm is $O(|V|^2)$.

5   Experimental Results

We report the experiment results obtained by applying the best LLV from top down and bottom up approaches on five datapath-intensive benchmarks, namely, IIR, FIR, Elliptic, Lattice, and Differential Equation Solver. Only functional unit sharing (resource optimization technique during high level synthesis) is assumed. As described in Sect. 3 the library is characterized *a priori* and the low leakage vectors sets saved. Top down and bottom up techniques process these low leakage vector sets to obtain a reduced set. The best LLV is further obtained by applying simulated annealing algorithm on the reduced set. The leakage power values are measured at the layout level using Synopsys Nanosim. We employ the Predictive Technology Models for 16 nm technology node generated by the online model generation tool available on the ASU PTM website [18]. The simulations were carried out on a SunOS workstation (16 CPUs, 96 GB RAM).

To obtain the experimental results, we initially vary the value of ε and determine the optimum (lowest) value for maximum leakage savings (i.e., leakage increase in any module up to ε % is tolerated). Figures 14 and 15 show the variation of leakage savings with tolerance in different designs for top down and bottom up approaches, respectively. From Fig. 14, it can be observed that the optimum tolerance value for top down approach is 10 % (i.e., leakage increase in any module up to 10 % is tolerated). The low leakage vector is captured within 10 % tolerance itself. Even if the tolerance is increased above 10 %, it is observed that leakage savings do not increase any further. From Fig. 15, the optimum tolerance value for bottom up approach is observed to be 15 %.

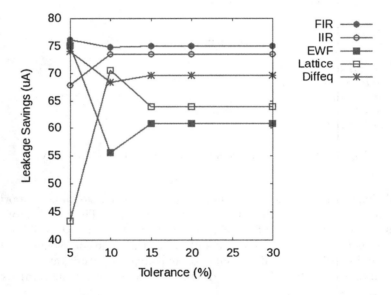

Fig. 14. Leakage vs. tolerance - top down approach.

Tables 1 and 2 report the results for top down and bottom up approaches respectively. Column 3 presents the leakage value obtained from interval propagation with simulated annealing. We can see a significant improvement compared to the random case in Column 2. Column 4 reports leakage savings. The top down approach achieved average leakage savings of 93.6 % for 10 % tolerance with no area overhead. On the other hand, bottom up approach achieved 89.2 % average leakage savings for 15 % tolerance with no area overhead.

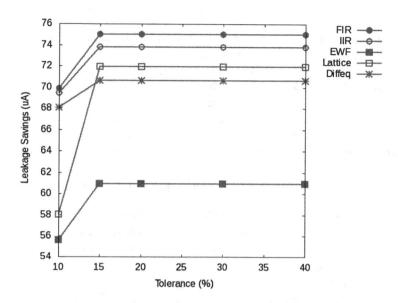

Fig. 15. Leakage vs. tolerance - bottom up approach.

Table 1. Power savings - top down approach.

Design	Leakage (μA)		Savings (%)
	Random	Top down	
Diffeq (2+, 5*)	197.9	16.42	91.70
EWF (26+, 8*)	654.0	64.13	90.19
FIR (4+, 5*)	220.9	9.95	95.50
IIR (4+, 5*)	266.8	11.94	95.50
Lattice (8+, 5*)	226.4	11.01	95.10

Table 2. Power savings - bottom up approach.

Design	Leakage (μA)		Savings (%)
	Random	Bottom up	
Diffeq (2+, 5*)	197.9	21.6	89.0
EWF (26+, 8*)	654.0	72.8	88.9
FIR (4+, 5*)	220.9	25.8	88.3
IIR (4+, 5*)	266.8	25.3	90.5
Lattice (8+, 5*)	226.4	23.9	89.4

Table 3. Speed up with interval propagation.

Design	Interval + SA		SA		Leakage improvement (%)	Speed up
	Leakage (μA)	Time (min)	Leakage (μA)	Time (min)		
Diffeq	20.60	12	18.75	170	+8.98	14x
EWF	55.24	13	71.62	812	−29.65	62x
FIR	16.50	2	16.30	247	+1.21	124x
IIR	16.55	18	14.46	244	+12.63	14x
Lattice	23.00	6	21.83	440	+5.09	73x

Table 4. Simulated Annealing (SA) Only vs. interval propagation + SA.

Design	Leakage with SA				Interval + SA	
	10 min (μA)	1h (μA)	2h (μA)	3h (μA)	Leakage (μA)	Time (min.)
Diffeq	32.08	27.65	25.24	22.20	20.60	12
EWF	99.12	83.50	87.18	85.95	55.24	13
FIR	34.74	31.80	33.10	26.06	16.50	2
IIR	45.53	27.56	29.90	28.16	16.55	18
Lattice	41.24	36.64	32.71	33.21	23.00	6

We conducted an experiment to compare the proposed interval arithimetic followed by pure SA based approach. Table 3 reports the simulation speed up obtained when we use simulated annealing on reduced set of intervals from top down propagation as opposed to pure simulated annealing. Columns 2 and 4 present the leakage values. Execution time is reported in columns 3 and 5 in Table 3. It shows that simulated annealing with top down propagation is much faster than simulated annealing alone to obtain a similar solution quality. The difference in solution quality is also presented in column 6 of Table 3. For EWF benchmark, a solution that is much better than pure simulated annealing solution is obtained with interval propagation and simulated annealing combined. For the rest of the benchmarks, the difference between solutions is small. Column 7 reports speed up resulting from IA with as much as 124X in case of FIR filter. The results of this experiment demonstrate that Interval Arithmetic greatly helps in finding a good low leakage vector quickly.

Table 4 compares the solution quality obtained by pure simulated annealing(SA) for 10 min, 1 h, 2 h, and 3 h with that by top down approach with simulated annealing (an average of 10 min). Columns 2–5 report the leakage obtained by pure SA. Column 6 reports the leakage obtained from top down approach. It is observed that the leakage found by interval propagation with SA in 10 min is better than the solution found by pure SA in 3 h. These results reiterate the efficacy of interval propagation based approach.

6 Conclusion

We have formulated the low leakage vector identification technique based on interval propagation and successfully demonstrated that significant subthreshold leakage savings can be obtained with no area overhead (i.e., no internal control points). We also proposed a self similarity based module characterization procedure that is scalable with module complexity. Both top down and bottom up approaches are equally effective (although in case of the benchmarks tested in this work, top down performs slightly better than bottom up approach).

References

1. SIA: International technology roadmap for semiconductors (itrs). http://www.itrs.net/(2010)
2. Abdollahi, A., Fallah, F., Pedram, M.: Leakage current reduction in CMOS VLSI circuits by input vector control. IEEE Trans. Very Large Scale Integr. (VLSI) Syst. **12**(2), 140–154 (2004)
3. Pendyala, S., Katkoori, S.: Interval arithmetic based input vector control for RTL subthreshold leakage minimization. In: 2012 IEEE/IFIP 20th International Conference on VLSI and System-on-Chip (VLSI-SoC), pp. 141–14, October 2012
4. Pendyala, S., Katkoori, S.: Self similarity and interval arithmetic based leakage optimization in RTL datapaths. In: 2014 22nd International Conference on Very Large Scale Integration (VLSI-SoC), pp. 1–6, October 2014
5. Mandelbrot, B.B.: Fractal Geometry of Nature. Freeman, New York (1983)
6. Barnsley, M.F.: Fractals Everywhere. Morgan Kaufmann, Orlando (2000)
7. Halter, J., Najm, F.: A gate-level leakage power reduction method for ultra-low-power CMOS circuits. In: Proceedings of the CICC, pp. 475–478 (1997)
8. Yuan, L., Qu, G.: A combined gate replacement and input vector control approach for leakage current reduction. IEEE Trans. Very Large Scale Integr. (VLSI) Syst. **14**(2), 173–182 (2006)
9. Gao, F., Hayes, J.: Exact and heuristic approaches to input vector control for leakage power reduction. IEEE Trans. Comput.-Aided Des. Integr. Circ. Syst. **25**(11), 2564–2571 (2006)
10. Radjassamy, R., Carothers, J.: Faster power estimation of CMOS designs using vector compaction - a fractal approach. IEEE Trans. Syst. Man Cybern. Part B: Cybern. **33**(3), 476–488 (2003)
11. Leland, W., Takku, M., Willinger, W., Wilson, D.: Statistical analysis and stochastic modeling of self-similar data traffic. In: Proceedings 14th International Teletraffic Congress, pp. 319–328 (1994)
12. Sullivan, J.: Wikimedia commons. http://commons.wikimedia.org/wiki/File%3AFractal_Broccoli.jpg
13. Eppstein, D.: Wikimedia commons. http://commons.wikimedia.org/wiki/File%3AH_tree.svg
14. Premarathne, U., Premaratne, U., Samarasinghe, K.: Network traffic self similarity measurements using classifier based hurst parameter estimation. In: 2010 5th International Conference on Information and Automation for Sustainability (ICIAFs), pp. 64–69 (2010)

15. Qian, B., Rasheed, K.: Hurst exponent and financial market predictability. In: Proceedings of the 2nd IASTED International Conference on Financial Engineering and Applications, Cambridge, MA, USA, pp. 203–209 (2004)
16. Falconer, K.: Fractal Geometry: Mathematical Foundations and Applications, 2nd edn. Wiley, New York (2003)
17. Moore, R.E.: Methods and applications of interval analysis. Siam, Philadelphia (1979)
18. Cao, Y.: Asu predictive technology model website. http://ptm.asu.edu
19. Zhao, W., Cao, Y.: New generation of predictive technology model for sub-45nm design exploration. In: 7th International Symposium on Quality Electronic Design, ISQED 2006, pp. 585–590, March 2006
20. Zhao, W., Cao, Y.: New generation of predictive technology model for sub-45 nm early design exploration. IEEE Trans. Electron Devices **53**(11), 2816–2823 (2006)
21. Evmorfopoulos, N., Stamoulis, G., Avaritsiotis, J.: A monte carlo approach for maximum power estimation based on extreme value theory. IEEE Trans. Comput. Aided Design Integr. Circuits Syst. **21**(4), 415–432 (2002)
22. Qiu, Q., Wu, Q., Pedram, M.: Maximum power estimation using the limiting distributions of extreme order statistics. In: Proceedings of the Design Automation Conference, pp. 684–689 (1998)

8T-SRAM Cell with Improved Read and Write Margins in 65 nm CMOS Technology

Farshad Moradi[⊠], Mohammad Tohidi, Behzad Zeinali,
and Jens K. Madsen

Integrated Circuits and Electronics Laboratory,
Department of Engineering, Aarhus University, Aarhus, Denmark
{moradi,m.tohidi,beze,jkm}@eng.au.dk

Abstract. SRAM operation at subthreshold/weak inversion region provides a significant power reduction for digital circuits. SRAM arrays which contribute to a large amount of power consumption for the processors in sub-100 nm technologies, however, cannot benefit from subthreshold operation. To this end, new SRAM technique on the circuit or architecture level is required. In this chapter, a novel 8T-SRAM cell is proposed which shows a significant improvement in write margin by at least 22 % in comparison to the standard 6T-SRAM cell at supply voltage of 1 V. Furthermore, read static noise margin of the proposed cell is improved by at least 2.2X compared to the standard 6T-SRAM cell. Although by the use of the proposed SRAM cell, the total leakage power is increased for superthreshold region, the proposed cell is able to work at supply voltages lower than 200 mV through which the total power consumption and the robustness of the cell are improved significantly. The proposed circuit is designed in 65 nm CMOS TSMC technology.

Keywords: SRAM · Subthreshold · Low-power · Write margin

1 Introduction

SRAM memories take up to 80 % of the total die area and up to 70 % of the total power consumption of high-performance processors [1]. Therefore, there is a crucial need for high-performance, low-leakage, and highly robust SRAMs. Unfortunately by scaling the CMOS technology, particularly under scaled supply voltages, both read and write stabilities are affected by the existing intra- and inter-die variations. Furthermore, due to the use of large number of small geometry transistors in a memory array, process variations have a significant impact—leading to possible read, write, and hold failures. Furthermore, in standard 6T SRAMs, the conflict between read and write stabilities is an inevitable design constraint that needs to be considered meaning that by improving the write margin, read margin is degraded and vice versa.

To improve the SRAM cell functionality, several solutions have been proposed from device to architecture level. For instance, the use of new devices such as FinFETs that leads to a significant performance improvement [2–5]. At the cell level, new cells such as 7T, 8T, 9T, 10T, and 11T [6–15] have been proposed with the focus on improving read static noise margin (RSNM) or write margin (WM). At the architecture

© IFIP International Federation for Information Processing 2015
L. Claesen et al. (Eds.): VLSI-SoC 2014, IFIP AICT 464, pp. 95–109, 2015.
DOI: 10.1007/978-3-319-25279-7_6

level, proposed read and write assist techniques in literature can improve SRAM robustness and performance while occupying less area compared to the cell techniques (e.g. 8T and 10T) and can be used with any type of SRAM [16, 17]. To understand the existing challenges in SRAM design let us explain the operation of standard 6T-SRAM cell.

The standard 6T-SRAM cell is shown in Fig. 1 that consists of two back-to-back inverters (includes two pull-up PMOS and two pull-down NMOS transistors) and two NMOS access transistors connected to the bitlines with the gates connected to the wordline. During read, wordline is asserted and the voltage difference between bitlines is sensed using a sense amplifier. The read cycle is done via access transistors and the pull-down transistors. Stronger pull-down transistors (PDL and PDR) and weaker access transistors improves RSNM. On the other side, stronger access transistors and weaker pull-up transistors improves WM. Through upsizing, the SRAM cell can operate at very low supply voltages (i.e. low VDD_{min}) with minimized threshold voltage variation with a penalty of increased area. However, continuously increasing process variations in sub-100 nm technologies has led to a pronounced degradation in stability of SRAM cells especially at lower voltages.

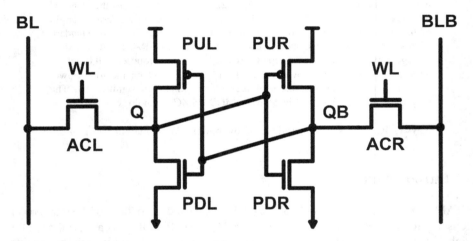

Fig. 1. 6T-SRAM cell using CMOS technology.

To overcome this issue, different cell techniques such as 8T-SRAM cell ameliorates the degraded robustness of the standard 6T-SRAM cell by separating read and write bitlines leading to a significant improvement in read static noise margin (RSNM) while the write margin is not affected. The standard 8T-SRAM cell is shown in Fig. 2. As it is seen, read and write cycles use different wordlines and bitlines. Noted, the standard 8T-SRAM cell uses a single-ended read scheme which reduces the swing of bitlines. The 8T-SRAM cell provides significantly improved RSNM (similar to the Hold Static Noise Margin (HSNM) of the standard 6T-SRAM cell) with similar access time, write time, and write margin. However, for the 8T-SRAM cell write assist techniques such as boosted wordline without affecting the read performance can be used.

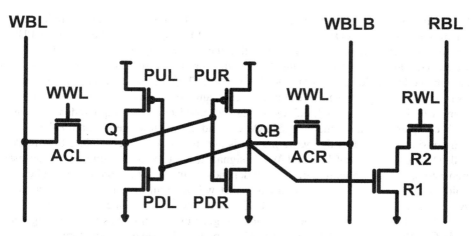

Fig. 2. Standard 8T-SRAM cell [13].

Therefore, proposing a new SRAM cell to improve both read and write margins under scaled supply voltages is crucial for ultra-low power applications with low penalty on area, access time, and leakage power consumption.

In this chapter, a novel 8T-SRAM cell is presented that improves both read and write operation margins. The proposed SRAM cell improves write and read noise margin by at least 22 % and 2.2X compared to the standard 6T-SRAM cell, respectively. Furthermore, this method reduces gate leakage while increases subthreshold leakage compared to the standard 6T-SRAM cell in 65 nm CMOS technology. In general, leakage power of the proposed cell increases by 67 % at $V_{DD} = 1$ V and 5.6 % at $V_{DD} = 300$ mV. The proposed design improves the leakage power by 3 % at $V_{DD} = 200$ mV. The threshold voltage of the transistors used in this paper is 300 mV.

The rest of this chapter is structured as follows: in Sect. 2, the new 8T-SRAM cell is presented and described in different modes of operation. In Sect. 3, the simulations results are presented and discussed. We conclude in Sect. 4.

2 The Proposed 8T-SRAM Cell

Figure 3 shows the proposed 8T-SRAM cell where two transistors, one NMOS and one PMOS are added to the standard 6T-SRAM cell while the mechanism of read is single-ended [18]. During read, only RWL is asserted while during write both WWL and RWL signals are set to high. In this SRAM cell structure, transistor PUC is used to improve the write margin of the circuit when a "1" is stored on the storage node Q. In this mode, when the value on QB is "0", the voltage on the drain of NF increases that weakens the drivability of PUC. Therefore, writing "0" on storage node becomes easier. When QB keeps "1", however, the write margin is not expected to be improved. In this case, to improve the write margin of SRAM cell, PUR is sized smaller than PUL that results in an improved write margin in this mode as well. During read, ACL turns on while ACR is kept in cut-off region. When Q holds a "0", transistors PDL and NF help to discharge the bitline capacitance to a level to be sensed by a sense amplifier. In this mode, transistors PDR, PUL, and ACR are OFF. Sizing down the transistor PDR will improve read margin due to the fact that the discharging path of QB to ground is weakened. Noted, the stacking effect lowers the current through the transistor PDR. In case the node Q holds a "1", transistor NF is OFF. Therefore, no discharging path exist from node Q to ground that results in significant improvement in read static noise margin (RSNM). In general, RSNM of the proposed circuit is improved by at least 2.2X compared to the standard 6T-SRAM cell and is similar to the standard 8T-SRAM cell considering this fact that write margin is not improved in the standard 8T-SRAM cell. During hold, both RWL and WWL signals are set to low turning off the access transistors. The data retention of this cell depends on the bit stored on the cell. When Q holds a "1" the node QB will be floating that will give an uncertainty of the circuit. Although, the level of voltage on node QB is not zero, due to the stacking effect of PDR-NF where the drain of the transistor NF goes to a level equals to the voltage on node QB, the transistor PDR will turn off completely. However, when storage node is holding a "0", the data retention improved due to the fact that both NF and PDR are ON that keeps "0" at node QB.

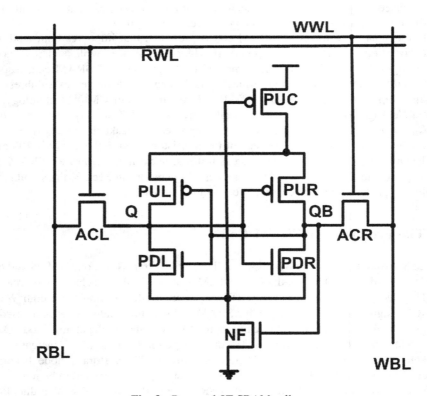

Fig. 3. Proposed 8T-SRAM cell.

Similar to the standard 8T-SRAM cell, the proposed cell uses a single-ended read approach which definitely reduces the swing of the output. However, different techniques can be used to compensate this effect such as a pseudo-differential sensing scheme that can be used for our proposed SRAM cell [19].

The simulation results for the circuit for different modes will be discussed in the next section.

3 Simulation Results and Comparison

Simulation results are done using 65 nm CMOS technology models at room temperature (i.e. 27° C) at different supply voltages from subthreshold to superthreshold to region. In this section, the proposed SRAM cell is simulated at different modes of operation.

To evaluate the read stability of an SRAM cell Read Static Noise Margin (RSNM) is used. RSNM is defined as the length of the side of the largest square that can fit into the lobes of the butterfly curve. Butterfly curve is obtained by drawing and mirroring the inverter characteristics while access transistors are ON and bitlines are precharged to V_{DD} [20]. For the proposed SRAM cell, however, only left side of the circuit defines the stability of the circuit. The reason is attributed to this fact that, when Q holds "1", increasing the value of QB even to very large values does not change the data stored on node Q. To this end, we simulate the proposed SRAM cell for cases Q = "0", WWL = "1", and RWL = "0" (i.e. CASE 1) and also Q = "1", WWL = "1", and RWL = "0" (i.e. CASE 2). The shadowed part of Fig. 4 shows the operation of the proposed SRAM cell when WWL is asserted and RWL signal is low. Here, we consider two cases. In CASE 1, node QB discharges via transistor ACR to ground that is a successful write while RWL is kept at "0". However, in CASE 2 where Q holds "1", although the voltage on node QB increases to 0.4 V, the value on node Q is not flipped. This proves a very high robustness of circuit even at very high input noises when Q stores "1". This concludes that single ended writing will fail (i.e. CASE 2) that leads us to turn on both access transistors during write cycle. The results for RSNM of the proposed SRAM cell compared to the standard 6T-SRAM cell at different supply voltages are shown in Fig. 5. As it is shown, 2.66 X improvements in RSNM is achieved by the use of the proposed 8T-SRAM cell compared to the standard 6T-SRAM cell. At lower supply voltages such as 200 mV, the proposed 8T-SRAM cell shows 4.86X improved RSNM. Due to this fact, the proposed SRAM cell is able to operate with a high margin at very low supply voltages (i.e. subthreshold/weak inversion region). However, the standard 8T-SRAM cell shows slightly better RSNM compared to the proposed 8T-SRAM cell.

To clarify the operation of the proposed circuit, the SRAM operation at different modes is shown in Fig. 6. As it is shown, during read, when Q holds "0", while the BL has been discharged to 300 mV, voltage on node Q is not increased higher than 0.2 V that is due to the stacking effect of transistors from node QB to ground and the small size of the transistor PDR in the cell (Fig. 6(b)). This confirms the robustness of the proposed circuit during read (i.e. RSNM). The successful writing "0" is shown in Fig. 6(a) when both RWL and WWL are set to high.

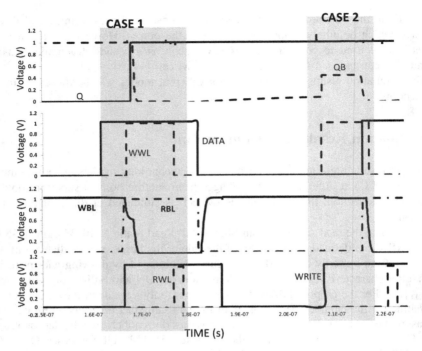

Fig. 4. Waveforms of the proposed 8T-SRAM cell (Shadowed part shows when WWL = "1" and QB = 1 or "0").

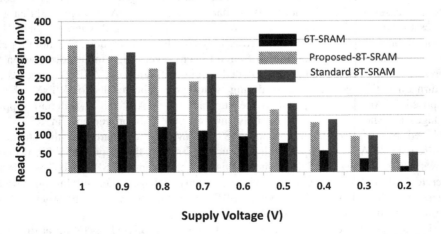

Fig. 5. RSNM results for the standard 6T-SRAM, 8T-SRAM and the proposed 8T-SRAM cell.

Write margin is another metric used to evaluate the stability of an SRAM cell in write mode. Different methods have been used to find the WM of an SRAM cell [21]. For the WM simulations, we choose the Word-Line (WL) voltage sweep method. In this method the bitline will be connected to the appropriate voltages to enable flipping

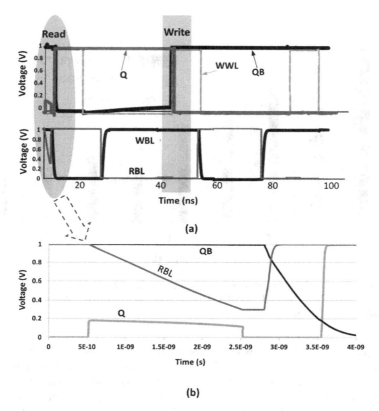

Fig. 6. (a) The proposed 8T-SRAM cell waveforms (b) read operation.

the data on the storage node. Then WL and WLB are swept from 0 V to 1 V and 1 V to 0 V, respectively. WM is calculated as the difference between V_{DD} and WL voltage when the data stored in the cell is flipped. Figure 7 illustrates the write margin of the proposed 8T-SRAM cell versus the standard 6T-SRAM cell. As it can be seen, when writing "0", the proposed 8T-SRAM improves the write margin between 28 %–73 % at different supply voltages. The proposed 8T-SRAM cell improves write margin by at least 21 % when writing "1". As it is shown in Fig. 7, improvement in write margin of the proposed circuit is increased at lower supply voltages enabling this circuit to work at extremely low supply voltages. Figure 8 shows an example of writing "0".

To achieve improvements in both read and write, the proposed 8T-SRAM cell must be sized carefully. To achieve the best write improvement when writing "1", PUR is sized smaller than PUL. In addition, improved read noise margin can be achieved by down-sizing the PDR transistor. The sizing of the proposed 8T-SRAM cell used is tabulated in Table 1.

Another important metric for An SRAM cell is leakage power consumption. To measure the leakage power consumption of the proposed SRAM cell compared to the standard 6T-SRAM cell, the leakage current of each transistor was measured that is

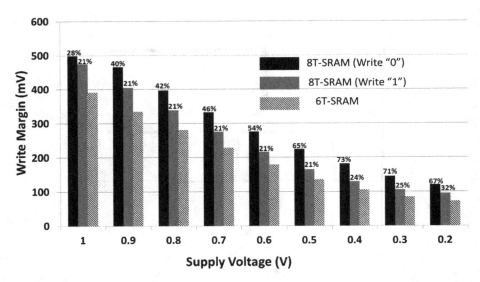

Fig. 7. Write margin of the proposed 8T-SRAM cell versus the standard 6T-SRAM cell when writing "0" and "1" (the standard 8T-SRAM provide negligibly smaller WM in comparison to the standard 6T-SRAM cell).

shown in Table 2. As it is shown the leakage through access transistors is reduced significantly that is attributed to the raised voltage level of storage node holding "0". However, the total leakage current of the proposed cell is increased when the stored bit is "1" while in case of Q = "0", the total leakage of the proposed cell is less than the standard 6T and 8T-SRAM cells. For this simulation a bitline capacitance of 200fF and the supply voltage of V_{DD} equals to 1 V at room temperature have been considered. To show the power degradation of the proposed SRAM cell at different supply voltage, we calculate the total power consumption of the proposed cell versus the standard 6T-SRAM and 8T-SRAM cells for V_{DD} = 1 V to V_{DD} = 200 mV. As it is shown in Fig. 9, leakage power of the proposed SRAM cell compared to the standard 6T-SRAM cell is degraded by 14.2 % and 67 % for supply voltages of 0.2 V and 1 V, respectively when the stored bit is "0" while for the case of Q="1", the proposed cell improves the leakage power by 34 % and 23 % at supply voltage of 1 V and 0.4 V, respectively. In comparison to the standard 8T-SRAM cell for the case of Q = "1", leakage current is degraded by 7 % to 21 % for VDD = 0.2 V and 1 V, respectively while for the case of Q = "0", the leakage current of the proposed cell increases by 20 % and 43 % for VDD = 0.2 V and 1 V, respectively.

In this part, the access time and the write time of the proposed circuit is explored in comparison with the standard 6T and 8T-SRAM cells [6]. Access time is measured as the time required for discharging the bitline voltage so that the difference between bitline voltage and V_{DD} (i.e. V_{sense}) can be sensed by the sense amplifier circuit. To this end, we simulate the proposed 8T-SRAM cell at supply voltage of V_{DD} = 300 mV at room temperature. Figure 10 illustrates the comparison between the proposed 8T-SRAM cell versus standard 6T-SRAM and the 8T-SRAM cells. As it is seen, the

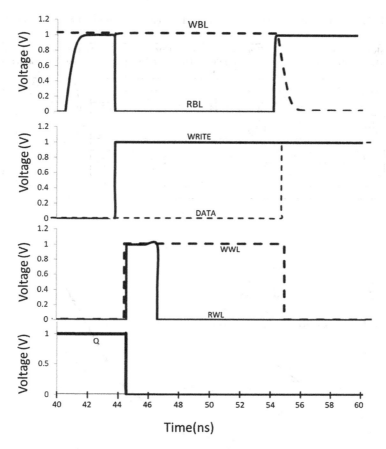

Fig. 8. Write "0" for the proposed 8T-SRAM cell.

Table 1. Sizing of the standard 6T, 8T and the proposed 8T-SRAM cells.

6T-SRAM cell		Proposed 8T-SRAM		Standard 8T-SRAM	
ACL, ACR	180n	ACL, ACR	180n	ACL, ACR	180n
PDR	230n	PDR	200n	PDR,PDL	200n
PUL	230n	PUL	150n	PUL	150n
PUR, PDR	150n	PUR	120n	PUR	150n
		PUC	150n	R1	180n
		PDL, NF	300n	R2	230n

maximum degradation is at lower supply voltage due to the weakened drivability of the transistors at lower supply voltages. The maximum degradation is at 200 mV (21 %) which improved by increasing the supply voltage. For instance, at $V_{DD} = 600$ mV, the access time degradation is only 4 % compared to the standard 6T and 8T-SRAM cells and all the circuit show similar access time at $V_{DD} = 800$ mV and above.

Table 2. The leakage current of the standard 6T and the proposed 8T SRAM cells.

6T-SRAM Current (nA). G:gate, D: Drain, and S: Source				Proposed 8T-SRAM Current (nA). G:gate, D: Drain, and S: Source				Standard 8T-SRAM Current (nA). G:gate, D: Drain, and S: Source			
Tr.	G	D	S	Tr.	G	D	S	Tr	G	D	S
ACL	0.323	0.017	0.15	ACL	0.36	0.084	0.209	ACL	0.1	1.3	1.16
ACR	0.153	1.802	1.853	ACR	0.144	0.178	0.187	ACR	0.23	0.098	0.104
PUL	0.563	4.191	4.767	PUL	0.462	2.95	3.428	PUL	0.115	1.13	1.01
PUR	0.208	1.856	1.66	PUR	0.122	1.132	0.979	PUR	0.31	2.69	2.68
PDL	0.234	2.361	2.103	PDL	0.246	1.497	1.73	PDL	0.52	2.72	3.24
PDR	1.47	4.455	5.892	PDR	0.887	3	2.02	PDR	0.114	1.37	1.24
				PUC	0.47	4.42	4.896	R1	1.10	3.90	1.13
				NF	0.001	4.967	5.025	R2	0.57	1.02	0.075

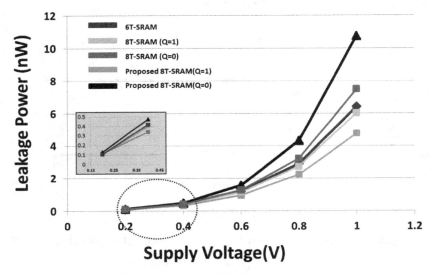

Fig. 9. Leakage power increase percentage for proposed 8T-SRAM cell versus the standard 6T-SRAM cell.

Another metric to compare different SRAM topologies is write time. In the proposed circuit due to the increased write margin, it is expected a faster data flipping on storage nodes during write cycle. Due to the asymmetry nature of the proposed SRAM cell, we simulate the cell for write "0" and write "1". Figure 11(a) and (b) illustrate the proposed SRAM cell behavior for both cases. As it is seen, the proposed SRAM cell provides faster write during write "0" compared to write "1" that is attributed to the weakened pull-up path through which the contention between PMOSs and access transistors is reduced. Figure 12 shows a comparison between the proposed SRAM cell versus the standard 6T and 8T SRAM cells at supply voltage of 600 mV. Here, the write time improvement percentages provided by the proposed cell over the standard

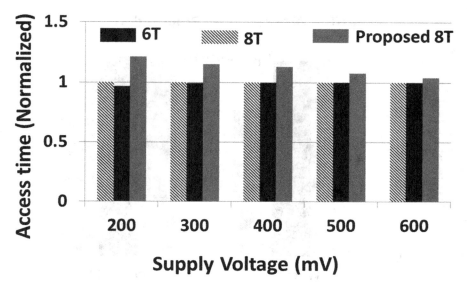

Fig. 10. Access time comparison for different SRAM cells (access time is normalized to the access time of the standard 6T-SRAM cell at different supply voltages).

6T and 8T SRAM cells during write "0" and write "1" are 25 % and 12 %, respectively. Noted, the improvement for write time at lower supply voltages is degraded due to the weakened driving current of transistors in the stacked configuration of the proposed SRAM cell. To this end, the use of low-Vth transistors can help to solve the low drivability of the stacked transistors with the penalty of area overhead.

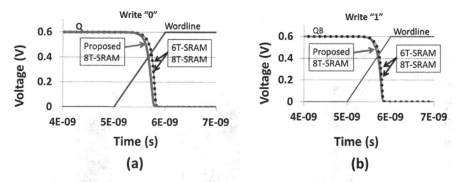

Fig. 11. (a) Write "0" and (b) write "1" for the proposed 8T-SRAM cell at V_{DD} = 0.6 V.

One of the main issues for the proposed 8T-SRAM cell is floating storage node (QB) when the stored data is "1". Therefore, a thorough discussion for the proposed cell is required to evaluate the cell operation. As mentioned, during hold, read "1", and write "1", the storage node QB is grounded which turns off the NF transistor disconnecting the floating node from ground. Therefore, the proposed circuit is simulated

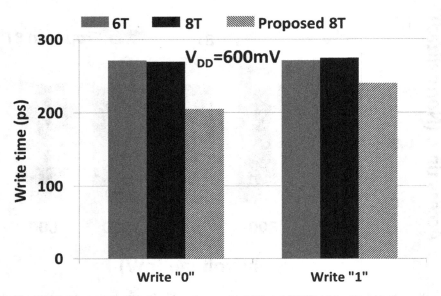

Fig. 12. Write time comparison between the standard 6T and 8T SRAM cells with the proposed 8T-SRAM cell.

for each cycle. During hold, the drain of NF is charged to a voltage equals to 53.5 mV which is equals to the voltage on node QB. The circuit was simulated for a long stay in hold time which shows the voltage on nodes QB and the drain of NF becomes equal and fixed at 53.5 mV. This leads to a turned-off transistor PDR which reduces the leakage current through storage node to ground. All three SRAM cells were simulated to measure their leakage current through storage nodes to ground under same condition.

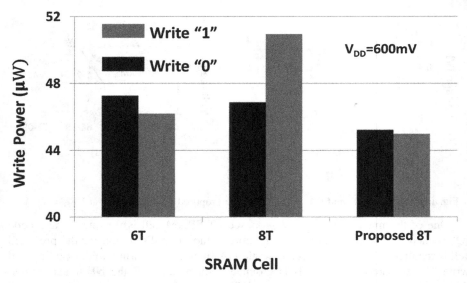

Fig. 13. Write power consumption for different SRAM cells.

During hold, we measured the leakage through transistors connected to ground to get an estimation of the total leakage when the node QB is floating. Simulation results show a fixed leakage current of 1.72 nA through pull-down transistors to ground while the standard 6T and 8T SRAM cells show a total leakage current of 2.59 nA and 2.63 nA through transistors connected to ground, respectively. However, as shown before, the total leakage power of the proposed circuit is higher than as for the standard 6T-SRAM cell when the stored data is "0".

During write "0", as explained in Sect. 2, the QB node is floating which helps to improve the write margin and write time. Based on this fact, the total write power is reduced, as well. To this end, the total power consumption of the standard 6T and 8T is compared with the proposed 8T-SRAM cell which is shown in Fig. 13. As it is seen, the proposed design provides minimum write power consumption during write "0" which is attributed to the floating node QB and drain of transistor NF.

During read due to the single-ended structure of the proposed circuit in which the node QB is decoupled from bitline, it will not affect the read process. Assuming that the

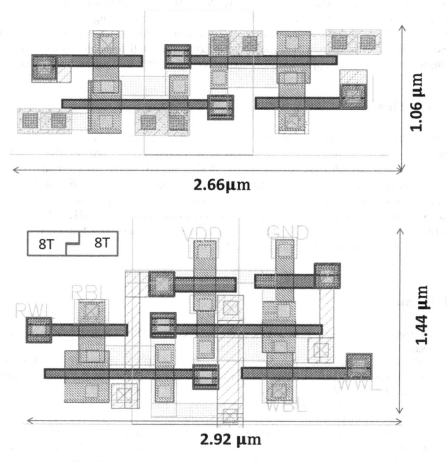

Fig. 14. Write power consumption for different SRAM cells.

voltage on node QB is 53.5 mV, it will continue to keep this voltage during read, as well. To evaluate the cells during read "1", the read power consumption of each circuit was measured. The standard 6T and 8T SRAM cells consume a read power of 119.46 nW and 1.9758 nW, respectively, while the proposed 8T-SRAM consumes 0.93 nW (930 pW). Consequently, we can claim that the floating node QB has no effect on the performance as well as it improves the power consumption during read and write.

Finally, the area of the proposed circuit in comparison to the standard 6T-SRAM cell is shown for a single cell. As it is shown in Fig. 14, the proposed technique increases the area by 49 % in comparison the standard 6T-SRAM cell. However, due to the L-shape of the cell layout, the total area overhead of the cell will be reduced. The standard 8T-SRAM cell, however, introduces 33 % area overhead in TSMC 65 nm technology.

All in all, the proposed SRAM cell, similar to the standard 8T-SRAM cell, improves read margin significantly while the write margin is improved, as well. Therefore, the proposed design has the advantages of improved write margin and write-time over the standard 6T and 8T-SRAM cells. Due to the asymmetric nature of the proposed SRAM cell, write margin improvement when writing "0" is larger than the case of "1". Therefore, as mentioned, by careful sizing of the transistors in our design, higher write margin (i.e. more symmetric write) will be achieved that enables designers to scale the supply voltage aggressively for ultra-low power applications.

4   Conclusions

In this chapter, a new 8T-SRAM cell was discussed which shows improvement in read and write margins by 2.2X and 22 %, respectively, compared to the standard 6T-SRAM cell. In addition, the proposed design improves the gate leakage power consumption while increases the subthreshold leakage compared to the 6T-SRAM cell. All in all, the proposed design improves read and write margins without any penalty in leakage power at subthreshold region compared to the standard 6T-SRAM cell. Furthermore, the proposed 8T-SRAM cell has a superior advantage of improved write margin in comparison to the standard 8T-SRAM cell.

References

1. Horowitz, M.: Scaling, power, and the future of MOS. In: IEDM Technical Digest, pp. 9–15, December 2005
2. Moradi, F., Gupta, S.K., Panagopoulos, G., Wisland, D.T., Mahmoodi, H., Roy, K.: Asymmetrically doped FinFETs for low-power robust SRAMs. IEEE Trans. Electron Devices 58(12), 4241–4249 (2011)
3. Collaert, N., De Keersgieter, A., Dixit, A., Ferain, I., Lai, L.-S., Lenoble, D., Mercha, A., Nackaerts, A., Pawlak, B.J., Rooyackers, R., Schulz, T., Sar, K.T., Son, N.J., Van Dal, M.J. H., Verheyen, P., von Arnim, K., Witters, L., De, M., Biesemans, S., Jurczak, M.: Multi-gate devices for the 32 nm technology node and beyond. In: Proceedings of 37th ESSDERC, pp. 143–146, 11–13 September 2007

4. Sachid, A.B., Hu, C.: Denser and more stable SRAM using FinFETs with multiple fin heights. IEEE Trans. Electron Devices **59**(8), 2037–2041 (2012)
5. Tawfik, S.A., Kursun, V.: Multi-threshold voltage FinFET sequential circuits. IEEE Trans. VLSI Syst. **19**(1), 151–156 (2011)
6. Verma, N., Chandrakasan, A.: A 256 kb 65 nm 8T subthreshold SRAM employing sense-amplifier redundancy. IEEE J. Solid-State Circuits **43**(1), 141–149 (2008)
7. Aly, R.E., Bayoumi, M.A.: Low-power cache design using 7T SRAM cell. IEEE Trans. Circuits Syst. II, Exp. Briefs **54**(4), 318–322 (2007)
8. Madiwalar, B., Kariyappa, B.S.: Single bit-line 7T SRAM cell for low power and high SNM. In: International Multi-Conference on iMac4s, pp. 223–228, March 2013
9. Wen, L., Li, Z., Li, Y.: Differential-read 8T SRAM cell with tunable access and pull-down transistors. Electron. Lett. **48**(20), 1260–1261 (2012)
10. Tu, M.H., Lin, J.-Y., Tsai, M.-C., Lu, C.-Y., Lin, Y.-J., Wang, M.-H., Huang, H.-S., Lee, K.-D., Shih, W.-C., Jou, S.-J., Chuang, C.-T.: A single-ended disturb-free 9T subthreshold SRAM with cross-point data-aware write word-line structure, negative bit-line, and adaptive read operation timing tracing. IEEE J. Solid-State Circuits **47**(6), 1469–1482 (2012)
11. Chang, I.J., Kim, J., Park, S.P., Roy, K.: A 32 kb 10T sub-threshold SRAM array with bit-interleaving and differential read scheme in 90 nm CMOS. IEEE J. Solid State Circuits **44**(2), 650–658 (2009)
12. Moradi, F., Wisland, D.T., Aunet, S., Mahmoodi, H., Tuan Vu, C.: 65 nm sub-threshold 11T-SRAM for ultra-low voltage applications. In: SOC Conference, IEEE International, pp. 113–118 (2008)
13. Calhoun, B.H., Chandrakasan, A.P.: Static noise margin variation for sub-threshold SRAM in 65 nm CMOS. IEEE J. Solid-State Circuits **41**, 1673–1679 (2006)
14. Moradi, F., Madsen, J.K.: Robust subthreshold 7T-SRAM cell for low-power applications. In: IEEE Midwest Symposium on Circuits and Systems (MWSCAS), pp. 893, 896, 3–6 August 2014
15. Moradi, F., Madsen, J.K.: Improved read and write margins using a novel 8T-SRAM cell. In: International Conference on Very Large Scale Integration (VLSI-SoC), pp. 1, 5, 6–8 October 2014
16. Moradi, F., Wisland, D.T., Mahmoodi, H., Berg, Y., Cao, T.V.: New SRAM design using body bias technique for ultra-low power applications. In: 11th International Symposium on Quality Electronic Design (ISQED), pp. 468, 471, 22–24 March 2010
17. Farkhani, H., Peiravi, A., Moradi, F.: A new asymmetric 6T SRAM cell with a write assist technique in 65 nm CMOS technology. Microelectronics Journal **45**, 1556–1565 (2014)
18. Moradi, F., Madsen, J.K.: Improved read and write margins using a novel 8T-SRAM cell. In: 2014 22nd International Conference on Very Large Scale Integration (VLSI-SoC), pp. 1, 5, 6–8 October 2014
19. Nalam, S., Chandra, V., Pietrzyk, C., Aitken, R., Calhoun, B.: Asymmetric 6T SRAM with two-phase write and split bitline differential sensing for low voltage operation. In: Proceedings 11th International Symposium Quality Electronic Design (ISQED), pp. 139–146, March 2010
20. Seevinck, E., List, F.J., Lohstroh, J.: Static-noise margin analysis of MOS SRAM cells. IEEE J. Solid-State Circuits **22**, 748–754 (1987)
21. Wang, J., Nalam, S., Calhoun, B.H.: Analyzing static and dynamic write margin for nanometer SRAMs. In: Proceedings of International Symposium Low Power Electron. Design, pp. 129–134, New York (2008)

On the Co-simulation of SystemC with QEMU and OVP Virtual Platforms

Alessandro Lonardi[1] and Graziano Pravadelli[1,2(✉)]

[1] Department of Computer Science, University of Verona, Verona, Italy
alessandro.lonardi@univr.it
[2] EDALab s.r.l., Verona, Italy
graziano.pravadelli@edalab.it

Abstract. Virtual prototyping allows designers to set up an electronic system level software simulator of a full HW/SW platform to carry out SW development and HW design almost in parallel. To achieve the goal virtual prototyping tools allow the co-simulation between an efficient instruction set simulator, mainly based on dynamic binary translation of the target code, and simulation kernels for HW models, described by means of traditional hardware description languages, like, for example, SystemC. In this context, some approaches have been proposed for co-simulation between QEMU and SystemC, both from EDA companies and academic research groups. On the contrary, no paper addresses integration between Open Virtual Platform (OVP) and SystemC. Indeed, OVP models and the related simulator can be integrated into SystemC designs by using TLM 2.0 wrappers and opportune OVP APIs. However, this solution presents some disadvantages, like the incapability of supporting cycle-accurate models, and the necessity of re-design, in terms of SystemC modules, all OVP components that should be integrated in the target platform. To avoid such drawbacks, and provide an easy way to port SystemC models from a QEMU-based to an OVP-based virtual platform and vice versa, this paper presents a common co-simulation approach that works for integrating SystemC components with both QEMU and OVP. Experimental results show the effectiveness of the proposed architecture.

1 Introduction

Virtual prototyping is today an essential technology for modelling, verification and re-design of full HW/SW platforms [1]. With respect to the serialized approach, where the majority of SW is developed and verified after the completion of the silicon design, with the risk of failing aggressive time-to-market requests, virtual prototyping guarantees a faster development process by implementing the software part almost in parallel with the hardware design (Fig. 1). This enables software engineers to start implementation months before the hardware platform

This work has been partially supported by the EU large-scale integrating project CONTREX (FP7-2013-ICT-10-611146).

L. Claesen et al. (Eds.): VLSI-SoC 2014, IFIP AICT 464, pp. 110–128, 2015.
DOI: 10.1007/978-3-319-25279-7_7

is complete. The core of virtual prototyping is represented by the virtual system prototype, i.e., an electronic system level (ESL) software simulator of the entire system, used first at the architectural level and then as a executable golden reference model throughout the design cycle. Virtual prototyping brings several benefits like, for example, efficient management of design complexity, decoupling of SW development from the availability of the actual HW implementation, and control of prototyping costs. More pragmatically, it enables developers to accurately and efficiently explore different solutions with the aim of balancing design functionality, flexibility, performance, power consumption, quality, ergonomics, schedule and cost.

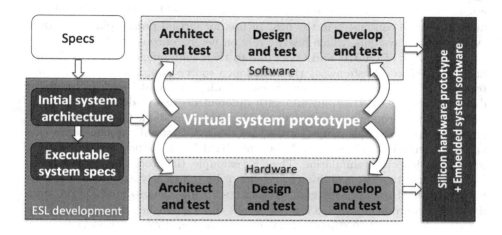

Fig. 1. The virtual prototyping approach.

A common aspect in modern virtual platform approaches is the use of an ISS that exploits DBT [2]. This technique has become the de facto standard to guarantee high speed and accuracy of cross-compiled software, thus many groups, both in industry and academia, have started to consider DBT as a key technology of their virtual prototyping solutions. Companies, like VaST (acquired by Synopsys) and Virtutech (acquired by Intel/Windriver) introduced virtual prototyping platforms for rapid development and fast execution of target software [3,4]. Meanwhile all of the three main EDA companies (Synopsys, Cadence, Mentor) have their own virtual prototyping platform [5–7]. All of them are using fast simulation technologies that are based on DBT. However, as they target to keep their markets, most of them did not support open standard interfaces. The technology itself is proprietary and provided under binary format, making it impossible to perform modifications within the models, i.e., addition of new features or annotations. Furthermore, most commercial products bind the customer to their own standard languages and features limiting the reuse of models towards and from other tools.

Taking an opposite view to this closed-source approach, several research groups have recently focused on QEMU [8], an open-source DBT-based virtualization platform that allows cross-platform operating system execution and provides a very fast emulation comparable to commercially available tools. As an alternative to QEMU, Imperas has proposed the Open Virtual Platform (OVP) initiative [9]. OVP, similarly to QEMU, offers a simulation kernel based on a code morphing DBT mechanism to guarantee very efficient simulation of full HW/SW systems. It includes several models of processors, peripherals and behavioural components that the software communicates with. One difference between QEMU and OVP is that the former is more targeted for *homogeneous* single/multi-core platforms, while OVP has been thought to better support *heterogeneous* MPSoC architectures. For this reason, it is likely that OVP will gain more and more consensus, in the near future, for virtual prototyping of modern cyber-physical systems, which heavily rely on heterogeneous architectures.

The advent of QEMU and OVP, due to their high efficiency and flexibility, has then replaced SystemC as the main open-source approach for virtual prototyping of full HW/SW systems. SystemC allows to model entire systems at different levels of abstractions and with different degrees of detail, however, its simulation performances are poor when accurate and realistic CPU models, good enough to run real operating systems, are desired. SystemC processes are executed sequentially and managed by a centralized kernel, which definitely represents a bottleneck for simulation. Thus, for example, the processing power offered by multi- and many-core architectures cannot be sufficiently exploited by adopting SystemC. However, SystemC guarantees to model customized (non standard) HW components with a level of details that cannot be achieved neither by QEMU nor by OVP. Furthermore, effective virtual prototyping approaches cannot exclude design reuse and bottom-up component-based design, where already defined (SystemC) models are integrated in new prototypes, to reduce the time to market. For this reason, several approaches, like [10–13], propose the use of QEMU, for efficient instruction set simulation, in combination with SystemC, for specification and reuse of customized HW components. In particular, [10] proposes a QEMU-SystemC approach developed by the GreenSoCs company which represents the main way for connecting SystemC models, as peripherals, to QEMU. On the contrary, Imperas supports the integration between SystemC and OVP by allowing the encapsulation of OVP models, wrapped by a TLM 2.0 interface, inside SystemC designs. However, such an encapsulation presents some disadvantages. First, it works natively only for TLM designs; the OVP user guide discourages from the integration of OVP models into non-TLM systems, highlighting the risk of incorrect results [14]. This prevents accurate simulation of RTL SystemC models. Secondly, encapsulation of OVP models inside SystemC modules is a quite complex operation, which does not allow a rapid reuse of SystemC components. In fact, all OVP models included in the target platform must be redesigned in terms of SystemC modules (through OVP APIs and TLM interfaces) to be co-simulated with the customized SystemC hardware. Furthermore, the porting of a SystemC component, originally linked inside a

QEMU-based platform, towards an MPSoC OVP-based platform would require a huge effort. Similar considerations apply in the opposite case, when porting from the OVP world to QEMU's one is desired.

To overcome these drawbacks, this paper, as an extension of [15], proposes a common architecture to integrate SystemC components in both QEMU and OVP-based virtual platforms. Starting from the idea presented in [10], our approach defines an efficient, shared-memory based architecture that allows the communication between a SystemC peripheral and a SW program, which runs either on a QEMU or on an OVP CPU model, through a common PCI virtual device bridge. In this way, porting of SystemC components from a QEMU-based to an OVP-based virtual platform is straightforward, since it requires only to redefine the virtual device in terms of either OVP or QEMU APIs. Finally, there is no limitation about the abstraction level at which SystemC models are implemented.

The rest of the paper is organized as follows. Section 2 briefly presents the main characteristics of QEMU and OVP, and it summarizes approaches for their co-simulation with SystemC. Section 3 describes the proposed common co-simulation architecture. Section 4 is devoted to experimental results. Finally, concluding remarks are reported in Sect. 5.

2   Background and Related Works

QEMU and OVP are two very popular open-source environments for rapid prototyping of virtual platforms. Both of them allow a very efficient emulation of several architectures and they can interface with many types of physical host hardware. QEMU is mainly intended for simulation of a fixed, defined single processor platform. OVP is more suited to model heterogeneous platforms with arbitrary shared and local memory configurations. Next subsections report a brief summary of their main characteristics and the state of the art related to their integration with SystemC.

2.1   QEMU

QEMU is a machine emulator relying on dynamic binary translation of the target CPU application code. Each instruction of the target CPU is translated into a set of micro-operations that are implemented by C functions for the host machine. Such C functions are then compiled to obtain a dynamic code generator which is called, at run time, to generate the corresponding code to be executed on the host machine. QEMU works at basic block level. Each block is translated, the first time it is encountered, into the corresponding code for the target CPU, then it is stored in a cache for future uses. In addition to such a common feature, different optimizations can be implemented to further keep execution speed close to native execution, like, for example, dynamic recompilation where some parts of the code are recompiled to exploit information that are available only at run time.

There is no a native way to integrate SystemC models into QEMU, thus some co-simulation approaches have been proposed in the past [10,12,13,16]. The intent of [10] is to facilitate the development of software and device drivers for whatever operating system without spending too much effort on modifying the virtual platform itself by plugging SystemC TLM 2.0 models into the QEMU-based virtual platform. This work is further extended in [13] where the authors introduce a checkpoint-based feature to save and restore the SystemC state into the simulator. Alternatively, in [12,16], the authors propose a QEMU/SystemC-based framework for virtual platform prototyping that cannot only estimate the performance of a target system, but also co-simulate with hardware models down to the cycle accurate level.

2.2   OVP

OVP is a virtual platform emulator released by Imperas for enabling the simulation of embedded systems running real application code. It includes a fast Just-In-Time (JIT) code morphing simulator engine (OVPsim), a set of APIs for modelling new platforms and components, like CPUs and peripherals, and a set of already designed models. An OVP platform is composed of one or more processors, memories, interconnections, and possibly some peripherals. A platform is modelled through the following sets of APIs:

- Innovative CPU Manager (ICM): ICM functions enable instantiation, interconnection and simulation of complex multiprocessor platforms composed of processors, memories and busses in arbitrary topology.
- Virtual Machine Interface (VMI): VMI functions are used to create new models of processors to be run inside the OVPsim. CPU instructions are mapped onto the JIT code morphing compiler primitives to speed-up the simulation.
- Behavioural Hardware Modelling (BHM): BHM functions allow to define behavioural models of hardware and software components that act as peripherals to the processors. They are executed by the Peripheral Simulation Engine (PSE) in a separate (protected) process with respect to OVPsim.
- Peripheral Programming Model (PPM): PPM functions are used in conjunction with BHM functions to model interfaces to the platform and connections (bus ports, net ports, etc.).

The use of OVP to model heterogeneous multiprocessor architectures is described in [17] through a set of case studies. A drag and drop interactive approach for MPSoC exploration using OVP is proposed in [18]. A technique exploiting OVP for development and optimization of embedded computing applications by handling heterogeneity at the chip, node, and network level is proposed in [19]. Heterogeneity is handled by providing an infrastructure to connect multiple virtual platforms like OVP and QEMU.

None of previous works considers co-simulation between an OVP-based virtual platform and external SystemC models. However, OVPsim platform models can be compiled as shared objects. Thus, they can be encapsulated in any simulation environment that is able to load shared objects, including SystemC. The

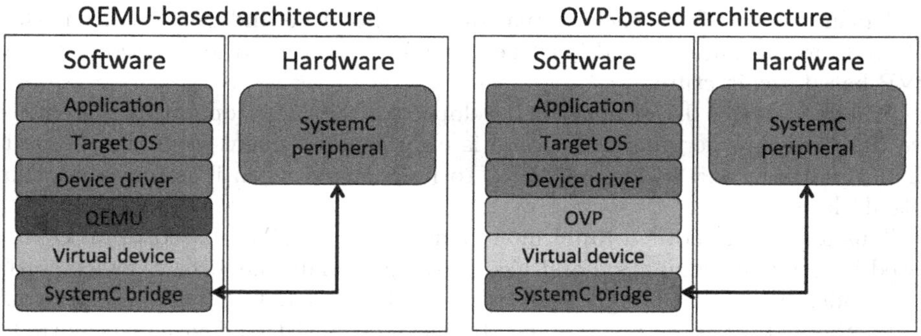

Fig. 2. Co-simulation architectures. Pink boxes indicate unchanged code between QEMU and OVP (Colour figure online).

integration with SystemC is enabled by the ICM APIs. OVP models and OVPsim can be encapsulated inside a SystemC design to create a virtual platform where SystemC components and OVP models simulate together under the control of the SystemC simulation engine. However, the OVP CPUManager is not intended for cycle-accurate or pin-level simulation. For this reason ICM APIs provide only loosely timed TLM 2.0 interfaces. Thus, integration of OVP models in a SystemC RTL system would require the definition of TLM-to-RTL transactors. However, the OVP user guide discourages from the integration of OVP models into non-TLM systems, highlighting the risk of incorrect results [14]. Moreover, as shown in our experimental results, simulation performances are heavily penalized when OVP is integrated inside SystemC.

3   Co-simulation Architecture

In this paper, the HW/SW co-simulation architecture depicted in Fig. 2 is proposed. Similarly to the approaches presented in [10,13], it reflects the traditional operating system-based stack where software applications interact with hardware peripherals through device drivers. The target platform, where software applications run, is emulated by using, indifferently, QEMU or OVP, and it is connected to a SystemC hardware peripheral through a *virtual PCI*[1] *device, a SystemC bridge* and a device driver for the target operating system.

The virtual PCI device, connected to the PCI bus of the virtual platform, acts as an interface between the SystemC simulator and the QEMU or OVP virtual platforms. The virtual device code is different for the QEMU-based and the OVP-based architectures, since it depends on the APIs exported by QEMU and OVP for modeling new devices.

The SystemC bridge consists of a set of functions that allow the communication with SystemC. The bridge is compiled as a C library linked to the

---

[1] The same approach can be adopted also for other kinds of buses, like for example AMBA.

implementation code of each virtual device, thus it is independent from the selected virtual platform and it is the same for both the QEMU-based and the OVP-based architectures.

Finally, a device driver must be developed for the target operating system to use the hardware peripheral. Its code is clearly independent from the selected virtual platform and it does not need to be changed when it is moved to the actual platform.

This approach allows a rapid interchange from a QEMU-based to an OVP-based SystemC co-simulation and vice versa, since only the virtual device must be re-coded moving from a QEMU virtual platform to an OVP virtual platform.

Further details about the SystemC bridge and the virtual device are reported, respectively in Sects. 3.1 and 3.2, while Sect. 3.3 describes how the device driver and the virtual device interact to implement the interrupt handling mechanism.

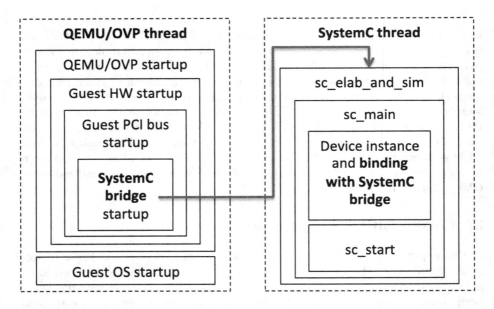

Fig. 3. Startup of the cosimulation between QEMU/OVP and SystemC.

3.1   SystemC Bridge

The SystemC bridge is a C++ class implementing a singleton design pattern that exposes a set of APIs towards the virtual device for interfacing with SystemC. Moreover, it manages the communication protocol and the synchronization mechanism between QEMU/OVP and SystemC. Since both QEMU and OVP are written in C, the bridge wraps the SystemC APIs through a set of C functions included in a library, which is statically linked to the SystemC runtime library.

The QEMU and the OVP virtual platforms[2] initially call a function implemented in the bridge to start the SystemC simulator. Until the SystemC runtime is operative, the virtual platform is blocked to prevent its premature request to the hardware device. Differently from [10], the SystemC simulator is run as a separate thread inside the same process where the QEMU emulator or OVP simulator is executed (Fig. 3), such that the communication between the two worlds is based on shared memory and thread synchronization primitives. This prevents the use of expensive interprocess communication mechanisms (like sockets). Then, the starting routine of the thread launches the SystemC *sc_main* function where the following steps are executed:

- instantiation and initialization of the SystemC device to be connected to the bridge; in particular, input and output ports of the device are registered in the bridge;
- unlocking of the semaphore that is blocking the virtual platform;
- starting of the SystemC simulator.

The SystemC bridge exports two functions (i.e., *sc_ioport_read* and *sc_ioport_write*) towards the virtual platform to allow reading from/writing to the SystemC module.

Read operations are performed by calling the *sc_ioport_read* function. This invokes the *read* method of the SystemC bridge on the target signal (*Systemc_To_VirtualPlatform_Signal*), which represents an output port for the SystemC device. The signal is implemented like a proxy for a *sc_core::sc_out* as reported in Fig. 4. In particular, it is an *SC_MODULE* with a method, *run*, which updates the signal value each time a change happens in the output port of the SystemC device. Then, the *read* method retrieves the current value of the signal each time the virtual platform calls the *sc_ioport_read* function, as reported in the sequence diagram of Fig. 5. To guarantee atomicity of operations, *read* and *run* methods are made mutually exclusive through the use of a mutex.

Write operations are performed in a similar way by invoking the *sc_ioport_write* function. As shown in the sequence diagram of Fig. 7, it calls the *write* method of the SystemC bridge on the target signal (*VirtualPlatform_To_Systemc_Signal*), which represents an input port for the SystemC device. Such a signal is implemented in a similar way with respect to the *Systemc_To_VirtualPlatform_Signal* (Fig. 6). The only difference is represented by the necessity of preventing concurrent write operations by the virtual platform, which would be missed by the SystemC runtime. This is obtained by using a mutex that is locked as soon as the *write* method is invoked and by a flag that is used to notify a pending write operation to the SystemC device. Then, the *run* method is executed at each clock cycle checking for a pending operation from the virtual platform; in case of its presence, the pending value is written to the

---

[2] In the following, we use the generic name *virtual platform* to refer, without distinction, to the QEMU as well as the OVP environment.

```
1    template <typename T>
2      SC_MODULE(Systemc_To_VirtualPlatform_Signal),
3      public Systemc_To_VirtualPlatform_Signal_Base {
4
5      SC_HAS_PROCESS(SystemC_To_VirtualPlatform_Signal);
6
7      Systemc_To_VirtualPlatform_Signal(
8        sc_core::sc_out<T>& port,
9        sc_core::sc_module_name name) : sc_module(name) {
10
11       SC_METHOD(run);
12       sensitive << signal;
13       port.bind(signal);
14     }
15
16     virtual uint64_t read() {
17       Scoped_Lock sl(mutex);
18       return static_cast<uint64_t>(native);
19     }
20
21     void run() {
22       Scoped_Lock sl(mutex);
23       native = signal.read();
24     }
25
26     virtual std::string name() const {
27       return sc_module::name();
28     }
29
30     private:
31       Mutex mutex;
32       T native;
33       sc_core::sc_signal<T> signal;
34   };
```

Fig. 4. Implementation of a SystemC to virtual platform signal to allow QEMU/OVP reading from the SystemC device.

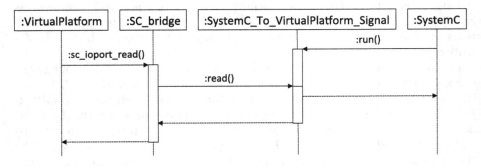

Fig. 5. Sequence diagram of a read operation from a SystemC device.

port of the SystemC device and the mutex is unlocked allowing further write operations from the virtual platform.

To optimize performance, time synchronization between QEMU/OVP and SystemC is not clock accurate, but it happens only when a call to a SystemC device is performed in order to update the SystemC time to be the same as

```
1    template <typename T>
2      SC_MODULE(VirtualPlatform_To_Systemc_Signal),
3      public VirtualPlatform_To_Systemc_Signal_Base {
4
5      SC_HAS_PROCESS(VirtualPlatform_To_Systemc_Signal);
6
7      VirtualPlatform_To_Systemc_Signal(
8        sc_core::sc_in<T>& port,
9        sc_core::sc_clock& clock_signal,
10       sc_core::sc_module_name name) : sc_module(name) {
11
12             is_vp_write = false;
13             SC_METHOD(run);
14             sensitive_pos << clock.pos();
15             clock.bind(clock_signal);
16             port.bind(signal);
17      }
18
19      virtual void write(uint64_t value) {
20        token.hold;
21        native = static_cast<T>(value);
22        is_vp_write = true;
23      }
24
25      void run() {
26        if (is_vp_write) {
27          signal.write(native);
28          is_vp_write = false;
29          token.release();
30        }
31      }
32
33      virtual std::string name() const {
34        return sc_module::name();
35      }
36
37      private:
38        Token token;
39        T native;
40        sc_core::sc_signal<T> signal;
41        bool is_vp_write;
42        sc_core::sc_in_clk clock;
43   };
```

Fig. 6. Implementation of a virtual platform to SystemC signal to allow QEMU/OVP
writing to the SystemC device.

QEMU time. This only guarantees that two subsequent operations do not inter-
fere with each other, which is a sufficient condition for functional verification
but not enough for other kind of analysis (e.g., power consumption/timing estimation). Future works will deal with a more accurate time synchronization.

3.2   Virtual Device

A device can be made visible to the QEMU and OVP virtual platforms by
implementing a virtual device. In our work, we considered PCI devices, however,
in a similar way other kinds of bus can be adopted. Differently from the SystemC
bridge, whose implementation code is the same for QEMU and OVP, the creation

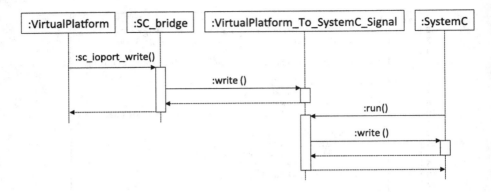

Fig. 7. Sequence diagram of a write operation to a SystemC device.

of a virtual device is tightly coupled to the APIs exported by the virtual platform. Thus, QEMU and OVP implementations will be described separately.

QEMU Virtual Device. The implementation of the QEMU virtual device is based on the PCI APIs. The device is plugged to the selected machine (in our experiments a Malta platform) and connected to a PCI bus. The device characteristics (name, parent class, size of the occupied memory, initialization routine) are described into a structure which is passed to the selected machine during the device registration phase. The initialization routine is executed when a new instance of the device is initialized. Its role consists of registering the I/O ports memory regions and starting the SystemC simulation through the SystemC bridge. The registration of the I/O ports memory region reserves a chunk of memory for the virtual device and retrieves the pointers to functions for reading/writing from/to the virtual device I/O ports that are mapped to the actual SystemC device I/O ports. Such function invokes the corresponding *sc_ioport_read* and *sc_ioport_write* of the SystemC bridge.

OVP Virtual Device. The implementation of the virtual device in OVP is split in two parts: the device and the intercepted functions. The device consists of a C application with a standard *main* function. It first executes a set of initialization activities (SystemC simulation, PCI configuration header, PCI memory regions); then it connects the PCI configuration port (necessary to read the PCI configuration header) and the PCI master bus. Finally, it registers some call back functions that are triggered at each read/write operation from/to the PCI I/O port regions. The interaction between the SystemC bridge and the virtual device is performed by means of a set of intercepted functions. The PSE simulator intercepts such functions through the Application Binary Interface (ABI), which specifies size, layout and alignment of data types, how an application should make a system call to the operating system, and the calling conventions (how arguments of a function are passed, and how return value is retrieved). In particular, there is an intercepted function for reading from the SystemC device and one for writing to the SystemC device. Their role consists in calling the corresponding *sc_ioport_read* and *sc_ioport_write* of the SystemC bridge.

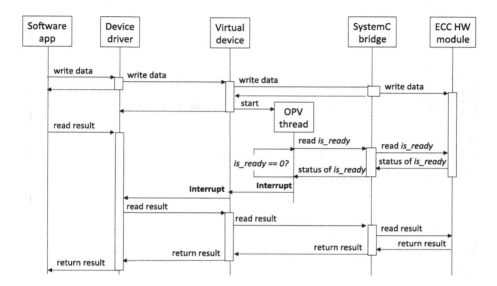

Fig. 8. Sequence diagram of the interrupt mechanism for ECC benchmark.

3.3   Interrupt Handling

The basic architecture described in the previous sections supports only I/O requests from the virtual platform to the SystemC device, while the second acts only as a slave. However, an effective virtual prototyping solution cannot forget to provide support for interrupt-based asynchronous communication, through which, for example, a device can notify the completion of a task to the CPU. To achieve this goal, an interrupt handling mechanism has been defined. Its implementation is composed of two parts, which does not involve the SystemC bridge: the first part is embedded in the device driver, the second in the virtual device. As an explanatory example, we refer to the interaction between a SW application and a SystemC module representing and error correction code (ECC) that we used in the experimental result section (see Sect. 4). Figure 8 shows the sequence diagram that describes these interactions. In particular, a write operation is performed on the ECC module and then a subsequent read operation is called. The device driver and the virtual device manage the correct sequencing of the two operations such that the *read* is executed only after the *write* has completed. The completion of the *write* is notified by the virtual device through an interrupt that is raised as soon as the *is_ready* line of ECC becomes high.

```
1   // variable declarations
2
3   // semaphore for unlocking read operation upon interrupt
4   struct semaphore readLock;
5
6   // device driver opening
7   static int open(struct inode* inode, struct file* file) { ... }
8
9   // device driver releasing
10  static int release(struct inode* inode, struct file* file) { ... }
11
12  // read operation callback
13  static ssize_t read(struct file* file, char* buf,
14      size_t count, loff_t* ppos)
15  {
16      // initializations and sanity checks
17      ...
18      // blocking via semaphore (unlocked by interrupt handler method)
19      wait(&readLock);
20      // read operation
21      ...
22  }
23
24  // write operation callback
25  static ssize_t write(struct file* file, const char* buf,
26      size_t count, loff_t* ppos)
27  {
28      // write operation
29      ...
30  }
31
32
33  // Interrupt handler method
34  static irqreturn_t irq_handler(int received_irq, void* dev_id) {
35      // data ready unlock semaphore
36      signal(&readLock);
37      return IRQ_HANDLED;
38  }
39
40  // Device driver initialization
41  static int __init init(void)
42  {
43      // variables and utilities initializations
44      ...
45
46      // Semaphore initalization and interrupt handler registration
47      sema_init(&readLock, 1);
48      if((err = request_irq(15, irq_handler,
49          IRQF_SHARED, DRV_NAME, (void*)(irq_handler))))
50      {
51          pr_err(''Cannot obtain irq, aborting'');
52          return -1;
53      }
54          return 0;
55  }
56
57  // other functions
58  ...
```

Fig. 9. Device driver implementation for ECC.

```
1    // Interrupt checking thread method
2    static void interruptCheckThread(void* data)
3    {
4       Uns32 result = 0;
5
6       while(1)
7       {
8          // wait until write operation is called on the device\\
9          bhmWaitEvent(threadEventHandle);
10         while(result == 0)   // Check if ECC is ready?
11         {
12            result = read_ecc_is_ready();
13            // yield for a while to avoid hogging the CPU
14            bhmWaitDelay(100);
15         }
16
17         // When ECC is ready send interrupt
18         ppmWriteNet(intPort, 1);
19         ppmWriteNet(intPort, 0);
20      }
21   }
22
23   // main: used as OVP peripheral constructor
24   int main(int argc, char **argv) {
25      // peripheral initializations
26      ...
27      // PCI initialization
28      pciHeaderInit();
29      pciMappingInit();
30      pciRegisterCallBack();
31      // Bus ports initializations
32      ppmOpenSlaveBusPort(''config'', config_window, sizeof(config_window));
33      pciConnectConfigSlavePort(PREFIX, NULL);
34
35      // initialization of the Interrupt line
36      intPort = ppmOpenNetPort(''sclinkInterrupt'');
37
38      // initialization of the interrupt checking thread
39      threadEventHandle = bhmCreateEvent();
40      threadHandle = bhmCreateThread(interruptCheckThread,
41                        NULL, threadName, &threadStackData[THREAD_STACK]);
42      bhmEventHandle finished = bhmGetSystemEvent(BHM_SE_END_OF_SIMULATION);
43      bhmWaitEvent(finished);
44      bhmMessage(''I'', PREFIX, ''Shutting down'');
45
46      terminate();
47      return 0;
48   }
```

Fig. 10. Interrupt handling inside the OVP virtual device for ECC.

Monitoring such a line is the role of a dedicated OVP thread, which is activated as soon as a new *write* is requested by the software application.

The device driver side is implemented in the traditional way. From the point of view of interrupt handling, it just requires the definition of a function that is called through the interrupt service routine when this is triggered by the arrival of the corresponding interrupt. For example, let us consider the piece of code reported in Fig. 9. It shows the skeleton of the device driver written for ECC. An interrupt is raised by the ECC module as soon as a write operation is concluded. As a consequence, the *irq_handler* function is executed (lines 34–38), which unlocks the *readLock* semaphore (line 36). Such a semaphore is used to block the *read* routine that waits till the ECC device is ready for a read operation (line 19).

Then, the most effort for implementing the interrupt handling resides in the virtual device side. The mechanism is the same for both QEMU and OVP, given that, on the virtual device side, either QEMU or OVP APIs are adopted. Figure 10 shows the skeleton for the OVP case. ECC raises an interrupt by fixing to 1 the line *is_ready* as soon as a write operation on the device is completed. At platform level, a signal is used to connect the virtual device to the interrupt lines provided by the platform chipset (line 36). When an interrupt is generated by the SystemC device, the interrupt is notified to the chipset through such a signal (lines 18–19). To catch the interrupt from the SystemC module, the virtual device creates an OVP thread (line 40–41) that cyclically checks the *is_ready* line of the SystemC module (lines 1–21). A waiting time is introduced between two consecutive checks to avoid hogging the CPU (line 14). The thread is finally suspended, to reduce its busy waiting activity, after the interrupt is raised till a new write operation is called on the ECC (line 9).

4   Experimental Results

Experimental results have been executed by setting up a virtual platform composed of a MIPS-based Malta platform and a SystemC RTL module connected through the PCI bus. The SystemC module implements an Error Correction Code (ECC) algorithm as an external hardware peripheral. Two versions of the platform have been implemented, one based on QEMU and one on OVP. The Malta platform is equipped with a MIPS 34Kf CPU running a Debian 6.0.9 with a 2.6.32.5 Linux kernel. The host machine is an Intel Core2Quad Q6600 @2.4 GHz with 4 GB of RAM, running Ubuntu 12.04, QEMU 1.0.50, OVP v20140127.0 and SystemC 2.3.0.

Experimental results concerning simulation times are reported in Table 1. A software application running on the target CPU has been required to ask the SystemC peripheral to compute the ECC a variable number of times (Column ITERATIONS. The experiment has been executed on the QEMU-SystemC and OVP-SystemC common architecture described in Sect. 3 (respectively, columns QEMU-SYSTEMC BRIDGE and OVP-SYSTEMC BRIDGE). Moreover, a virtual platform has been implemented by wrapping the OVP modules of the Malta platform into a SystemC design by following the official guidelines reported in the OVP documentation [14] (columns OVP WRAPPED INTO SYSTEMC). This requires also to implement a transactor to convert the RTL interface of the ECC module towards a TLM 2.0 interface. Two different sets of experiments have been executed by setting the clock period of the SystemC RTL peripheral, respectively to 10 ms (left part of the table) and 1 ns (right part of the table). This different setting negatively impacted on the results of the official OVP-SystemC schema, since it was not able to carry on the simulation for clock periods lower than 10 ms. The simulation blocked during the initialization phase. Indeed, OVP guidelines explicitly state that CPU manager is based on the TLM

2.0 loosely time model, and it is not intended for cycle-accurate simulation of RTL components. Attempting to use other models gives incorrect results. On the contrary, with a period of 1 ms the simulation works correctly, but the simulation time is negatively affected with respect to the co-simulation schemas proposed in this paper.

Table 1. Comparison of simulation times between the SystemC-QEMU/OVP common co-simulation architecture proposed in this paper and the native way of integrating OVP into SystemC described in the OVP guidelines [14].

Iterations	SystemC clock set at 10 ms			SystemC clock set at 1 ns		
	Boot	Boot & run	Run	Boot	Boot & run	Run
QEMU-SystemC bridge						
5,000	80.54 s	92.84 s	12.30 s	79.79 s	91.18 s	11.39 s
10,000		103.11 s	22.57 s		102.45 s	22.66 s
50,000		191.07 s	110.53 s		197.65 s	117.86 s
100,000		314.65 s	234.11 s		305.84 s	226.05 s
OVP-SystemC bridge						
5,000	85.50 s	125.07 s	39.57 s	79.95 s	123.68 s	43.73 s
10,000		170.19 s	84.69 s		171.41 s	91.46 s
50,000		475.60 s	390.10 s		474.30 s	394.43 s
100,000		899.92 s	814.42 s		903.76 s	823.81 s
OVP wrapped into SystemC [14]						
5,000	101.83 s	458.46 s	356.63 s	-	-	-
10,000		835.62 s	733.79 s	-	-	-
50,000		3808.38 s	3706.55 s	-	-	-
100,000		7509.38 s	7407.55 s	-	-	-

The table reports the time required to boot and shut down the virtual platform without running the application (Boot)[3], the time required to boot, run the application and shut down (Boot & run), and finally, the time referred to only the run of the application (Run). This final value is the most interesting, since it includes the time required for the communication between the QEMU/OVP virtual platform and the SystemC peripheral. There is a significant difference in the communication time. This is highlighted in Table 2, where a comparison between the OVP-SystemC co-simulation proposed in this paper and the native way of integrating OVP into SystemC described in the OVP guidelines is reported, taking the QEMU-SystemC architecture, which is the fastest, as reference for the simulation time. Columns of the table report the simulation

---

[3] As expected, the boot time is not influenced by the iteration number in all the three schemas.

Table 2. Comparison between the OVP-SystemC co-simulation proposed in this paper and the native way of integrating OVP into SystemC described in the OVP guidelines [14], taking the QEMU-SystemC architecture as reference for the simulation time.

ITERATION	SystemC clock set at 10 ms			SystemC clock set at 1 ns		
	QEMU-SC SIM. TIME	OVP-SC MUL. FAC.	OVPW-SC MUL. FAC.	QEMU-SC SIM. TIME	OVP-SC MUL. FAC.	OVPW-SC MUL. FACT
BOOT						
5,000	80.54 s	1.1x	1.3x	79.79 s	1.0x	-
10,000						
50,000						
100,000						
RUN						
5,000	12.30 s	3.2x	29.0x	11.39 s	3.8x	-
10,000	22.57 s	3.8x	32.5x	22.66 s	4.0x	-
50,000	110.53 s	3.5x	33.x5	117.86 s	3.3x	-
100,000	234.11 s	3.5x	31.6x	226.05 s	3.6x	-

time for the QEMU-based architecture (QEMU-SC SIM. TIME), and its ratio (multiplication factor) with respect to the simulation time of the OVP-SystemC archichture based on the SytemC bridge (OVP-SC MUL. FAC.) and the architecture proposed in [14] (OVPW-SC MUL. FAC.). While boot time (columns BOOT) is almost similar among the three approaches, the communication with the SystemC peripheral introduces an higher overhead in the OVP-based platforms rather than in the QEMU one (columns RUN). However, it is worth noting that the overhead is much higher by adopting the co-simulation proposed in [14] with respect to using the bridge-based architecture proposed in this paper. This shows that the architecture described in this paper is more efficient with respect to wrapping OVP models into SystemC.

5   Conclusions

In this paper, we present a common architecture to integrate SystemC with both QEMU and OVP. The architecture is based on a SystemC bridge, which manages the communication protocol and the synchronization mechanism between QEMU/OVP and SystemC, and a virtual device, which acts as an interface between the SystemC simulator and the QEMU or OVP world. Interrupt handling is also supported. The bridge is the same for both QEMU and OVP, while only the virtual device must be coded according to the APIs exported by QEMU and OVP. This allows to rapidly reuse SystemC components from a QEMU-based to an OVP-based virtual platform and vice versa.

Experimental results highlighted that the QEMU-based approach is almost 4 times faster than the corresponding OVP-based approach. However, compared to the official way of integrating SystemC with OVP reported in the OVP guidelines, the OVP co-simulation approach proposed in this paper is one order of magnitude faster. Furthermore, we support cycle-accurate simulation of RTL (as well as TLM) models, while only TLM 2.0 loosely timed models work properly with the official OVP-SystemC co-simulation schema.

Future works will be mainly devoted to the definition of a more precise timing synchronization. Currently, synchronization between QEMU/OVP and SystemC is not clock accurate. A further extension will be related to the possibility of instantiating an arbitrary number of SystemC components. In the current approach, this requires to run a separate instance of the SystemC simulation kernel for each SystemC model.

Acknowledgements. The authors would like to thank Filippo Cucchetto and Stefano Angeleri for their contribution in applying the proposed architecture to the case study reported in experimental results.

References

1. Hellestrand, G.: Enhance communications platform design with virtual systems prototyping. http://www.embeddedintel.com/special_features.php?article=115
2. Ebcioglu, K., Altman, E., Gschwind, M., Sathaye, S.: Dynamic binary translation and optimization. IEEE TCOMP **50**(6), 529–548 (2001)
3. VaST's new CoMET 5 systems engineering environment for architectural design and exploration avoids chip respins and speeds development. http://www.businesswire.com/news/home/20040524005033/en/VaSTs-CoMET-5-Systems-Engineering-Environment-Architectural.VNKYKsbS5U8
4. Wind River Simics. http://www.windriver.com/products/simics/simics_po_0520.pdf
5. Synopsys, CoMET-METeor. http://www.synopsys.com/Systems/VirtualPrototyping/Pages/CoMET-METeor.aspx
6. Graphics, M..: Vista virtual prototyping. http://www.mentor.com/esl/vista/virtual-prototyping/
7. Cadence, Virtual system platform. http://www.cadence.com/products/sd/virtual_system/
8. Bellard, F.: QEMU, a fast and portable dynamic translator. In: Proceedings of USENIX ATEC, pp. 41–46 (2005)
9. http://www.ovpworld.org/
10. Monton, M., Carrabina, J., Burton, M.: Mixed simulation kernels for high performance virtual platforms. In: ECSI FDL, pp. 1–6 (2009)
11. Becker, M., Di Guglielmo, G., Fummi, F., Mueller, W., Pravadelli, G., Xie, T.: RTOS-aware refinement for TLM2.0-based HW/SW designs. In: Proceedings of ACM/IEEE DATE, pp. 1053–1058 (2010)
12. Chiang, M.-C., Yeh, T.-C., Tseng, G.-F.: A QEMU and SystemC-based cycle-accurate ISS for performance estimation on SoC development. IEEE TCAD **30**(4), 593–606 (2011)
13. Monton, M., Engblom, J., Burton, M.: Checkpointing for virtual platforms and SystemC-TLM. IEEE TVLSI **21**(1), 133–141 (2013)

14. Using OVP models in SystemC TLM2.0 platforms (2013). http://www.ovp world.org/using-ovp-models-with-osci-systemc-tlm20-platforms-to-gain-200-500-mips-performance
15. Cucchetto, F., Lonardi, A., Pravadelli, G.: A common architecture for co-simulation of SystemC models in QEMU and OVP virtual platforms. In: Proceedings of IEEE VLSI-SOC, pp. 1–6 (2014)
16. Yeh, T.-C., Chiang, M.-C.: On the interface between QEMU and SystemC for hardware modeling. In: Proceedings of IEEE ISNE, pp. 73–76 (2010)
17. Rekik, W., Ben Said, M., Ben Amor, N., Abid, M.: Virtual prototyping of multi-processor architectures using the open virtual platform. In: Proceedings of IEEE ICCAT, pp. 1–6 (2013)
18. Marchesan Almeida, G., Bellaver Longhi, O., Bruckschloegl, T., Hubner, M., Hessel, F., Becker, J.: Simplify: a framework for enabling fast functional/behavioral validation of multiprocessor architectures in the cloud. In: Proceedings of IEEE IPDPSW, pp. 2200–2205 (2013)
19. Jung, Y., Park, J., Petracca, M., Carloni, L.: netShip: a networked virtual platform for large-scale heterogeneous distributed embedded systems. In: Proceedings of ACM/EDAC/IEEE DAC, pp. 1–10 (2013)

Statistical Evaluation of Digital Techniques for $\Sigma\Delta$ ADC BIST

Matthieu Dubois[1,2], Haralampos-G. Stratigopoulos[1,2], Salvador Mir[1,2], and Manuel J. Barragan[1,2(✉)]

[1] TIMA, CNRS, 38000 Grenoble, France
[2] TIMA, Université Grenoble-Alpes, 38000 Grenoble, France
manuel.barragan@imag.fr

Abstract. Digital techniques for an embedded dynamic test of $\Sigma\Delta$ ADCs have been recently presented in the literature. These techniques are based on the use of $\Sigma\Delta$ streams for the stimulation of the ADC. Binary and ternary test stimuli have been proposed. In this chapter, we aim at the validation of these embedded test techniques, comparing the results obtained with the different types of digital stimuli with a standard high-resolution analog sinusoidal stimulus. This validation is done in terms of the expected yield loss and test escapes of the proposed embedded techniques. However, performing this validation at the design stage demands extensive computational resources, which may render electrical simulations infeasible. Thus, we propose an advanced simulation framework for this validation. The proposed simulation strategy relies on a combination of transistor-level simulations, behavioral simulations, and statistical tools.

1 Introduction

The standard approach for characterizing the dynamic performance of an analog-to-digital converter (ADC), i.e. signal-to-noise ratio (SNR), signal-to-noise-and-distortion ratio (SNDR), etc., requires the application of a full-scale sinusoidal analog test stimulus at the input of the ADC and the collection of a high number of output samples to accurately compute the spectrum of the ADC response [1,2]. The resolution of the sinusoidal analog test stimulus is required to be at least two or three bits above the resolution of the ADC, such that the noise and distortion at the output are predominantly due to the ADC. The test resources for generating the test stimulus and for storing and processing the digital samples of the ADC response can be found in any modern Automatic Test Equipment (ATE). Yet, a built-in test approach where test stimulus generation and response evaluation are instead implemented on-chip would greatly reduce test costs, since the ATE requirements would be relaxed and the test throughput would be increased. However, implementing these test resources on-chip with low overhead circuitry remains a challenging task. Especially, the on-chip generation of a high-resolution analog sinusoidal test stimulus is extremely challenging and has led to the search

© IFIP International Federation for Information Processing 2015
L. Claesen et al. (Eds.): VLSI-SoC 2014, IFIP AICT 464, pp. 129–148, 2015.
DOI: 10.1007/978-3-319-25279-7_8

for equivalent digital techniques. $\Sigma\Delta$ ADCs in particular offer this possibility and are the focus of this chapter.

In this line, an idea that has been thoroughly explored in the literature is the use of $\Sigma\Delta$ digital bitstreams to encode a high-resolution analog sinusoidal test stimulus. As it is schematically depicted in Fig. 1, the starting point is to use an ideal $\Sigma\Delta$ modulator in software that converts a high-resolution analog sinusoid to a bitstream [6]. The bitstream is divided in sub-bitstreams of length N and the sub-bitstream with the highest resolution (i.e. highest SNR, SNDR, etc.) is selected to be periodically reproduced through a circular shift register. Bitstreams can also be generated by on-chip digital oscillators, but their design is not as straightforward [9,10]. The bitstream can be converted to a high-resolution analog sinusoid by passing it through a 1-bit digital-to-analog converter (DAC), which could simply be a digital buffer, followed by a low-pass filter to remove the quantization noise. Although this solution is applicable for a built-off test where the 1-bit DAC and the low-pass filter are placed on the load board [12], it is not applicable for a built-in test since the low-pass filter is far more complex than the $\Sigma\Delta$ modulator itself [13].

Interestingly, in the case of switched-capacitor (SC) $\Sigma\Delta$ ADCs, the bitstream can be fed directly into the modulator by adding simple circuitry at its input [7,17,18]. Typically, a 1-bit DAC is merged into the first integrator in the $\Sigma\Delta$ modulator, and used to convert the bitstream to the analog reference voltages of the modulator. Figure 2 shows an efficient implementation of this approach into a generic SC integrator. As it can be seen, the injection of the $\Sigma\Delta$ bitstream only requires the addition of four switches, which is a negligible modification in the overall design of the modulator.

However, the direct application of the bitstream to the input of the ADC will overload the modulator, unless the reference voltages of the 1-bit DAC are

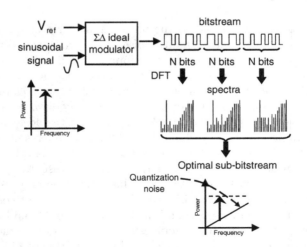

Fig. 1. Generation of optimized $\Sigma\Delta$ digital bitstreams.

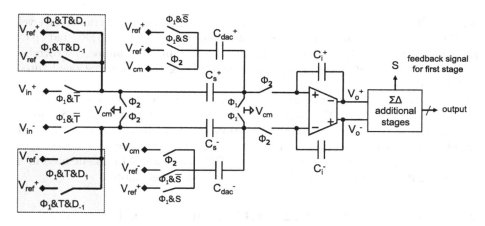

Fig. 2. Injection of binary stimulus $\{D_{-1}, D_1\}$ into the first stage of a generic switched-capacitor $\Sigma\Delta$ modulator.

adequately attenuated. Unfortunately, by attenuating these reference voltages we also scale down the amplitude of the encoded sinusoid. The maximum amplitude that can be encoded in the bitstream is in fact less than the actual dynamic range of the ADC and, thereby, we do not test the dynamic performances of the ADC at full scale. Especially for measuring SNDR, the amplitude of the test stimulus has to be as close as possible to full scale such that the harmonic distortion introduced by the ADC under test is amply manifested [15].

A solution to this problem has been proposed in [8]. More specifically, the input switched-capacitor network of the modulator is reconfigured in test mode in such a way that it accepts multiple bitstreams delayed from each other. This reconfiguration is shown to attenuate the noise power of the test stimulus, thus the modulator starts overloading for a test stimulus with a much higher amplitude than before. However, this comes at the expense of modifying significantly the input stage of the modulator.

An elegant approach to overcome this issue was presented in [3]. A test stimulus is encoded in a ternary stream that is composed of three levels $\{-1, 0, 1\}$. The ternary stream is converted to a three-level analog signal directly at the input stage of the modulator. The conversion does not require reconfiguration of the input stage and is achieved through the addition of only four switches, that is, just as in the case of applying a digital bitstream. The proposed approach presents minimal overhead and allows measuring SNDR for amplitudes close to full scale.

In this chapter, we present a review of dynamic testing of $\Sigma\Delta$ ADCs based on a ternary test stimulus and we develop a simulation framework to validate this test approach. This chapter extends and improves the techniques and strategies previously presented by the authors in [4]. The proposed simulation framework allows us to compare the ternary test stimulus against the bitstream and high-resolution sinusoidal test stimuli, in order to show its feasibility and accuracy. Our simulation framework relies on a combination of transistor-level and behavioral-level simulations to generate instances of the $\Sigma\Delta$ ADC that span the whole feasible design space. In this way, we are able to examine the correlation between the test decisions obtained by applying the aforementioned three test stimuli.

The rest of the chapter is organized as follows. Section 2 presents our strategy for dynamic test of $\Sigma\Delta$ ADCs based on a ternary test stimulus. Section 3 discusses an efficient on-chip implementation. Section 4 describes our proposed simulation framework for validating our test strategy, while Sect. 5 demonstrates its application on a second-order SC $\Sigma\Delta$ ADC that has been implemented in a 130 nm CMOS technology. Finally, Sect. 6 concludes the chapter.

2 Dynamic Test of $\Sigma\Delta$ ADCs Using Digital Ternary Stimuli

Our test approach is a fully-digital, low-cost BIST strategy for measuring the Signal-to-Noise and Distortion Ratio (SNDR) of $\Sigma\Delta$ ADCs, originally proposed in [3,18]. Figure 3 shows the general block diagram of the BIST strategy. The BIST circuitry is mainly composed of two digital blocks, namely the Stimulus Generator, and Response Analyzer. During test mode, the $\Sigma\Delta$ ADC under test is disconnected from the main signal path and is connected to the Stimulus Generator and the Response Analyzer. The Stimulus Generator provides an optimized digital ternary stimulus to the input whereas the Response Analyzer computes the SNDR based on a simplification of the sine-wave fitting algorithm. In the following subsections, we discuss the theoretical basis of the ternary stimulus and its optimization, as well as the theoretical basis of the response analysis strategy. An efficient on-chip implementation is discussed in Sect. 3.

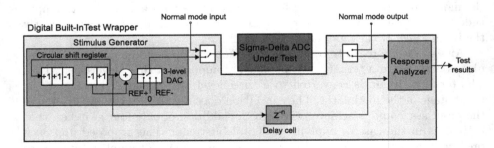

Fig. 3. General block diagram of the BIST strategy for $\Sigma\Delta$ ADCs.

2.1 Ternary Stimulus: Theoretical Basis

Our test strategy for the dynamic test of $\Sigma\Delta$ ADCs is based on the injection of a high-linearity ternary stimulus that is composed of three levels $\{-1, 0, 1\}$ at the input of the modulator of the $\Sigma\Delta$ ADC under test. The ternary stimulus is generated in the digital domain by adding a $\Sigma\Delta$ encoded binary bitstream with a delayed version of itself, as shown in Fig. 4.

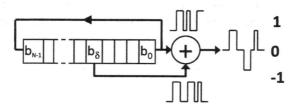

Fig. 4. Ternary stream construction.

From a spectral point of view, the Discrete Fourier Transform (DFT) of a length-N bitstream $\{b_0, \cdots, b_{N-1}\}$ is given by

$$B(k) = \sum_{n=0}^{N-1} b_n \cdot e^{-j\frac{2\pi \cdot n}{N}k}, \quad k = 0, \cdots, N-1. \tag{1}$$

The N periodic extension leads to a spectrum made by N lines located at $f_k = kf_s/N$, where f_s is the sampling frequency. The DFT of the circular-shifted bitstream delayed by δ samples $\{b_\delta, \cdots, b_{N-1}, b_0, \cdots, b_{\delta-1}\}$ is obtained by applying the time shift theorem to (1)

$$B_\delta(k) = B(k) \cdot e^{-j\frac{2\pi}{N}\delta k}, \quad k, \delta = 0, \cdots, N-1. \tag{2}$$

The DFT of the ternary stream is then obtained by averaging the DFT of the original bitstream and the DFT of the circular-shifted version of it and by using the linearity property of the DFT

$$T(k) = \frac{B(k)}{2} \left(1 + e^{-j\frac{2\pi}{N}\delta k}\right), \quad k, \delta = 0, \cdots, N-1. \tag{3}$$

The Power Spectral Density (PSD) of the bitstream and the ternary stream are given by

$$S_B(k) = \|B(k)\|^2 \tag{4}$$

$$S_T(k) = S_B(k) \cdot cos^2 \left(\frac{\pi k \delta}{N}\right) \tag{5}$$

$$k, \delta = 0, \cdots, N-1.$$

Therefore, for $\delta = 1, \cdots, N-1$, $k = 0, \cdots, N-1$, the amplitude of the spectra of the ternary stream is lower than the amplitude of the spectra of the bitstream, i.e. $S_T(k) < S_B(k)$, and the cumulative PSD of the ternary stream $Pq_T(n) = \sum_{k=2}^{n} S_T(k)$ is less than the cumulative PSD of the bitstream

$Pq_B(n) = \sum_{k=2}^{n} S_B(k)$, i.e. $Pq_T(n) < Pq_B(n)$, $n = 2, \cdots, N-1$. This is shown graphically in Fig. 5 for $\delta = 1$. As it can be observed, the spectra of the ternary stream presents a high frequency filter behaviour and the quantization noise power of the ternary stream is about 6 dB less than the quantization noise power of the bitstream. In other words, the ternary stream overloads less the modulator compared to the bitstream and, thereby, offers the possibility of testing the $\Sigma\Delta$ ADC closer to full scale.

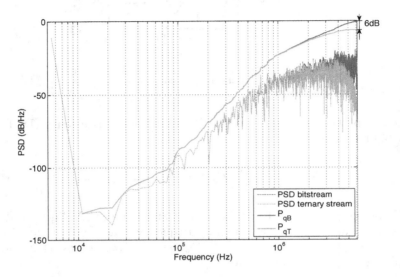

Fig. 5. Power spectral density and cumulative power spectral density of a bitstream and a ternary stream for $\delta = 1$.

The fundamental of the ternary stream is given from (3) for $k = 1$

$$T(1) = \frac{B(1)}{2} \cdot \left(1 + e^{-j\frac{2\pi}{N}\delta}\right)$$
$$= B(1) \cdot cos\left(\frac{\pi \cdot \delta}{N}\right) \cdot e^{-j\frac{\pi}{N}\delta}, \qquad (6)$$
$$\delta = 0, \cdots, N-1.$$

If we denote by A_T and Φ_T the amplitude and the phase of the fundamental of the ternary stream and by A_B and Φ_B the amplitude and the phase of the fundamental of the bitstream, then from (6)

$$A_T = A_B \cdot \left|cos\left(\frac{\pi \cdot \delta}{N}\right)\right| \qquad (7)$$

$$\Phi_T - \Phi_B = -\frac{\pi}{N}\delta \qquad (8)$$
$$\delta = 0, \cdots, N-1.$$

Therefore, when $\delta \ll N$, $A_T \approx A_B$ and $\Phi_T \approx \Phi_B$, i.e. the amplitude and the phase of the fundamental encoded in the ternary stream are practically the same with the amplitude and the phase of the fundamental encoded in the bitstream. As δ increases, A_T decreases with respect to A_B and the phase difference $\Phi_T - \Phi_B$ moves away from zero. These relationships are plotted in Fig. 6.

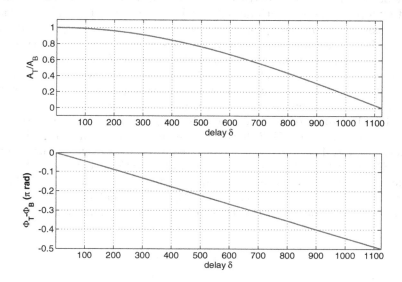

Fig. 6. Encoded signal amplitude and phase versus delay δ (for $\delta = 1$ to N/2).

2.2 Ternary Stimulus Optimization

For a meaningful dynamic test, the in-band noise and harmonic distortion of the ternary test stimulus have to be smaller than the noise and distortion originated by the $\Sigma\Delta$ ADC under test. Typically, the SNDR of the test stimulus should be at least 3 effective number of bits (ENOB) higher than the SNDR specification of the $\Sigma\Delta$ ADC. Moreover, the power of the test stimulus has to be as small as possible to avoid overloading the $\Sigma\Delta$ modulator. The ternary stimulus has to be optimized so as to fulfill these requirements.

The spectral quality of the ternary stimulus is defined by two parameters: the initial bitstream and the delay parameter δ. Concerning the initial bitstream, our optimization loop simulates an ideal $\Sigma\Delta$ modulator of one order higher than the $\Sigma\Delta$ modulator under test using a pure sinusoidal input signal of an amplitude A_T. From the output of this ideal $\Sigma\Delta$ modulator, the algorithm selects several bitstreams of length N equal to the period of the input signal and it records their total power $P_B = P_{q_B}(N-1)$. Next, for each bitstream, it computes the SNDR and the total power of the resulting ternary stream $P_T = P_{q_T}(N-1)$ for different values of δ. The objective of the optimization loop is to select a ternary stream that has a SNDR larger than the SNDR specification of the $\Sigma\Delta$ modulator by at least 3 ENOB and a low power P_T or, equivalently, a large ratio P_B/P_T.

As an example of the described optimization procedure, Fig. 7 plots the SNDR of the ternary stream versus the ratio P_B/P_T for different initial bitstreams of length $N = 2252$, extracted from an ideal third-order $\Sigma\Delta$ modulator excited by a pure sinusoid with amplitude $A_T = -8\,\mathrm{dBFS}$. Five different values of δ were considered in the optimization. For a given δ, the large SNDR variations stem from using different initial bitstreams to generate the ternary stream. For a given initial bitstream, we obtain different ratios P_B/P_T by varying δ. It can be seen that the highest P_B/P_T is achieved for $\delta = 1$. In particular, for this choice of δ, the total power of the ternary test stimulus is 5 times lower than the total power of the bitstream from which it is generated. Furthermore, from Fig. 8, which is a zoom onto the upper right corner of Fig. 7, it can be seen that for a given δ the highest SNDR does not necessarily correspond to the best possible ratio P_B/P_T. Thus, amongst the bitstreams that result in a ternary stream with an SNDR at least 3 ENOB higher than the SNDR specification of the $\Sigma\Delta$ modulator under test, we select the sequence that has the best ratio P_B/P_T. Assuming an SNDR specification of 106 dB, the optimal bitstream circled in Fig. 8 has an SNDR of 109.5 dB with a ratio P_B/P_T of around 5.25.

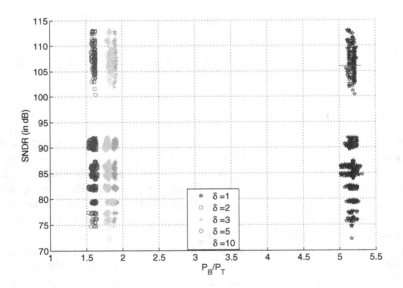

Fig. 7. SNDR of the ternary stream versus the power ratio P_B/P_T as a function of the delay parameter δ.

Finally, this algorithm is repeated for different input signal amplitudes A_T, in order to generate optimized test stimuli that cover the whole dynamic range

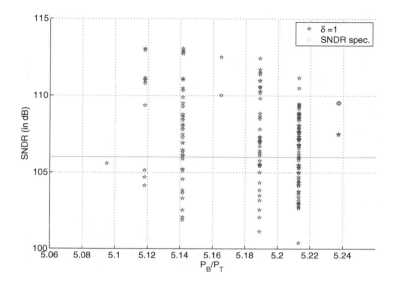

Fig. 8. Selection of a ternary stream that has an appropriate SNDR.

of the $\Sigma\Delta$ ADC under test. Figure 9 plots the SNDR of the ternary stream as a function of the input signal amplitude A_T. In all cases, the SNDR of the ternary stream exceeds the SNDR specification of the $\Sigma\Delta$ modulator by more than 3 ENOB. A ternary stream that encodes a sinusoid with full scale amplitude cannot be obtained since the bitstream generator will be overloaded. However, this is not a concern since the $\Sigma\Delta$ modulator under test itself is overloaded for amplitudes very close to the full scale.

2.3   Response Evaluation: Theoretical Basis

The analysis of the ADC response is performed by a simplified version of the sine-wave fitting algorithm. This simplification is based on the fact that our test stimulus and reference signal have the same frequency and they are completely synchronized, which saves us from computing the phase of the test response. This synchronization between the response and reference signals is easily achieved in the digital domain by designing the delay cell in Fig. 3 to match the delay introduced by the $\Sigma\Delta$ modulator. Next, we describe in detail the proposed response evaluation algorithm.

In a first step, the algorithm computes the DC component of the response signal as

$$DC = \frac{1}{N} \sum_{i=1}^{N} S_{out}(i), \tag{9}$$

where $S_{out}(i)$ are the samples of the ADC output (i.e. the signal under evaluation) and N is the number of samples considered in the evaluation.

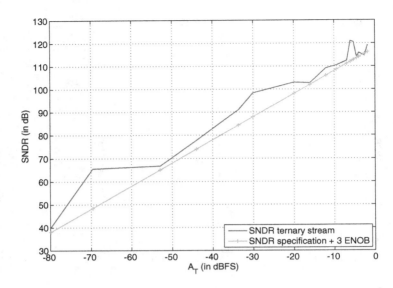

Fig. 9. SNDR of the optimized ternary stream for different input signal amplitudes A_T.

In a second step, the algorithm computes the point-to-point correlation of the response and reference signals as

$$Correl = \sum_{i=1}^{N} S_{out}(i)S_{ref}(i), \qquad (10)$$

where $S_{ref}(i)$ are the samples of the reference signal.

The amplitude of the response signal is related to the computed correlation as

$$A = \frac{2}{NA_{ref}} Correl, \qquad (11)$$

where A_{ref} is the amplitude of the reference signal, which is known *a priori*. Once the amplitude of the response signal has been computed, the algorithm continues by adjusting the reference signal to the amplitude and DC values obtained

$$S_{ref,adj}(i) = \frac{A}{A_{ref}} S_{ref}(i) + DC. \qquad (12)$$

Finally, the algorithm computes the noise and distortion power in the response signal, denoted by P_{error}, by comparing the samples of the ADC output with the samples of the adjusted reference signal

$$P_{error} = \frac{1}{N} \sum_{i=1}^{N} \left(S_{out}(i) - S_{ref,adj}(i) \right)^2. \qquad (13)$$

With the obtained P_{error} it is straightforward to compute the SNDR of the response signal as

$$SNDR = 10\log\frac{A^2/2}{P_{error}}. \tag{14}$$

Finally, by performing a comparison with a preloaded threshold, the BIST can provide a go/no-go output signal. Specifically, from (14)

$$Go/No\text{-}Go = \begin{cases} 1, & \text{if } \frac{A^2}{2} \geqslant P_{error}10^{SNDR_{spec}/10} \\ 0, & \text{if } \frac{A^2}{2} < P_{error}10^{SNDR_{spec}/10} \end{cases} \tag{15}$$

where the threshold value $SNDR_{spec}$ is the actual SNDR specification limit.

3   Efficient On-chip Implementation

The ternary stimulus can be efficiently generated on-chip while the response analysis is a purely digital algorithm, making the proposed strategy overall very suitable for a full BIST implementation, as illustrated in the general block diagram in Fig. 3.

Specifically, the ternary stimulus generator, although it is mostly digital, requires the introduction of a mixed-signal element, i.e. a 3-level DAC, to interface the digital ternary stimulus to the analog $\Sigma\Delta$ modulator. Figure 10 shows two different possible implementations for the digital part of the ternary stimulus generator. Figure 10(a) shows a strategy where the ATE is occupied for a

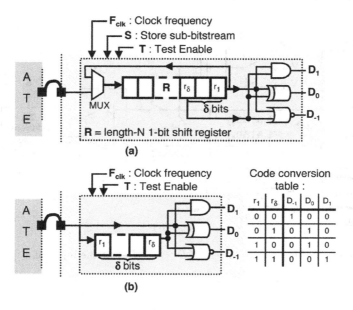

Fig. 10. On-chip generation of the ternary stream.

very small time interval to store in an on-chip shift register the length-N bitstream. During the testing phase, the bitstream circulates in the shift register and three logic gates are used to generate $\{D_{-1}, D_0, D_1\}$ that correspond to the three states $\{-1, 0, 1\}$ of the ternary stream. Another possibility, which incurs a lower area overhead, is to provide periodically the bitstream directly from the ATE, as shown in Fig. 10(b). This last implementation is attractive in the case where the bitstream can be generated on-chip using a digital resonator.

Concerning the injection of the digital ternary stimulus into the analog input of the modulator, the necessary Digital-to-Analog interface can be easily merged into the input section of a SC $\Sigma\Delta$ modulator. Figure 11 shows an implementation example for a generic fully-differential SC $\Sigma\Delta$ modulator. This implementation exploits the inherent linearity of 1-bit DACs built by two switches to perform the conversion. The test is enabled for $T = 1$. The states 1 and -1 are converted to a positive ΔV_{ref} and a negative $-\Delta V_{ref}$ differential voltage, respectively. To preserve the linearity of the test stimulus, the 0 state must correspond to the middle point between ΔV_{ref} and $-\Delta V_{ref}$, that is, the null differential voltage. Thus, the state 0 must be implemented by generating a null differential voltage at the input of the sampling capacitors, which corresponds to fully discharging the sampling capacitors. This can be achieved by switching the sampling capacitors to the common-mode voltage V_{cm} during the sampling phase, as shown in Fig. 11. Notice that the injection of the 0 state makes use of existing switches while the injection of the 1 and -1 states requires the addition of only four additional switches that are in the highlighted area. Finally, concerning the response analysis algorithm, its fully-digital implementation can be synthesized using standard digital design techniques and is out of the scope of this chapter.

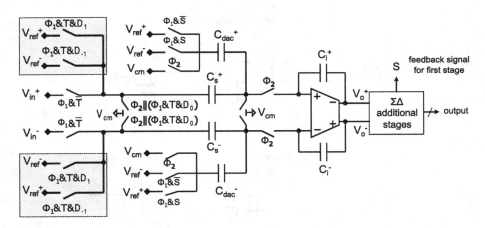

Fig. 11. Injection of the ternary stream $\{D_{-1}, D_0, D_1\}$ at the input of a SC $\Sigma\Delta$ modulator.

4   Simulation Framework

A key point for proving the feasibility of any embedded test strategy is to assess the resultant yield loss and test escapes. Yield loss is defined as the probability that a circuit will fail the test given that it is functional and test escape is defined as the probability that a circuit will pass the test given that it is faulty. In our analysis, we exclude catastrophic defects in the calculation of test escape since they are easily detectable and we focus exclusively on process variations which can bring the circuit outside the nominal specification range and are much more challenging to detect. In this case, we refer to parametric faults. The validation step has to be performed before deploying the proposed test technique into production, and, thereby, needs to rely necessarily on Monte Carlo simulations.

However, transistor-level Monte Carlo simulations may imply an important computational effort, depending on how fast the particular circuit under test can be simulated and also on the yield of the fabrication process. If the fabrication process has a natural parametric fault level in the range of a few hundreds of ppms (parts per million), then a small-scale Monte Carlo simulation will produce very few samples, if any at all, in the pass-fail boundary. In this case, a correct estimation of the test metrics, such as yield loss and parametric test escape, would require a prohibitively large number of Monte Carlo runs. Furthermore, regarding the case of $\Sigma\Delta$ ADCs, a single transistor-level simulation to compute the SNDR performance with an acceptable level of confidence could take days to complete. In short, direct transistor-level Monte Carlo simulations for estimating test metrics are computationally infeasible for our case study. Next, we propose a simulation framework for validation of the proposed test technique that overcomes this issue by relying in a combination of transistor-level simulations, behavioral-level simulations, and statistical tools.

The proposed simulation framework is schematically depicted in Fig. 12. Instead of simulating the complete $\Sigma\Delta$ ADC, in a first step we are going to break down the circuit into different building blocks. These building blocks are comparatively much smaller than the complete circuit and can be efficiently simulated at transistor-level. We then carry out an initial set of Monte Carlo runs for each building block separately, but using the same seed for each batch of simulations, such that the same sequence of process parameter vectors (e.g. the same netlists) are simulated for each batch of simulations. These simulations are, in any case, performed at the design stage by the designers to evaluate the robustness of the design, so they do not increase the design effort. The set of performances extracted from these simulations are used as behavioral parameters in a high-level behavioral model of the complete circuit. This way, we can efficiently estimate the effect of process parameter variations on the performance of the complete circuit.

The initial number of Monte Carlo runs needs to be low enough to keep the simulation time constrained, so it is unlikely that these simulations yield any samples of the complete circuit that have an SNDR close to the specification limit. In fact, it is likely that the majority of the samples will have an SNDR around the nominal value. To produce extreme variations that can bring the circuit out of specification, we propose to use a classical design of experiment technique in the behavioral parameter space. Specifically, we perform a Latin-Hypercube Sampling (LHS) in order to evenly cover the complete feasible behavioral parameter space. This way, we can easily draw vectors of behavioral parameters that correspond to extreme process parameter variations. By feeding these extreme behavioral parameters to the behavioral model, we can then produce extreme instances of the complete circuit that have an SNDR far from the nominal value.

5   Case Study

The following subsections describe the simulation framework and the obtained simulation results for a second-order SC $\Sigma\Delta$ modulator that has been implemented in a 130 nm CMOS technology [18]. This modulator is designed for audio ADC applications that must have 16 bits of resolution or, equivalently, an output SNDR of at least 96 dB.

5.1   Behavioral Model

$\Sigma\Delta$ ADCs are usually simulated by means of a behavioral model, since one transistor-level simulation may take several days to complete. The proposed behavioral model captures the main non-idealities of the individual sub-blocks composing the ADC by performing transistor-level simulations of the isolated blocks. Given that the decimation filter is not affected by parametric deviations since it is a digital circuit operating at moderate frequencies, only the non-idealities of the blocks of the $\Sigma\Delta$ modulator are considered. For the same reason, we do not include in this case study the on-chip response analysis block. Being a purely digital algorithm, it has been emulated in software. We consider the following non-idealities in the first integrator stage: finite amplifier open-loop gain and unity gain frequency, limited slew-rate, output saturation levels, kT/C noise, amplifier thermal noise, and clock jitter. Most non-idealities in the second integrator stage are of much less relative importance since they are attenuated due to the noise shaping. The only non-ideality that we consider for this stage is the output saturation levels. Finally, we consider the offset of the output comparator. The behavioral model derivation is explained in detail in [5,11,16]. The complete behavioral model, depicted in Fig. 13, is built and simulated in Matlab Simulink®. A single behavioral simulation to calculate SNDR with an accuracy of 0.1 dB lasts about 10 s on an Intel Core2 2.40 GHz PC.

5.2   Fault-Free Case

A vector of nominal behavioral parameters is extracted from transistor-level simulations of the sub-blocks that synthesize the $\Sigma\Delta$ modulator. The behavioral model is simulated for three different test stimuli: an ideal analog sinusoid that corresponds to a standard test, an optimized ternary stream where the ideal

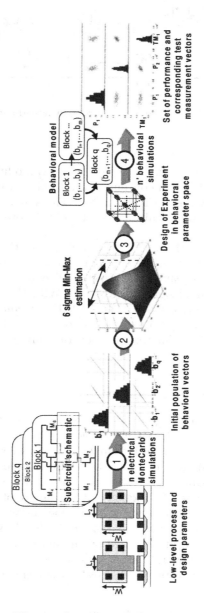

Fig. 12. Simulation framework.

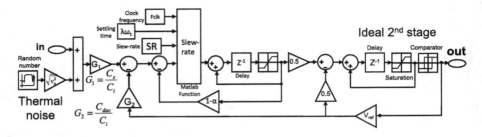

Fig. 13. Behavioral model for the second-order switched-capacitor $\Sigma\Delta$ modulator under study.

analog sinusoid serves as the input to the ideal $\Sigma\Delta$ modulator in software, and the selected bitstream from the output of the ideal $\Sigma\Delta$ modulator in software from which the ternary stream is generated. The simulations are repeated for different amplitudes of the ideal analog sinusoid, in order to cover the whole input dynamic range.

Figure 14 plots the SNDR versus the amplitude of the ideal analog sinusoid which is also the amplitude of the sinusoid encoded in the ternary stream and bitstream. The ternary stream and bitstream allow us to estimate correctly the SNDR until an input amplitude of -12 dBFS. With the bitstream we begin to underestimate significantly the SNDR at -8 dBFS. In contrast, with the ternary stream, we estimate SNDR with a maximum difference of 3 dB until -4.5 dBFS at which point the $\Sigma\Delta$ modulator starts overloading even for the ideal analog sinusoidal stimulus.

5.3   Nominal and Extreme Variations

According to the simulation guidelines in Sect. 4, first, the $\Sigma\Delta$ modulator is divided into sub-blocks and, for these sub-blocks we extract the behavioral parameters that capture the pertinent information. Then, we run $n = 10^3$ transistor-level Monte Carlo simulations of each sub-block using the same seed to obtain n vectors of behavioral parameters. A Monte Carlo analysis samples by definition the statistically likely cases. To examine the accuracy of the proposed built-in test technique across the feasible space of parameters, we perform a LHS of size $n' = 10^3$ in the space of behavioral parameters defined by minimum and maximum values that are fixed at 6σ based on the initial Monte Carlo sample [14]. This synthetic set of behavioral parameter vectors span beyond the most likely feasible space to emulate instances that exhibit extreme variations.

5.4   Parametric Test Metrics Estimation

Behavioral simulations were carried out for each of the $n + n'$ behavioral parameter vectors considering three different test stimuli: an ideal analog sinusoid with amplitude -4.5 dBFS which corresponds to the highest SNDR in Fig. 14,

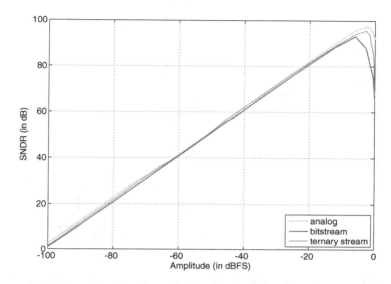

Fig. 14. SNDR across the dynamic range obtained with the standard analog test and by using the bitstream and ternary stream as test stimuli.

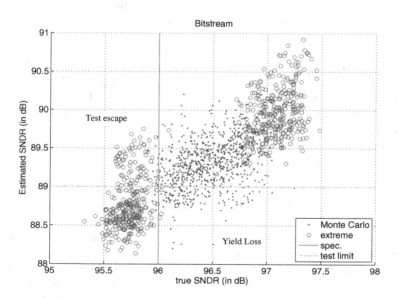

Fig. 15. SNDR estimates obtained by applying the bitstream compared to the true SNDR values obtained by applying the standard analog test stimulus.

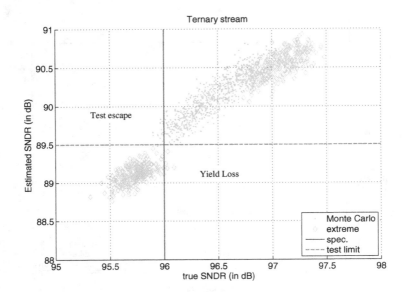

Fig. 16. SNDR estimates obtained by applying the ternary stream compared to the true SNDR values obtained by applying the standard analog test stimulus.

an optimized ternary stream where an ideal analog sinusoid with amplitude −12 dBFS serves as the input to the ideal $\Sigma\Delta$ modulator in software, and the selected bitstream from the output of the ideal $\Sigma\Delta$ modulator in software from which the ternary stream is generated.

Figure 15 projects the $n + n'$ instances onto the space defined by the true SNDR obtained by applying the ideal analog sinusoidal stimulus and the estimated SNDR obtained by applying the bitstream. Similarly, Fig. 16 shows the same result for the ternary stream. The solid points in Figs. 15 and 16 correspond to the n Monte Carlo instances while the circles in Fig. 15 and the diamonds in Fig. 16 correspond to the n' samples derived by LHS. The Monte Carlo instances are distributed around the nominal point while the extreme samples derived by LHS are distributed away from the nominal point at the upper right and lower left corners of the scatter plot. The SNDR specification of the $\Sigma\Delta$ modulator under test is fixed at 96 dB and it is shown in Figs. 15 and 16 with a vertical line. As it can be seen, most of the n Monte Carlo instances lie on the right side of the line, i.e. they satisfy the specification. Looking at the distribution of instances along the y-axis, we observe from Figs. 15 and 16 that the SNDR obtained by applying the bitstream presents a much larger variation and has a lower mean value compared to the case of the ternary stream. This is explained by the fact that the bitstream overloads the $\Sigma\Delta$ modulator under test to a larger degree compared to the case of the ternary stream. It can also be seen that the ternary stream results in SNDR estimates that correlate well with the true SNDR while for the bitstream the correlation is less apparent.

Test limits on the estimated SNDR can be placed to achieve the best trade-off between parametric test escape and yield loss. A possible selection of test limits is shown in Figs. 15 and 16 with the horizontal lines. Since the ternary stream leads to a better correlation between the true and estimated SNDR as opposed to the bitstream, we observe that the test escape and yield loss is much lower. Regarding the bitstream, any placement of the test limit will result inadvertently to test escape and/or yield loss.

6   Conclusion

In this chapter, we described a BIST technique for the SNDR performance of $\Sigma\Delta$ ADCs together with an advanced simulation framework for its thorough validation. The BIST technique is nearly fully digital with minimal modifications in the analog part of the ADC. It relies on the injection of a ternary stream test stimulus at the input of the ADC. It is shown that a ternary stream is more efficient than a bitstream in terms of stimulus dynamic range, as well as in terms of the resultant parametric test metrics, such as test escape and yield loss. Moreover, the actual values of the SNDR and the estimates obtained by applying a ternary stream correlate very well, which makes the proposed BIST practically equivalent to the standard test using a high-resolution analog sinusoid supplied from the ATE.

References

1. IEEE standard for digitizing waveform recorders. IEEE Std 1057–2007 (Revision of IEEE 1057–1994), pp. 1–142 (2008)
2. IEEE standard for terminology and test methods for analog-to-digital converters. IEEE Std 1241–2010 (Revision of IEEE Std 1241–2000), pp. 1–139 (2011)
3. Dubois, M., Stratigopoulos, H.G., Mir, S.: Ternary stimulus for fully digital dynamic testing of SC $\Sigma\Delta$ ADCs. In: IEEE International Mixed-Signals, Sensors, and Systems Test Workshop, pp. 5–10 (2012)
4. Dubois, M., Stratigopoulos, H.G., Mir, S., Barragan, M.J.: Evaluation of digital ternary stimuli for dynamic test of $\Sigma\Delta$ ADCs. In: 2014 22nd International Conference on Very Large Scale Integration (VLSI-SoC), pp. 1–6, 6–8 Oct 2014
5. Dubois, M., Stratigopoulos, H., Mir, S.: Hierarchical parametric test metrics estimation : A $\Sigma\Delta$ converter BIST case study. In: Proceedings of the IEEE International Conference on Computer Design, pp. 78–83 (2009)
6. Dufort, B., Roberts, G.W.: On-chip analog signal generation for mixed-signal built-in self-test. IEEE J. Solid-State Circuits **34**(3), 318–30 (1999)
7. Hong, H.C.: A design-for-digital-testability circuit structure for $\Sigma\Delta$ modulators. IEEE Trans. Very Large Scale Integr. (VLSI) Syst. **15**(12), 1341–1350 (2007)
8. Hong, H.C., Liang, S.C.: A decorrelating design-for-digital-testability scheme for $\Sigma\Delta$ modulators. IEEE Trans. Circuits Syst. I Regul. Pap. **56**(1), 60–73 (2009)
9. Hong, H.C., Liang, S.C., Song, H.C.: A cost effective BIST second-order $\Sigma\Delta$ modulator. In: Proceedings of IEEE Workshop on Design and Diagnostics of Electronic Circuits and Systems, pp. 1–6 (2008)

10. Lu, A., Roberts, G., Johns, D.: A high-quality analog oscillator using oversampling DA conversion techniques. In: Proceedings of the IEEE International Symposium on Circuits and Systems, pp. 1298–1301 (1993)
11. Malcovati, P., Brigati, S., Franscesconi, F., Maloberti, F., Cusinato, P., Baschirotto, A.: Behavioral modeling of switched-capacitor sigma-delta modulators. IEEE Trans. Circuits Syst. I Fundam. Theory Appl. **50**(3), 351–364 (2003)
12. Mattes, H., Sattler, S., Dworski, C.: Controlled sine wave fitting for ADC test. In: Proceedings of the IEEE International Test Conference, pp. 963–971 (2004)
13. Mir, S., Rolindez, L., Domigues, C., Rufer, L.: An implementation of memory-based on-chip analogue test signal generation. In: Proceedings of the IEEE Asia and South Pacific Design Automation Conference, pp. 663–668 (2003)
14. Mutlu, A., Rahman, M.: Statistical methods for the estimation of process variation effects on circuit operation. IEEE Trans. Electron. Packag. Manuf. **28**(4), 364–375 (2005)
15. Norsworthy, S.R., Schreier, R., Temes, G.C.: Delta-Sigma Data Converters: Theory, Design, and Simulation. Wiley IEEE Press, New York (1997)
16. Oliaei, O.: Thermal noise analysis of multi-input SC-integrators for delta-sigma modulator design. In: Proceedings of the IEEE International Symposium on Circuits and Systems, vol. 4, pp. 425–428 (2000)
17. Ong, C.K., Cheng, K.T., Wang, L.C.: A new sigma-delta modulator architecture for testing using digital stimulus. IEEE Trans. Circuits Syst. I Regul. Pap. **51**(1), 206–213 (2004)
18. Rolindez, L., Mir, S., Carbonero, J.L., Goguet, D., Chouba, N.: A stereo $\Sigma\Delta$ ADC architecture with embedded SNDR self-test. In: Proceedings of the IEEE International Test Conference (2007). (paper 32.1)

A Parallel MCMC-Based MIMO Detector: VLSI Design and Algorithm

Dominik Auras[✉], Uwe Deidersen, Rainer Leupers,
and Gerd Ascheid

Institute for Communication Technologies and Embedded Systems,
RWTH Aachen University, 52056 Aachen, Germany
auras@ice.rwth-aachen.de
http://www.ice.rwth-aachen.de

Abstract. Stochastic detection for multi-antenna (MIMO) systems promises communications performance close to max-log detection for certain SNR regimes, especially when the system iterates between detector and channel decoder following the Turbo Principle. In this work, we propose a parallel VLSI architecture for soft-input soft-output Markov chain Monte Carlo based stochastic MIMO detection. It features runtime adaptability to varying channel conditions, effectively allowing us to adjust the invested effort. Besides the details of our area-throughput efficient design, like the low-level algorithm and micro-architecture design, we also provide an extensive data set from our experiments regarding the detector's communications performance and relate it to our VLSI implementation results. The provided data analysis highlights the architecture's run-time adaptability and demonstrates how we can trade off throughput for improved communications performance.

1   Introduction

With the wide-spread adoption of MIMO (multi-antenna) technology in current and future wireless communication systems, such as those based on the IEEE 802.11n standard [1], academia and industry are searching for MIMO detectors with reasonable implementation complexity and algorithmic performance. Especially for systems using bit-interleaved coded modulation with iterative decoding (BICM-ID) [2], a major challenge for VLSI implementation is the required soft-input soft-output (SISO) detector, since optimal detection has an exponential complexity.

Iterative MIMO decoding can yield impressive algorithmic performance gains in terms of significantly reduced signal-to-noise ratio (SNR) requirements to achieve a certain fixed error rate [3]. This SNR gain has several possible uses amongst others: we can extend the transmission range, we can serve more users (i.e. tolerating more interference), we can lower the transmission power to save energy (and at the same time reduce interference to other users), or transmit at a higher throughput in the same bandwidth.

ⓒ IFIP International Federation for Information Processing 2015
L. Claesen et al. (Eds.): VLSI-SoC 2014, IFIP AICT 464, pp. 149–169, 2015.
DOI: 10.1007/978-3-319-25279-7_9

Possible detectors can be roughly put into two categories: linear detectors, e.g. MMSE-filter based [4–6], and non-linear detectors e.g. [3,7–9]. Basically, linear detectors try to suppress noise using linear filtering, then decode the estimate. In contrast to this, non-linear detectors perform a search, e.g. a randomly guided one, in the space of possibly transmitted data vectors. Stochastic detection based on Markov chain Monte Carlo (MCMC) methods [10] belongs to this class. It enables small configurable detectors that can cover a large design space. Furthermore, when iterating between detector and channel decoder, MCMC detection shows a communications performance close to max-log detection for certain SNR regimes [10].

To date, only some research effort has been directed towards this field. There exist only a handful of publications on MCMC detector architectures at the moment [11–14]. None of them correlates communications performance with VLSI implementations results.

Related Work. An MCMC-based SISO MIMO detector ASIC design supporting independent parallel Gibbs Samplers is presented in [12]. Amongst other things, [12] introduces an initialization scheme for the completely recursive, and thus simplified, computation of the detector states, and shows how to reuse the circuitry to draw independent first samples. However, a multiplier in the timing critical path yields a limited throughput and a relatively large area consumption.

In [11], the authors propose an MCMC-based SISO MIMO detector architecture mapped on an FPGA. It features one multiplier-free Gibbs Sampler pipelined at the symbol vector level. The architecture uses a simple recursive metric computation, but requires one dot-product per cycle. The first sample of every chain needs to be generated externally.

The hybrid soft-output only MCMC detector architecture [14] combined with a hard-output fixed-complexity sphere detector (FSD) features parallel multiplier-free Gibbs Samplers that start with the best candidates found by the FSD. However, the design requires the QR-decomposition of the channel matrix, and the results are only given in terms of operation counts.

Contribution. We present a complete redesign of the MCMC-based MIMO detector architecture presented in [12], with multiplier-free Gibbs Samplers and further architectural improvements that result in a significant area reduction and timing improvement. Post-layout area and clock period reduce by about 50 % and 40 % respectively. In extension to our previous publication [13], we additionally provide our detector's communications performance results and present an analysis showing how to trade off throughput for improved communications performance at run-time.

Outline. First, we introduce the general concept of MCMC-based MIMO detection (Sect. 3), describe the implemented algorithm (Sect. 4), then we propose the redesigned architecture (Sect. 5). Subsequently, we explicitly highlight the differences to the reference design [12] in Sect. 6. Our implementation results are

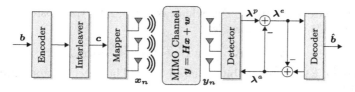

Fig. 1. Assumed MIMO BICM-ID System Model. Detector and decoder iteratively exchange information to improve the final decoding result.

presented in Sect. 7. The analysis of the communications performance results is explained in Sect. 8.

2 System Model

We consider a spatial-multiplexing $N_t \times N_r$ MIMO system with BICM-ID, as depicted in Fig. 1. A message $b \in \{0,1\}^{N_b}$ is encoded with rate $r = N_b/N_c$ and interleaved, yielding the code word $c \in \{0,1\}^{N_c}$. Let $\mathcal{X} \subset \mathbb{C}$ be a modulation alphabet with $K = \log_2 |\mathcal{X}|$ bits per symbol. The code word is partitioned into multiple subvectors $c_n \in \{0,1\}^{KN_t}$. They are subsequently mapped to symbol vectors $x_n \in \mathcal{X}^{N_t}$ that are transmitted independently. Assuming a frequency-flat fading channel characterized by $H_n \in \mathbb{C}^{N_r \times N_t}$, the received symbol vector at time n is $y_n = H_n x_n + w_n$ where $w_n \in \mathbb{C}^{N_r}$ is a white Gaussian noise process with $\mathbb{E}[w_n w_n^H] = N_0 I_{N_r}$. In the remainder, the time index n is dropped for convenience. Using iterative MIMO decoding following the Turbo Principle [15], detector and channel decoder exchange extrinsic information $\lambda^e = \lambda^p - \lambda^a$ in terms of log-likelihood ratios (LLRs), where λ^p are the detector's posterior LLRs and λ^a are the prior LLRs fed back from the decoder.

3 MCMC-Based MIMO Detection

The Markov chain Monte Carlo based MIMO detector class that we consider performs a randomly guided search in the space $c \in \{0,1\}^{KN_t}$. It starts with a random candidate, then walks around randomly. On its way, it evaluates and saves metric values of the current candidates, which are later used to approximate the posterior LLRs. The random process (Monte Carlo) from which it draws new candidates evolves recursively (Markov chain). By design the search converges towards candidates of high probability [10].

We select independent first samples $c^{(q,0)} \in \{0,1\}^{KN_t}$, one per chain $q = 1 \ldots N_q$, either randomly from the prior distribution $c^{(q,0)} \sim p(c) = f(\lambda^a)$ or given by an external hard-output detector $c^{(q,0)} = c^{\text{ext}}$ (usually for at most one chain). Every sample $s = 1 \ldots N_s$ is drawn in KN_t steps. The algorithm sequentially replaces every bit with 0 and 1, computes the metric for those two candidates, then selects one of them as the next partial sample.

Let $\varphi : \{0,1\}^{N_t K} \mapsto \mathcal{X}^{N_t}$ be a rule that maps bit labels onto symbol vectors $x \in \mathcal{X}^{N_t}$. We define the metric

$$\mu(c) = -\frac{1}{N_0} \|y - H\varphi(c)\|^2 - c^T \lambda^a \tag{1}$$

for the candidate $\boldsymbol{c} \in \{0,1\}^{KN_t}$, which is related to the posterior probability $P(\boldsymbol{c}|\boldsymbol{y}, \boldsymbol{H}, \boldsymbol{\lambda}^a)$. Furthermore, let

$$\boldsymbol{c}_{b\beta} = (c_1, \ldots, c_{b-1},\ \beta\ , c_{b+1}, \ldots, c_{KN_t}) \tag{2}$$

be the vector $\boldsymbol{c}$ with the b-th bit replaced by β. The detector approximates the posterior LLRs as

$$\lambda_b^p \approx \max_{q,s} \mu(\boldsymbol{c}_{b0}^{(q,s)}) - \max_{q,s} \mu(\boldsymbol{c}_{b1}^{(q,s)}) \tag{3}$$

where we search for the two maxima for every bit over all chains and samples.

4   Low-Level Algorithm

The presented algorithm implements the max-log variant of the Rao-Blackwellized MCMC detection algorithm with uniform sampling described in [10]. Its basic idea is to recursively compute the metric in Eq. (1) by tracking the changes while drawing bits [12]. First, we introduce the basic concepts required for understanding the algorithm, then describe the algorithm in detail. For the theoretic background, the reader is kindly referred to [10, 12].

4.1   Basic Concepts

Matched Filter. The algorithm in [12] replaces $\boldsymbol{H}$ with the Gram matrix $\boldsymbol{R} = \boldsymbol{H}^H \boldsymbol{H}$ and the received symbol vector $\boldsymbol{y}$ with the matched filter output $\boldsymbol{y}^{\mathrm{mf}} = \boldsymbol{H}^H \boldsymbol{y}$ in the metric. This does not influence the posterior LLR calculation, however it allows to use the symmetry $\boldsymbol{R} = \boldsymbol{R}^H$.

Gibbs Sampler (GS). We realize the Markov chains with Gibbs Sampling. To this end, the GS draw bits sequentially according to an approximation of the marginal distribution $P(c_b|c_1, \ldots, c_{b-1}, c_{b+1}, \ldots, c_{KN_t})$. The state of the q-th GS at the s-th sample after drawing the b-th bit is denoted as

$$\boldsymbol{c}_b^{(q,s)} = (c_1^{(q,s)}, \ldots, c_b^{(q,s)}, c_{b+1}^{(q,s-1)}, \ldots, c_{KN_t}^{(q,s-1)}) \tag{4}$$

and thus contains bits from the previous sample $\boldsymbol{c}^{(q,s-1)}$ and the current sample $\boldsymbol{c}^{(q,s)}$.

Common Starting Point. All chains start with $\boldsymbol{c}^{(-1)}$, which maps onto $\boldsymbol{x}^{(-1)}$ with $x_t = 1 + j$, i.e. we have $\varphi(\boldsymbol{c}^{(-1)}) = \boldsymbol{x}^{(-1)}$. This concept enables the initialization of parallel independent Gibbs Samplers [12].

Symbol Deltas. When the GS state changes, at most one bit is different. We introduce the notation

$$\begin{aligned} |\Delta|_b^2 (\boldsymbol{c}) &= |\varphi_n(\boldsymbol{c}_{b1})|^2 - |\varphi_n(\boldsymbol{c}_{b0})|^2 \\ \Delta_b(\boldsymbol{c}) &= \varphi_n(\boldsymbol{c}_{b1}) - \varphi_n(\boldsymbol{c}_{b0}) \end{aligned} \tag{5}$$

where φ_n is the mapping rule for the n-th antenna, and the b-th bit belongs to the n-th antenna.

Recursive Dot-Product. The algorithm tracks the current value of

$$S = y^{\mathrm{mf}} - \tilde{R}\varphi(c_b^{(q,s)}) \tag{6}$$

where $\tilde{R}$ is the matrix R with the diagonal set to zero. Starting from $S^{(-1)} = y^{\mathrm{mf}} - \tilde{R}x^{(-1)}$, it updates S recursively when $c_b^{(q,s)}$ changes.

Recursive Metric Computation. We introduce an arbitrary offset such that $\mu(c^{(-1)}) = 0$, which cancels out in Eq. (3). Let the distance update be

$$\delta_b^{(q,s)} = \mathrm{Re}\{r_{nn}\}\,|\Delta|_b^2\,(c^{(q,s-1)}) - 2\mathrm{Re}\{S_n^*\Delta_b(c^{(q,s-1)})\} \tag{7}$$

where the b-th bit belongs to the n-th antenna, then the metric update is

$$\Delta\mu = \frac{1}{N_0}\delta_b^{(q,s)} + \lambda_b^a \tag{8}$$

which we either subtract from or add to the current metric $\mu(c^{(q,s)})$, depending on the bit flip direction, if the b-th bit changes.

Log-Domain Bit Probability. The term

$$\gamma = \frac{1}{\eta N_0}\delta_b^{(q,s)} + \lambda_b^a \tag{9}$$

expresses the probability of the next bit being 1 in the log-domain, where the temperature parameter η mitigates lock-in effects in the high-SNR regime [10]. For the conversion to the linear domain, we apply a piece-wise linear approximation to logistic$(\gamma) = 1/(1+e^{-\gamma})$ as in [11,12]. To this end, the GS simply limits γ to the range $[-4, 4)$ and compares $-\gamma$ to a uniformly distributed pseudo-random number $u \sim U(-4, 4)$ in the same range.

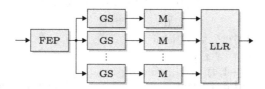

Fig. 2. Partitioning of the low-level algorithm: Front-end Processing, Gibbs Sampler, Metric Update, LLR Computation

4.2 Overall Algorithm Design

Figure 2 depicts the algorithm partitioned into four different parts: the *Front-end Processing* (FEP), that transforms the channel observations, the parallel *Gibbs Samplers* (GS) realizing the Markov chains, the *Metric Update* (M) tracking the current metric state, and the *LLR Computation*, which searches for the two maximum metric values per bit.

4.3   Front-end Processing

First, choose $\Gamma = 2^\alpha/(\eta N_0)$ with α such that $\Gamma \in [0.5, 1)$. We assume $\eta = 2$. The FEP computes

$$R = \Gamma H^H H$$
$$S^{(-1)} = \Gamma H^H y - \tilde{R} x^{(-1)} \tag{10}$$

as described in Sect. 4.1 (Recursive Dot-Product) but scaled by Γ.

4.4   Gibbs Sampler

Algorithm 1 describes how the GS sequentially draws bits of the candidate sequence $c^{(q,s)}$. GS and Metric Update share the term $\delta_b^{(q,s)}$ computed in line 6. Note the back-shifting with α to compensate the normalization of Γ. For the first sample ($s = 0$), only the prior LLRs are used, in order to draw $c^{(q,0)} \sim \lambda^a$ (line 7). The saturation in line 8 produces a threshold in the range $[-4, 4)$ (cf. Sect. 4.1 (Log-Domain Bit Probability)). The comparison to a uniformly distributed pseudo-random number in the same range (line 13) yields the new bit value. Afterwards, we need to update the S state (lines 14–16).

Algorithm 1. Gibbs Sampler

input: $S^{(-1)}, R, c^{\text{ext}}, \lambda^a$, Chain Index q
output: $c_b^{(q,s)}, c_b^{(q,s-1)}, \delta_b^{(q,s)}$

1 $c^{(q,-1)} = c^{(-1)}$
2 $S \leftarrow S^{(-1)}$
3 **for** $s = 0$ **to** N_s **do**
4   **for** $b = 1$ **to** $N_t K$ **do**
5        $n \leftarrow \lfloor (b-1)/K \rfloor + 1$
6        $\delta_b^{(q,s)} = \left[\mathrm{Re}\{r_{nn}\} |\Delta|_b^2 (c^{(q,s-1)}) - 2\mathrm{Re}\{S_n^* \Delta_b(c^{(q,s-1)})\} \right] 2^{-\alpha}$
7        $\gamma \leftarrow \lambda_b^a + \begin{cases} 0 & \text{if } s = 0 \\ \delta_b^{(q,s)} & \text{otherwise} \end{cases}$
8        $\gamma \leftarrow \text{saturate}(-4, 4, \gamma)$
9   draw $u \sim U(-4, 4)$
10   **if** $s = 0$ **and** $q = 1$ **then**   /* first sample, first chain */
11          $c_b^{(q,s)} = c_b^{\text{ext}}$
12   **else**
13          $c_b^{(q,s)} = \text{sign}(u + \gamma)$
14       $\Delta S_t \leftarrow r_{tn} \Delta_b(c^{(q,s-1)}) \quad \forall t = 1 \ldots N_t, t \neq n$
15   **if** $c_b^{(q,s-1)} \neq c_b^{(q,s)}$ **then**
16          $S_t \leftarrow S_t + \begin{cases} \Delta S_t & \text{if } c_b^{(q,s-1)} = 1 \\ -\Delta S_t & \text{if } c_b^{(q,s-1)} = 0 \end{cases} \forall t \neq n$

4.5 Metric Update

Algorithm 2 recursively computes the current candidate's metric $\mu(c_b^{(q)})$, using the state $\mu^{(q)}$, and produces the two metrics for the current bit $\mu(c_{b0/1})$. As stated earlier, we arbitrarily set the metric for the common starting point to zero (line 1). Lines 4 to 9 show the underlying metric update. Of the two possible states, one is identical to the current state, and thus has the same metric value (line 4). The other one is updated according to the direction of the bit flip (lines 6 and 8). In line 9, we select one of the two as the new current metric. It remains unaltered if the bit does not change.

Algorithm 2. Metric Update

    input: $c_b^{(q,s)}, c_b^{(q,s-1)}, \delta_b^{(q,s)}, \boldsymbol{\lambda}^a$, Chain Index q
    output: $\mu(c_{b0}^{(q,s)}), \mu(c_{b1}^{(q,s)})$

1 $\mu^{(q)} \leftarrow 0$
2 **for** $s = 0$ **to** N_s **do**
3   **for** $b = 1$ **to** $N_t K$ **do**
4       $\mu(c_{b0}^{(q,s)}) = \mu(c_{b1}^{(q,s)}) = \mu^{(q)}$
5   **if** $c_b^{(q,s-1)} = 0$ **then**
6         $\mu(c_{b1}^{(q,s)}) = \mu(c_b^{(q,s-1)}) - (\eta \delta_b^{(q,s)} + \lambda_b^a)$
7   **else**
8         $\mu(c_{b0}^{(q,s)}) = \mu(c_b^{(q,s-1)}) + (\eta \delta_b^{(q,s)} + \lambda_b^a)$
9       $\mu(c_b^{(q,s)}) = \begin{cases} \mu(c_{b0}^{(q,s)}) & \text{if } c_b^{(q,s)} = 0 \\ \mu(c_{b1}^{(q,s)}) & \text{if } c_b^{(q,s)} = 1 \end{cases}$
10     $\mu^{(q)} \leftarrow \mu(c_b^{(q,s)})$

4.6 LLR Computation

Algorithm 3 searches for the maximum metrics among all chains, then compares these local maxima with the current global maxima. It excludes the $s = 0$ step, which is the transition from $c^{(-1)}$ to $c^{(q,0)}$, from the search (line 3). The computation of the extrinsic LLRs in line 7 is included, as it can be easily implemented in hardware.

Algorithm 3. LLR Computation

    input: $\mu(c_{b0}^{(q,s)}), \mu(c_{b1}^{(q,s)}), \boldsymbol{\lambda}^a$
    output: $\boldsymbol{\lambda}^e$

1 $\mu_{b0}^{\max} \leftarrow -\infty \quad \forall b = 1 \ldots N_t K$
2 $\mu_{b1}^{\max} \leftarrow -\infty \quad \forall b = 1 \ldots N_t K$
3 **for** $s = 1$ **to** N_s **do**   /* Note: ignore input for $s = 0$ */
4   **for** $b = 1$ **to** $N_t K$ **do**   /* For every bit index */
5       $\mu_{b0}^{\max} \leftarrow \max(\mu_{b0}^{\max}, \max_q(\mu(c_{b0}^{(q,s)})))$
6       $\mu_{b1}^{\max} \leftarrow \max(\mu_{b1}^{\max}, \max_q(\mu(c_{b1}^{(q,s)})))$

7 $\lambda_b^e = \mu_{b0}^{\max} - \mu_{b1}^{\max} - \lambda_b^a \quad \forall b = 1 \ldots K N_t$

---

5   VLSI Architecture

5.1   Overview

The macro pipeline of FEP-Circuit and MCMC core, shown in Fig. 3, constitutes the proposed MCMC detector. Both components require multiple clock cycles per input vector, but double buffering between FEP and Core ensures that the computations can overlap. The MCMC core in turn contains four stages connected via registers. The stages exchange information in every clock cycle. They effectively run in a pipeline manner.

The FSM and the multiplexers (e.g. λ_b^a, and for the column of $\boldsymbol{R}$) are part of the Mux stage. There are N_p GS-Circuits implementing Algorithm 1. For every GS-Circuit, there is one corresponding M-Circuit executing Algorithm 2. The L-Circuit performs the LLR Computation in Algorithm 3. Every GS/M-Circuit can run several chains sequentially. For example $N_q = 8$ chains can be run on $N_p = 4$ GS/M-Circuits by executing two chains sequentially per GS/M-Circuit. We can also turn off some GS/M-Circuits, e.g. run $N_q = 4$ chains on $N_p = 8$ GS/M-Circuits with four inactive circuits.

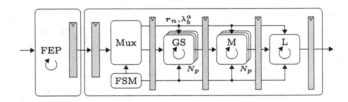

Fig. 3. Architecture design of the MCMC detector. The n-th column $\boldsymbol{r}_n$ of $\boldsymbol{R}$ and λ_b^a are selected in the Mux stage.

5.2   FEP-Circuit

The architecture, depicted in Fig. 4, contains in total five multipliers. Using four of these, the dot-product for the terms $\boldsymbol{H}^H \boldsymbol{y}$ and $\boldsymbol{R} = \boldsymbol{H}^H \boldsymbol{H}$ requires N_r cycles per complex entry. We need only the lower triangular of $\boldsymbol{R}$ due to $\boldsymbol{R}^H = \boldsymbol{R}$. The architecture computes either one complex off-diagonal entry, or two real diagonal entries in parallel. The fifth multiplier alternatingly multiplies real and imaginary parts with $\Gamma = \frac{2^\alpha}{N_0 \eta}$. In parallel, we multiply the entries of $\boldsymbol{R}$ with $x_t^{(-1)} = 1 + j$ (cf. Sect. 4.1 (Common Starting Point)) using only adders and multiplexers, and accumulate the results to obtain $\boldsymbol{S}$.

5.3   GS/M-Circuit

Figure 5 depicts the GS-Circuit. The $|\Delta|^2$-multiplier, depicted in detail in Fig. 6(a), exploits the limited range of $|\Delta|^2 \in \{-3, -2, \dots, 3\} \times \{8, 16\}$ which

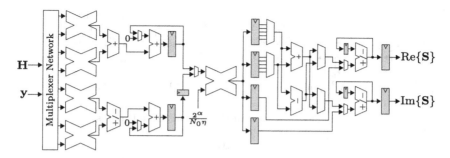

Fig. 4. FEP-Circuit

assumes only 14 different values for 4-/16-/64-QAM. The factor Δ is either purely real or imaginary. We define $|\Delta| = |\mathrm{Re}\{\Delta\}| + j|\mathrm{Im}\{\Delta\}|$. Then we have $\mathrm{Re}\{S_n^*|\Delta|\} = \mathrm{Re}\{S_n\}\mathrm{Re}\{|\Delta|\} + \mathrm{Im}\{S_n\}\mathrm{Im}\{|\Delta|\}$. For 4-/16-/64-QAM this assumes only the four values $\{1, 3, 5, 7\} \times 2$, which greatly simplifies the Δ-multiplier (Fig. 6(b), only shifts, adders and multiplexers). The control of the subsequent adder-subtractor ① considers if $\Delta < 0$ and if Δ is imaginary to decide whether to add or subtract. To generate the independent first samples, the multiplexer ② ensures $\gamma = \lambda_b^a$. For the external initialization, we have the multiplexer ③ that selects $c_b^{(q,s)} = c_b^{\mathrm{ext}}$. The circuit uses a 32-bit maximum length Galois-LFSR that generates one 32-bit word per clock cycle. The timing critical path of the whole MCMC detector starts in the $|\Delta|^2$-control, goes through the multiplexers in the $|\Delta|^2$-multiplier towards $c_b^{(q,s)}$, then finishes in the write-enable control for the S registers.

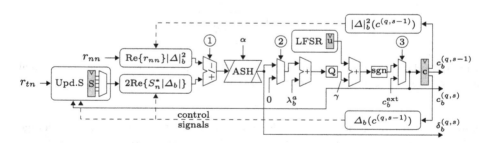

Fig. 5. GS-Circuit. The arithmetic shifter (ASH) reverts the normalization of Γ.

The M-Circuit, shown in Fig. 7, implements Algorithm 2 using a write-enabled register for the current metric, which is updated when we flip the current bit. The multiplication with η is implemented as a constant shift.

Update-S-Circuit. The Update-S-Circuit shown in Fig. 8 has $(N_t - 1)$ complex-valued Δ-multipliers, i.e. $2(N_t - 1)$ times Fig. 6(b). Using the multiplexers ③

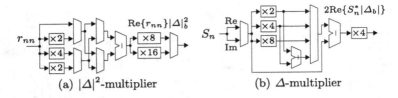

(a) $|\Delta|^2$-multiplier   (b) Δ-multiplier

Fig. 6. Detailed view of the simplified multipliers

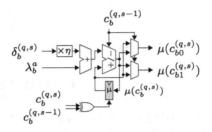

Fig. 7. M-Circuit

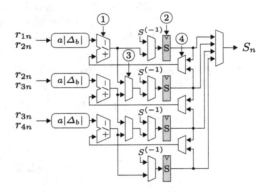

Fig. 8. Update-S-Circuit. Example for $N_t = 4$ antennas. All units exist for the real and for the imaginary parts respectively (not drawn).

and ④, we can update all N_t elements of S, however only $N_t - 1$ change per clock cycle. The entries of R e.g. r_{1n}, r_{2n} are selected in the Mux stage. Similar to the GS-Circuit, the adder-subtractor control ① considers $\Delta < 0$, if $|\Delta|$ is imaginary, and additionally the old bit $c_b^{(q,s-1)}$ and if the input needs to be conjugated, i.e. $\mathrm{Im}\{r_{tn}\} = -\mathrm{Im}\{r_{nt}\}$. The write-enabled S registers are updated if the current bit flips. This control ② is part of the aforementioned critical path.

5.4   L-Circuit

The L-Circuit shown in Fig. 9 contains two register files (RFs) for the current maximum metrics with KN_t entries each. We use tokens propagating alongside the data to indicate whether a value is valid. The Compare Select (CS) elements select the maximum of the valid inputs. The registers also store tokens per entry, which are reset to zero when the processing of a symbol vector starts. After the scalar subtractor, we saturate the extrinsic LLRs to limit their dynamic range. The saturation has a positive influence on the communications performance.

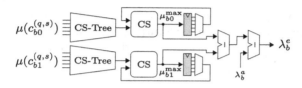

Fig. 9. L-Circuit

6   Differences to Reference Architecture

The proposed architecture is a complete redesign of [12]. This section explicitly highlights the architectural modifications. The original and new timing critical path are located in the GS-Circuit.

Multiplier-Free Gibbs Sampler: Similar to [11], we move the multiplication with $1/(\eta N_0)$ out of the GS into the FEP, by scaling R and S with Γ. This removes the multiplier from the detector's critical path, but increases the required word lengths.

Dynamic Scaling: The normalization of $\Gamma \in [0.5, 1)$ allows to use smaller word lengths, mitigating the previously mentioned increase. Consequently, we need an arithmetic shifter in the GS-Circuit at the previous location of the multiplier, which reverts the normalization.

Pipelined Input Multiplexers: Our MCMC detector selects the column of R and the entry of λ^a in the new Mux stage in front of the GS stage. While this removes those multiplexers from the detector's critical path, it adds an additional latency cycle.

Reduced Update-S-Circuit: We remove two Δ-multipliers (one per real and imaginary part) from the Update-S-Circuit, since in every cycle one of the entries of S does not change. This requires multiplexers for the resource sharing, which are however not in the critical path and are smaller than the removed Δ-multipliers.

Shared Maximum Metric Register File: The RFs are moved from the M-Circuit [12] to the L-Circuit. This reduces the required RFs from N_p to one.

We also add a pipeline register after the L-Circuit to improve timing, which requires another extra latency cycle. Also, our M-Circuit in Fig. 5 has one adder-subtractor instead of two adders, similar to [11].

Adder-Subtractor Units: These new units right after the Δ-multipliers in the GS- and the Update-S-Circuit, replace the original adders and the conditional negation units. The control selects addition or subtraction depending on the sign of Δ, if Δ is imaginary, the old bit $c_b^{(q,s-1)}$ and if $\text{Im}\{r_{tn}\} = -\text{Im}\{r_{nt}\}$.

Simplified Delta Multiplier: Our Δ-multipliers, used for γ and S, compute the absolute value $|\Delta|$. This removes one multiplexer stage from the critical path.

Postponed Conjugation: We are storing only the lower half of R. Due to the hermitian property of R, we have $\text{Im}\{r_{tn}\} = -\text{Im}\{r_{nt}\}$. The control of the subsequent adder-subtractor units considers the required negation, instead of an explicit conjugation [12].

7 Results

With the word lengths given in Sect. 7.1 and the throughput equations in Sect. 7.2, we first compare our model to the reference architecture [12] based on gate-level synthesis results, then we present post-layout results for different design-time variants of our architecture. Section 8 presents the algorithmic evaluations.

7.1 Simulation Setup

A 802.11n-like 4×4 MIMO system is considered assuming a spatially uncorrelated Rayleigh channel, perfect channel knowledge and a max-log BCJR decoder. For all results, we assumed a rate-5/6 tail-biting binary convolutional code with generator polynomials 0133 and 0171 and puncturing, a random interleaver and 64-QAM modulation ($K = 6$). The frame length of 2160 information bits equals the interleaver's length, which is one OFDM symbol for this setup. For every data point, we simulated at least 10^5 frames. The average signal-to-noise ratio (SNR) per receive antenna is defined as $\text{SNR} = \mathbb{E}[\|\boldsymbol{Hx}\|^2]/(N_r N_0)$. The required word lengths for an SNR loss of $\leq 0.1\,\text{dB}$ compared to the floating-point model at a frame error rate (FER) of $10\,\%$ are: [integer.fractional] $\boldsymbol{y}$ [7.8], $\boldsymbol{H}$ [3.8], $\boldsymbol{\lambda}^a$ [5.4], $1/N_0$ [6.11], $\boldsymbol{R}$ [6.10], $\boldsymbol{S}$ [9.9], δ [17.6], μ [19.5], γ [3.29], $2^\alpha \delta$ [14.6], α [4.0], $\boldsymbol{\lambda}^e$ [8.4]. All are signed, per entry, and for real and imaginary part identical. The first chain ($q = 0$) is always initialized with the result of an hard-output zero-forcing MIMO detector. We assume $N_q = 8$ chains with $N_s = 8$ samples per chain (i.e. $N_{gs} = 64$ in [12]) for the next three sections, but vary those parameters in Sect. 8.

7.2   Architecture

Our parameterized architecture implementation currently supports up to 4×4 MIMO and 64-QAM. MIMO mode and QAM scheme can be configured at run-time within the supported range, which in turn can be configured at design-time. Each GS/M-pair can process up to 16 chains sequentially, with up to 16 samples per chain. The FEP-Circuit requires

$$n_{\text{fep}} = N_r \left((N_t + 1) N_t / 2 + \lceil N_t / 2 \rceil \right) + 3 \tag{11}$$

cycles for its computation. This is slightly faster than the FEP-Circuit in [12]. The MCMC core runs for

$$n_{\text{gs}} = \frac{N_q}{N_p} (N_s + 1) K N_t + 5 \tag{12}$$

cycles. Compared to [12], we need two extra latency cycles (cf. Sect. 6 (Pipelined Input Multiplexers)). The code bit throughput of the architecture is $\theta_c = \frac{K N_t}{n_{\text{gs}}} f_{\text{clk}}$ assuming $n_{\text{gs}} \geq n_{\text{fep}}$ and sufficient input data.

7.3   Synthesis Results

We synthesized the design with Synopsys Design Compiler I-2013.12-SP2 in topographical mode using a 1.0 V standard-performance standard cell library for the UMC 90 nm SP-RVT LowK CMOS process. One gate-equivalent (GE) is the area of one 2-input drive-1 NAND gate. Figure 10 compares the four instances $N_p = \{1, 2, 4, 8\}$ to [12]. While the most efficient design in [12] has an AT_{exec}-product of 181.7 kGEµs, our proposed design achieves 50.0 kGEµs, which is 3.6 times more efficient.

Table 1. MCMC detector synthesis results

Component		This Work	[12]
FEP-Circuit		16.0 kGE	11.0 kGE
GS-Circuit	8x	10.7 kGE	16.9 kGE
M-Circuit	8x	0.9 kGE	12.2 kGE
L-Circuit	$N_p = 8$	13.3 kGE	3.3 kGE
Miscellaneous		5.0 kGE	17.9 kGE
Update-S-Circuit (cont. in GS)		5.2 kGE	7.7 kGE
Total	$N_p = 8$	127.1 kGE	265.0 kGE
Clock frequency		526 MHz	312 MHz
Cycles ($N_q = N_s = Np = 8$)		221	219
Average Throughput		57.4 Mbit/s	34.2 Mbit/s
Area efficiency		0.45 Mbit/s/kGE	0.13 Mbit/s/kGE

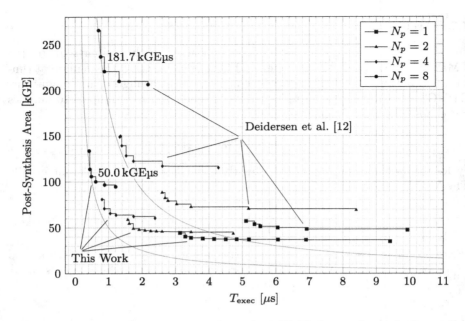

Fig. 10. Area vs. execution time based on the MCMC detector's synthesis results, comparing this work to [12], assuming $N_t = 4$, $K = 6$

Table 1 lists the synthesis results for our fastest design instance and the reference design [12]. The FEP is larger (5 kGE), while the GS is smaller (-6.2 kGE per GS), since we moved the multiplier from the GS to the FEP. The additional area of the new arithmetic shifter is partially compensated for by the other improvements. The Update-S-Circuit becomes smaller (-2.5 kGE) since we save one complex Δ-multiplier and use $|\Delta|$ now. The saving effect is larger than the additional area from the multiplexers required for the resource sharing. The M-Circuit exhibits only about 7.4 % of the original area, since we moved the RFs to the L-Circuit, which consequently became larger (10 kGE). The remainder of the area (-12.9 kGE) is occupied amongst others by the $\boldsymbol{R}$ column multiplexers. The area is reduced because the multiplexers are no longer in the timing critical path.

In total, the redesigned architecture takes on only about 48 % of the original area for $N_p = 8$. The saving depends on the number of GS/M-Circuits. The critical path was shortened by about 40 %, i.e. the maximum clock frequency increased from 312 MHz to 526 MHz.

7.4 Layout Results

A layout was obtained with Cadence SoC Encounter 9.1 for each configuration's fastest design instance in order to further study the proposed architecture's implementation complexity and to enable more precise comparison with future related work. All following area figures are taken from the layout results, depicted in Fig. 11. The consumed area slightly increased, while the achievable clock frequency decreased. It is interesting that the throughput mainly depends on the number of parallel GS/M-Circuits and the chain parameters, i.e.

$$\theta_c = \frac{KN_t}{n_{\text{gs}}} f_{\text{clk}} \approx \frac{N_p}{N_q(N_s + 1)} f_{\text{clk}} \tag{13}$$

as can be seen in Fig. 11.

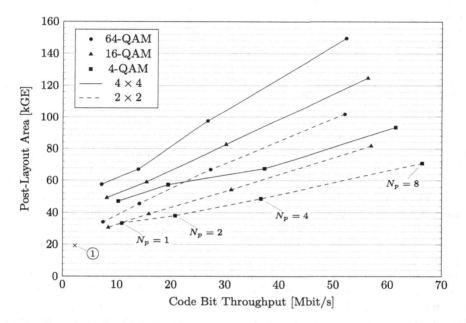

Fig. 11. Area vs. throughput based on the MCMC detector's layout results. For each design-time configuration, the ASIC with the fastest clock is shown. As an example, the 16-QAM 2×2 design supports one or two antennas and 4- or 16-QAM at run-time.

The largest instance, for 64-QAM, $N_t = 4$ and $N_p = 8$, requires 149.5 kGE or 0.47 mm^2 and achieves a maximum clock frequency of 479 MHz, yielding a code bit throughput of 52 Mbit/s. The fastest instance in terms of throughput supports 4-QAM, $N_t = 2$ and has $N_p = 8$ GS/M-Circuits. It occupies in total an area of 70.7 kGE or 0.22 mm^2 and runs at 664 MHz, which results in a throughput of 66 Mbit/s.

To determine the smallest instance, which should be the lower corner of the covered design space, ① in Fig. 11, we synthesized the detector with $N_t = 2$, 4-QAM and one GS/M-Circuit for a target of 100 MHz. This ASIC consumes 19.2 kGE or 0.06 mm^2, runs at 165 MHz and yields a 2.27 Mbit/s throughput. The FEP-Circuit and MCMC core require 10.9 kGE and 8.3 kGE respectively. Further word length optimizations could yield additional area reductions.

Table 2. Comparison to other reported MIMO detectors

	This work	[12]	[6]	[5]	[4]	[8]	[7]	[9]	[16]
Ant. Cfg.	$\leq 4 \times 4$	$\leq 4 \times 4$	4×4	4×4	4×4	4×4	$\leq 4 \times 4$	4×4	4×4
Mod. Order	≤ 64	≤ 64	≤ 64	≤ 64	≤ 64	64	≤ 64	16	64
Algorithm	MCMC	MCMC	EPIC	MMSE	MMSE	FCSD	STS-SD	Trellis	K-Best
SO/SISO	SISO	SISO	SISO	SISO	SISO	SISO	SISO	SISO	SO
Technology	90 nm	90 nm	90 nm	90 nm	90 nm	90 nm	90 nm	65 nm	65 nm
Core Area [mm^2]	0.47	–	1.08	1.5	–	2.61	–	1.58	0.57
TP Θ_c [Mbit/s]	avg. 52^a	avg. 34.2^a	733	757	833	2200	avg. 51.1^b	1228^c	1444^c
Preproc. [kGE]	–^{d}	–^{d}	345.8	384.2^e	178.3	–^{f}	–^{f}	–^{f}	–^{f}
Detection [kGE]	149.5	265				555	175	1097	298
Eff. [Mbit/s/kGE]	0.34	0.13	2.11	1.97	4.67	3.96	0.29	1.12	4.85

^{a}We assume $N_s = 64, N_{gs} = 8, N_p = 8$ [12].
^{b}We assume 100 visited nodes per symbol vector [5].
^{c}Scaled to 90 nm CMOS technology assuming $t_{pd} \sim 1/s$.
^{d}Area for optional initial detection not included.
^{e}Area for chip IO interface excluded.
^{f}Area for required QRD not included. circuitry.

Table 2 compares our work to a selection of reported MIMO detector implementations. We make three observations. First, in terms of hardware efficiency expressed in Mbit/s/kGE, the MCMC detector resides in about the same order of magnitude as the single-tree-search sphere decoder (STS-SD) [7], though our architecture is more than two times more efficient than our reference architecture [12]. The MCMC detector exhibits a deterministic run-time, which eases the receiver system design, while the SD can in principle always achieve near-capacity performance at the cost of a strongly varying run-time. Secondly, the MCMC detectors (and the STS-SD) are about one order of magnitude less efficient than the linear [4,5], iterative-linear [6] detectors, and most notably the fixed-complexity sphere decoder (FCSD) [8], which achieves close-to-optimal communications performance at a deterministic run-time. In this perspective, the FCSD [8] is the best choice. In case that a particularly small implementation is needed, the MCMC might have an advantage, depending on how well the FCSD scales. Lastly, there are three cases for the preprocessing circuitry. Some implementations include it [4–6], it is optional for the MCMC detectors [12], and definitely required for the other reported work [7–9,16]. This of course makes the area-throughput efficiency comparison difficult.

8   Algorithmic Considerations

In this section, we put the code bit throughput θ_c, as an implementation property of our architecture, in relation to our design's communications performance in terms of SNR required to achieve a 10 % frame error rate. With this data, we can determine for example appropriate run-time parameters, or an appropriate run-time strategy to adapt them. Depending on the optimization criterion, the parameter choices might be different. Possible criteria are for example spectral efficiency or energy efficiency (as future work, we plan to perform energy estimations). The first part of this section gives a general overview, while the second part explains in more detail the iterative receiver figures.

In the remainder, we use the post-layout implementation results of the 64-QAM, $N_t = 4$, $N_p = 8$ instance that runs at 479 MHz. The simulation setup that we select resembles the highest-throughput mode of the 802.11n standard, which requires a high SNR. However, our experiments show that the MCMC-based detection performs best in a mid-range SNR regime, in combination with lower-order modulation schemes. Thus this can be considered as kind of a worst-case scenario for the MCMC detector.

We assume the same simulation setup as in Sect. 7.1. Additionally, we perform up to two detector-decoder iterations, i.e. per frame, we execute the MCMC detector and BCJR decoder twice. This gives us four run-time parameters: the number of chains N_{q1} and samples N_{s1} in the first iteration and respectively N_{q2}, N_{s2} for the second iteration. The short-hand notation GS$_1$8x6 denotes $N_{q1} = 8$ and $N_{s1} = 6$, similarly we use GS$_2N_{q2}$xN_{s2}. We simulated the parameter set $N_{q1/2} \in \{8, 16\}$ and $N_{s1/2} = \{1, 2, \ldots, 16\}$. Thus all $N_p = 8$ GS/M-Circuits are always active. The total number of samples per iteration defined as $N_{gs1/2} = N_{q1/2} \cdot N_{s1/2}$ is our measure for the invested effort.

Figure 12 shows four curves: two for the first iteration, and two for the second. The last part of this section explains how we determine the two second-iteration curves. They are pareto-optimal in terms of SNR versus throughput.

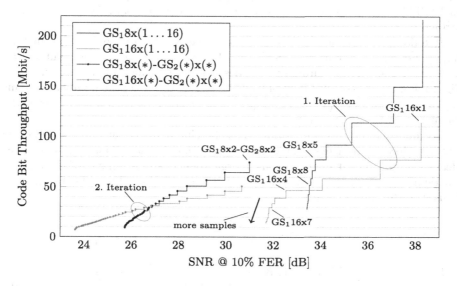

Fig. 12. Code bit throughput over SNR required to achieve a 10 % frame error rate

Clearly in Fig. 12, we can identify the existence of a run-time tradeoff between SNR and throughput. As could be expected, more effort (i.e. more samples, more chains) results in a better algorithmic performance (lower SNR). An SNR gain has several possible uses amongst others: we can extend the transmission range, we can serve more users (more interference), or we can also lower the transmission power to save energy (and reduce interference to other users).

In the non-iterative case (first iteration), we observe a vanishing gain beyond five samples, both for eight and 16 chains. At around 33.5 dB, it is better to use 16 instead of eight chains. Interestingly, this switches from $GS_1 8x8$ at 33.52 dB to $GS_1 16x4$ at 32.53 dB. The total number of samples for both configurations is 64, but we gain about 1 dB SNR while approximately maintaining the throughput. It is not completely identical due to the pipeline delays of the architecture.

Instead of using $GS_1 8x6$ after $GS_1 8x5$, a good decision would be to switch to the second iteration, therefore never using 16 chains in the non-iterative case. This yields a large SNR gain of about 2.7 dB at a similar throughput. At this transition point, we switch from $GS_1 8x5$ to $GS_1 8x2$-$GS_2 8x2$. The throughputs drops slightly from 77.15 Mbit/s to 74.65 Mbit/s. With $N_{gs1} = 40$ compared to $N'_{gs1} + N'_{gs2} = 32$, the MCMC detector's effort remains very similar.

MCMC-based detection benefits greatly from iterative MIMO decoding. Switching from one to two iterations yields SNR gains as large as 6 dB. While in the first iteration we achieve only about 31.7 dB, all SNR operating points of the second iteration are lower than 31 dB. A possible explanation is that the guidance from the channel decoder, in terms of prior LLRs, is the contributing factor for this. It helps the MCMC-based detection in two ways: we select the initial samples $c^{(q,0)} \sim p(c) = f(\lambda^a)$, and the transition probability γ depends on λ^a. This seems to let the chains converge faster (in less samples) to interesting regions.

It follows a closer look on the second iteration. There are four parameters, $N_{q1/2}$ and $N_{s1/2}$. For a given SNR, we determine the parameter combination that yields the highest throughput. These pareto-optimals points are shown in Fig. 13. For the two second-iteration curves in Fig. 13, we fix the number of chains in the first iteration $N_{q1} = 8$ and $N_{q1} = 16$ respectively, then optimize over the remaining three parameters.

For our calculations, we assume that the channel decoder and the buffering between decoder and detector cause no additional delay. This is a somewhat ideal scenario, since it might give us a large area consumption e.g. of the buffers, but definitely provides us with an upper bound for the achievable throughput. Thus, the throughput is given as

$$\theta_{c,2} = \frac{K N_t}{n_{gs,1} + n_{gs,2}} f_{clk} \qquad (14)$$

with $n_{gs,1/2} = \frac{N_{q1/2}}{N_p} \left(N_{s1/2} + 1 \right) K N_t + 5$ and fixing $N_p = 8$ here.

We observe that more effort is required in the first iteration. For example, around 27 dB, the two configurations $GS_1 8x7$ and $GS_2 8x4$ are in use, i.e. $N_{gs1} = 56$ total samples for the first iteration, and $N_{gs2} = 32$ for the second.

At about 26.8 dB, we switch from eight to 16 chains in the first iteration. It appears that multiple short chains are favorable for the first iteration. Only at around 24 dB, the detector should switch from eight to 16 chains in the second

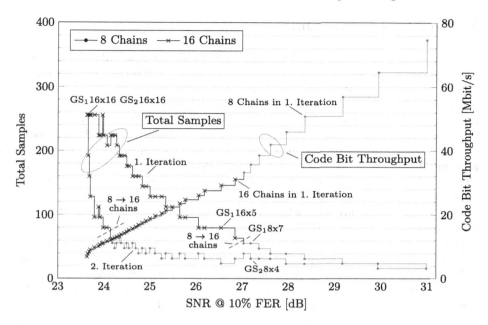

Fig. 13. Iterative receiver: two detector-decoder activations per symbol vector. For the throughput curve, dots and crosses denote if eight or 16 chains are used in the first of the two iterations. For the two total samples curves, the dots and crosses likewise denote if eight or 16 chains are used in the respective iteration. The figure shows only the pareto-optimal points in terms of SNR versus throughput determined from the data set with two iterations.

iteration. It is also the point where the effort significantly rises (near 23.6 dB), especially for the second iteration. This could be an indication for switching to three iterations.

From a pure SNR-throughput perspective, we can say that two iterations are better than a single. As previously stated, we observe large SNR gains from iterating, and the best non-iterative operating point is off by about 0.7 dB compared to the worst second-iteration point. However, this of course ignores the hardware cost caused by the required buffering and the increased throughput requirement on the detector and decoder architectures. A realistic comparison depends on the overall objective, i.e. lowest energy, small area, best spectral efficiency, and on additional constraints, like minimum supported bandwidth. While this is out of scope here, we think that our data outlines the run-time adaptability of the MCMC-based MIMO detection architecture. It also shows that it performs particularly well in iterative receivers, therefore it could be a reasonable candidate to consider in the design of such a system.

9   Conclusions and Outlook

We have presented synthesis and layout results of the proposed MCMC detector architecture. The area reduction of up to 52 % and the shorter clock period by up to 40 % indicate that the proposed architectural modifications to the reference design are effective. Our extensive data set for the communications performance further highlights the available tradeoff between signal-to-noise ratio and architecture throughput. With its run-time adaptability covering a large design space, our detector is effectively able to cope with a lot of channel conditions at the appropriate effort. Though being a stochastic detector, its completely deterministic run-time eases scheduling at the system level, i.e. inside a complex iterative receiver.

Still, the architecture suffers from a relatively low but deterministic throughput, which stems from the MCMC detection method itself. The main advantage appears to be its simple scalability through N_p and configurability through N_t and K. This allows the architecture to cover a large design space. Practically, only the availability of sufficient data might limit the architectural parallelism.

As future work, we plan to correlate algorithmic performance with energy consumption, which might reveal another tradeoff capability of the proposed design.

Acknowledgements. This work has been supported by the Ultra High-Speed Mobile Information and Communication (UMIC) Research Centre, RWTH Aachen University.

References

1. IEEE standard for information technology- local and metropolitan area networks-specific requirements–part 11: Wireless LAN medium access control (MAC) and physical layer (PHY) specifications amendment 5: Enhancements for higher throughput. IEEE Std 802.11n-2009, pp. 1–565 (2009)
2. Guillén i Fàbregas, A., Martinez, A., Caire, G.: Bit-interleaved coded modulation. Found. Trends Commun. Inf. Theory **5**(1–2), 1–153 (2008). http://dx.doi.org/10.1561/0100000019
3. Hochwald, B., ten Brink, S.: Achieving near-capacity on a multiple-antenna channel. IEEE Trans. Commun. **51**(3), 389–399 (2003)
4. Auras, D., Leupers, R., Ascheid, G.: A novel reduced-complexity soft-input soft-output mmse mimo detector: algorithm and efficient vlsi architecture. In: 2014 IEEE International Conference on Communications (ICC), pp. 4722–4728, June 2014
5. Studer, C., Fateh, S., Seethaler, D.: ASIC implementation of soft-input soft-output MIMO detection using MMSE parallel interference cancellation. IEEE J. Solid-State Circ. **46**(7), 1754–1765 (2011)
6. Auras, D., Leupers, R., Ascheid, G.: A novel class of linear mimo detectors with boosted communications performance: algorithm and VLSI architecture. In: 2014 IEEE Computer Society Annual Symposium on VLSI (ISVLSI), pp. 41–47, July 2014

7. Witte, E.M.: Efficiency and flexibility trade-offs for soft-input soft-output sphere-decoding architectures. Ph.D. thesis, RWTH Aachen University (2013)
8. Chen, X., He, G., Ma, J.: VLSI implementation of a high-throughput iterative fixed-complexity sphere decoder. IEEE Trans. Circ. Syst. II: Express Briefs **60**(5), 272–276 (2013)
9. Sun, Y., Cavallaro, J.: Trellis-search based soft-input soft-output MIMO detector: algorithm and VLSI architecture. IEEE Trans. Sig. Process. **60**(5), 2617–2627 (2012)
10. Senst, M., Ascheid, G.: A rao-blackwellized markov chain monte carlo algorithm for efficient MIMO detection. In: Proceedings of the IEEE ICC, pp. 1–6 (2011)
11. Laraway, S., Farhang-Boroujeny, B.: Implementation of a markov chain monte carlo based multiuser/MIMO detector. IEEE Trans. Circ. Syst. I, Reg. Pap. **56**(1), 246–255 (2009)
12. Deidersen, U., Auras, D., Ascheid, G.: A parallel VLSI architecture for markov chain monte carlo based MIMO detection. In: Proceedings of the ACM GLSVLSI, pp. 167–172 (2013)
13. Auras, D., Deidersen, U., Leupers, R., Ascheid, G.: VLSI design of a parallel MCMC-based MIMO detector with multiplier-free gibbs samplers. In: Claesen, L., Claesen, L., Sanz, M.T., Reis, R., Sarmiento-Reyes, A. (eds.) VLSI-SoC 2014. IFIP AICT, vol. 464, pp. 1–6. Springer, Heidelberg (2015)
14. Yuan, F.L., Yang, C.H., Markovic, D.: A hardware-efficient VLSI architecture for hybrid sphere-MCMC detection. In: Proceedings of the IEEE GLOBECOM, pp. 1–6 (2011)
15. Hagenauer, J.: The turbo principle in mobile communications. In: Proceedings of the International Symposium on Nonlinear Theory and its Applications, Xian, China (2002)
16. Patel, D., Smolyakov, V., Shabany, M., Gulak, P.: VLSI implementation of a WiMAX/LTE compliant low-complexity high-throughput soft-output K-Best MIMO detector. In: Proceedings of 2010 IEEE International Symposium on Circuits and Systems (ISCAS), pp. 593–596 (2010)

Real-Time Omnidirectional Imaging System with Interconnected Network of Cameras

Kerem Seyid[(✉)], Ömer Çogal, Vladan Popovic,
Hossein Afshari, Alexandre Schmid,
and Yusuf Leblebici

Ecole Polytechnique Fédérale de Lausanne (EPFL), Lausanne, Switzerland
kerem.seyid@epfl.ch

Abstract. The Panoptic camera is an omnidirectional multi-aperture visual system which is realized by mounting multiple imaging sensors on a hemispherical frame. In this chapter, we will present a novel distributed and parallel implementation of the real-time omnidirectional vision reconstruction algorithm of the Panoptic Camera, for camera modules with processing, memory and interconnectivity features. A methodology for the arrangement of camera modules with interconnectivity feature into a target interconnection network topology will be introduced. A unique custom-made multiple-FPGA hardware platform designed for the implementation of an interconnected network of a 49 camera prototype Panoptic system will be explained. A novel way to represent the omnidirectional data obtained from the Panoptic Camera and real-time high dynamic range (HDR) video application which is realized by the system will be presented.

Keywords: Field programmable gate arrays · Smart cameras · Real-time systems · Omnidirectional imaging · Telepresence · High dynamic range

1 Introduction

A trend in constructing high-end computing systems consists of parallelizing large numbers of processing units. A similar trend is observed in digital photography, where multiple images of a scene are used to enhance the performance of the capture process. The technique is called a multi-view imaging (MVI) and has attracted increasing attention due to the dropping cost of digital cameras [1]. Novel research themes and applications such as increasing image resolution [2], obtaining high dynamic range images [3,4], object tracking/recognition, environmental surveillance, industrial inspection, 3DTV, and free viewpoint TV (FTV) [5] are receiving increasing attention.

Most developed camera array systems are bulky and not easily portable platforms. Their control and operation depend on multi-computer setups. In addition, image sensors on camera arrays are usually mounted on planar surfaces

© IFIP International Federation for Information Processing 2015
L. Claesen et al. (Eds.): VLSI-SoC 2014, IFIP AICT 464, pp. 170–197, 2015.
DOI: 10.1007/978-3-319-25279-7_10

which prohibits them from covering the full view of their environment. Full view or panoramic imaging finds application in various areas such as autonomous navigation, robotics, telepresence, remote monitoring and object tracking. Several solutions for acquiring omnidirectional images and their application have been presented in [6].

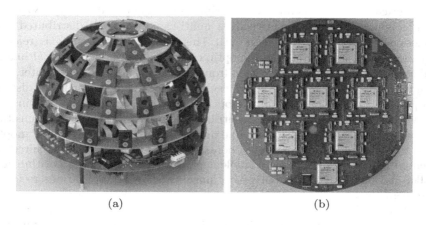

(a)   (b)

Fig. 1. (a) Built Panoptic prototype with 5 floors and 49 cameras. The sphere diameter of the prototype is $2r_\odot = 30\,\mathrm{cm}$. (b) Top view of the Panoptic Media FPGA-based development platform.

Early systems for capturing multiple views were based on a translating [7] or rotating [8] high-resolution camera for capturing, while rendering was carried out in post processing. The latter concept requires a long acquisition time. These ideas were later extended to a dynamic scene by using a linear array of still cameras [9]. For capturing large data sets, researchers focused on arrays of video cameras. In addition to the synchronization of the cameras, very large data rates present new challenges for the implementation of these systems. The first camera array systems were only built for recording and later post processing on Personal Computers [10]. Other such systems [11,12] were built with real-time processing capability for low resolution and low frame rates. A general-purpose camera array system was built at Stanford University [13] with limited local processing at the camera level. This system was developed to support recording of large amounts of data and subsequent intensive offline processing, but not for real-time operations.

In [14,15], real-time systems with six cubically arranged cameras are presented. These systems utilise high resolution imagers with a low number of cameras. Another six-camera panorama system with high resolution output is presented in [16]. Google Street View is one example of high resolution and increased number of cameras. The system in [17] is a 360° imaging system comprising 15 5 MP cameras, which covers 80 % of its surroundings. Lately, a novel system consisting of 44 5 MP cameras has been presented in [18], which offers an output resolution over 82 MP with offline processing. Another camera system which is able to acquire an image frame with more than 1 Gigapixel resolution was developed [19]. The system uses a very complex lens system comprising a parallel array of micro cameras to acquire the image. Due to the extremely high resolution of the image, it suffers from a very low frame rate, even at low output resolution. Recently, a method for implementing bio-inspired cameras with hemispherical view is presented in [20]. However, it is limited to only 180 pixels.

An original approach for creating a multi-camera system distributed over a spherical surface is presented in [21]. This multi-camera system is referred to as the Panoptic camera. The Panoptic camera is an omnidirectional imager capable of recording light information from any direction around its center. It is also a polydioptric system [22] where each CMOS camera sensor has a distinct focal plane. The previously built Panoptic system is explained detailed in [21]. The system is implemented with a centralized approach, where data acquisition and data processing reside on the same unit. Figure 1 depicts the new Panoptic Media Platform of 5 floors and 49 cameras. The new prototype and architecture presented in this chapter aim to implement the reconstruction algorithm in a parallel and distributed fashion, where image processing applications reside at the camera level.

First, omnidirectional vision reconstruction algorithm will be presented in Sect. 2. Detailed explanations of the distributed and parallel implementation of vision reconstruction are given in Sect. 3. A definition of an interconnected network of cameras and a methodology to solve the camera assignment problem is given in Sect. 4. The details of a custom-made FPGA platform designed for the practice of the concept of an interconnected network of cameras are given in Sect. 5 with implementation and imaging results. An immersive way for visualizing the omnidirectional data is presented in Sect. 6. A real-time 360° high dynamic range (HDR) video application with Panoptic Camera is presented in Sect. 7. Future work is presented in Sect. 8.

2   Omnidirectional Vision Reconstruction Algorithm

The omnidirectional vision of a virtual observer located anywhere inside the hemisphere of the Panoptic structure can be reconstructed by combining the information collected by each camera in the light ray space domain (or light field [23]).

In this process, the omnidirectional view is estimated on a discretized spherical surface S_d of directions. The surface of this sphere is discretized into an equiangular grid with N_θ latitudes and N_ϕ longitudes samples, where each sample represents one pixel. Figure 2(a) shows a pixelized sphere with sixteen pixels for N_θ and N_ϕ each. A unit vector $\omega \in S_d$, represented in the spherical coordinate system $\omega = (\theta_\omega, \phi_\omega)$, is assigned to the position of each pixel. Comparison of different pixel distributions over the sphere are discussed in Sect. 3.2.

The construction of the virtual omnidirectional view $\mathcal{L}(q, \omega) \in R$, where q determines the location of the observer, is performed in two steps. The first

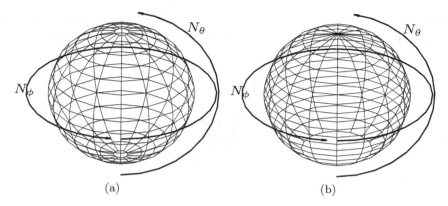

Fig. 2. Discretized sphere surface with $N_\theta = 16$ latitudes and $N_\phi = 16$ longitudes (256 pixels) (a) equi angular and (b) equal density pixelation.

step consists of finding a pixel in each camera image frame that corresponds to the direction defined by ω. The second step consists of blending all pixel values corresponding to the same ω into one. The result is the reconstructed light ray $\mathcal{L}(q, \omega)$.

To reconstruct the omnidirectional view, all the cameras having an ω in their angle of view are first determined. To extract the light intensity in that direction for each contributing camera, a pixel in the camera image frame has to be found. Due to the rectangular sampling grid of the cameras, the ω does not coincide with the exact pixel grid locations on the camera image frames. The pixel location is chosen using the nearest neighbour method, where the pixel closest to the desired direction is chosen as an estimate of the light ray intensity. The process is then repeated for all ω and results in the estimated values $\mathcal{L}(c_i, \omega)$, where c_i is the radial vector directing to the center position of the ith contributing camera's circular face. Figure 3(b) shows an example of the contributing cameras for a random pixel direction ω depicted in Fig. 3(a). The contributing position A_ω of the camera A, providing $\mathcal{L}(c_A, \omega)$ is also indicated in Fig. 3(b).

The second reconstruction step is performed in the space of light rays given by direction ω and passing through the camera center positions. Under the assumption of Constant Light Flux (CLF), the light intensity remains constant on the trajectory of any light ray. Following the CLF assumption, the light ray intensity for a given direction ω only varies in its respective orthographic plane. The orthographic plane is a plane normal to ω. Such plane is indicated as the "ω-plane" in Fig. 3(c), and represented as a gray-shaded circle (the boundary of the circle is drawn for clarity purposes). The light ray in direction ω recorded by each contributing camera intersects the ω-plane in points that are the projections of the cameras focal points on this plane. The projected focal points of the contributing cameras in ω direction onto the ω-plane are highlighted by hollow points in Fig. 3(c). Each projected camera point P_{c_i} on the planar surface is assigned the intensity value $\mathcal{L}(c_i, \omega)$, that is calculated in the first step.

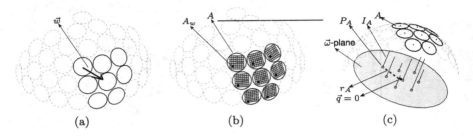

Fig. 3. (a) Cameras contributing to the direction ω direction, (b) contributing pixel positions on the image frame of the contributing cameras for direction ω.

As an example, the projected focal point of camera A onto the ω-plane (*i.e.*, P_A) in Fig. 3(c) is assigned the intensity value I_A. The virtual observer point inside the hemisphere (*i.e.*, q) is also projected onto the ω-plane. The light intensity value at the projected observer point (*i.e.*, $\mathcal{L}(q, \omega)$) is estimated by one of the blending algorithms, taking into account all $\mathcal{L}(q, \omega)$ values or only a subset of them. In the given example, each of the eight contributing camera positions shown with bold perimeter in Fig. 3(c) provides an intensity value which is observed into direction ω for observer position $q = 0$. The observer is located in the center of the sphere and indicated by a bold dot. A single intensity value is resolved among the contributing intensities through a blending procedure on its respective ω-plane.

When applying the nearest neighbour (NN) technique in the second reconstruction step, the light intensity at the virtual observer point for each ω direction is set to the light intensity value of the best observing camera for that direction. The nearest neighbour technique is expressed in (1) in mathematical terms:

$$j = \mathrm{argmin}_{i \in I}(r_i)$$
$$\mathcal{L}(q, \omega) = \mathcal{L}(c_j, \omega) \tag{1}$$

where $I = \{i | \omega \cdot t_i \geq \cos(\frac{\alpha_i}{2})\}$ is the index of the subset of contributing cameras for the pixel direction ω. A pixel direction ω is assumed observable by the camera c_i if the angle between its focal vector t_i and the pixel direction ω is smaller than half of the minimum angle of view α_i of camera c_i. The length r_i identifies the distance between the projected focal point of camera c_i and the projected virtual observer point on the ω-plane. The camera with the smallest r distance to the virtual observer projected point on the ω-plane is considered the best observing camera. As an illustration, such distance is identified with r_A and depicted by a dashed line for the contributing camera A in Fig. 3(c).

Different brightness levels between cameras and misalignment causes sharp transition among the cameras. In order to resolve this transition problems, several other blending techniques were proposed. For example, the linear blending scheme incorporates all the cameras contributing into a selected $\boldsymbol{\omega}$ direction through a linear combination [24]. This is conducted by aggregating the weighted intensities of the contributing cameras. The weight of a contributing camera is the reciprocal of the distance between its projected focal point and the projected virtual observer point on the $\boldsymbol{\omega}$-plane, *i.e.*, r_A in Fig. 3(c). The weights are also normalized to the sum of the inverse of all the contributing cameras distances. The linear blending is expressed in (2) in mathematical terms.

$$\mathcal{L}(\boldsymbol{q}, \boldsymbol{\omega}) = \frac{\sum\limits_{i \in I} w_i \cdot \mathcal{L}(c_i, \boldsymbol{\omega})}{\sum\limits_{i \in I} w_i} \tag{2}$$

$$w_i = \frac{1}{r_i}$$

Apart from nearest neighbour interpolation and linear interpolation techniques, other novel algorithms such as Gaussion Blending [25], Restricted Gaussian Blending [26] and a probabilistic approach for omnidirectional image reconstruction is presented in [27].

For detailed discussion camera arrangement on spherical surface, different blending approaches, camera orientation and multiple camera calibration, the reader is referred to [21].

3   Distributed and Parallel Implementation

The system presented in [28] is implemented using a centralized approach where a single unit is responsible for data acquisition and data processing from multiple image sensors. The real-time implementation of multi-camera systems applications with a high number of cameras, high image sensor resolutions and the current image sensor architectures demands a high amount of hardware resources, and depending on the target application it might also demand high computing performances. This can create bottlenecks in such multi-sensor systems and limits the scalability. The number of cameras that can be connected to a single node is limited by the I/O constraints. For instance, interfacing 49 standard CMOS imagers with a single unit will not be feasible in terms of pin count. Furthermore, for high number of cameras and high camera resolutions, the memory bandwidth requirement increases significantly where a single unit will not be able to overcome the total bandwidth demand. Parallel processing approaches aim to overcome these limitations by distributing signal processing tasks and memory bandwidth usage among several signal processing blocks. This technique creates possibility of constructing higher resolution images beyond centralized approach. Moreover, parallel approaches are faster implementations compared to centralized approaches, which creates the possibility of creating higher resolution images beyond centralized approach. Due to the constraints posed by technology, the distributed and parallel approach can be a feasible solution for the real-time realization of such systems.

If tasks are distributed properly among many processors, the computation time will decrease significantly. In order to distribute the tasks among the nodes, it is required to enhance the features of customary cameras to include processing and communication capabilities. The processing capability enables the camera module to perform local processing down to pixel level, while communicating features permit information exchange among the camera modules. In contrast to previous centralized approaches pertaining to omnidirectional light-field reconstruction algorithms, a novel distributed and parallel algorithm for image reconstruction is implemented. Assuming that all cameras have signal processing capability and communication media that permits a communication with other cameras and a central unit, omnidirectional vision reconstruction algorithms can be realised in a distributed manner among camera nodes.

In the distributed and parallel implementation of the Panoptic Camera, each camera constructs a portion of the omnidirectional vision with the help of neighbouring cameras. For a distributed implementation of the omnidirectional algorithm, each ith camera must possess the knowledge of its covering directions and the information of the other contributing cameras for all of these directions. This information can be extracted by the internal and external calibration processes of the Panoptic system. After extracting the camera parameters, such as camera direction vectors and coordinates on spherical surface, angle of views (AOV) of each camera, etc., each camera can construct its responsible portion of omnidirectional view independently.

For instance, in the nearest neighbour technique, the best viewing camera for each ω is selected. Hence in this technique, each camera constructs a unique set of observation directions. The set of observation directions of each camera has no intersection with the other cameras of the Panoptic system in the nearest neighbour method. Therefore, camera modules can be limited to observe solely their own set of directions and construct their portions of omnidirectional vision, independently from each other.

In the linear interpolation technique, similar to the nearest neighbour technique, each camera can still be assigned to the task of vision reconstruction for its particular partition. For this purpose, each camera would need the information about which other cameras contribute to the particular ω and the intensity values obtained by the contributing cameras. For a constant set of ω directions, these parameters are only required to be calculated once and are stored in a local memory for real-time access. The distributed implementation of the algorithm is summarized in Algorithm 1. The required information can be calculated once by the central unit and updated to the local memory of the camera modules. Alternatively, each camera module can calculate its own required information using its own processing features.

In the initialization process, the set of best observing directions for each camera is extracted. Furthermore, other contributing cameras for each coverage direction and their weights used in the second interpolation step are extracted. After the initialization process, each camera has the knowledge of which ω to construct, which other cameras are contributing to the same ω and, depending

---

Algorithm 1. Distributed Reconstruction Algorithm for Camera Nodes

---
1: calculate calibration data
2: calculate weights
3: **for all** best observing directions **do**
4:    $P_m := read\_pixel\_from\_memory$
5:    $p_{contr,2..n} := request\_pixels\_from\_contributing\_cameras$
6:    $C := W_m \cdot P_m + \sum_2^n P_{s,n}$
7:    send C to central unit
8: **end for**
9: **for all** other observing directions **do**
10:    wait for request from principal camera
11:    $P_s := read\_pixel\_from\_memory$
12:    $P_{s,out} := W_s \cdot P_s$
13:    send $P_{s,out}$ to principal camera
14: **end for**

---

on the interpolation type, what are the camera weights contributing to the final level of interpolation. Assuming cameras have processing capabilities, the missing variables to construct the light field are the light intensity values obtained by the other cameras. This creates the necessity of a communication scheme among the camera modules.

The distributed and parallel implementation of omnidirectional reconstruction algorithm is explained in detail in Algorithm 1. Firstly, the initialization phase is conducted. For each camera, all observing directions (ω) and weights for the chosen interpolation technique are extracted. Then, for each new frame, camera creates its responsible portion of the final omnidirectional image. For all best observing directions, cameras read from the memory the corresponding pixel light intensity value (P_m) and weight (W_m). In the meantime, the camera module requests contributing light intensity values from the other cameras which observes the same direction. Each camera sends the light intensity value multiplied by the weight. After obtaining all values, the camera sends the sum of all intensity values to the central unit for display.

For directions other than the best observing ones, cameras still possess the weight and light intensity values. When a new light intensity request comes from the best observing camera, the camera reads the light intensity value (P_s) and weight (W_s). Afterwards it reconstructs the light intensity value $P_{s,out}$ for given direction and sends the value to the best observing camera

3.1   Processing Demands

The proposed architecture in [28] performs the omnidirectional vision reconstruction in a pipeline flow for both the nearest neighbour and the linear interpolation techniques. Assuming that the memory used in the system can sustain consecutive access cycles, F_{clk} for the presented real-time omnidirectional vision reconstruction architecture is derived from (3) as follows:

$$N_{acs} \times F_{ps} + T_{lat} \leq F_{clk} \qquad (3)$$

For approximations, the latency term T_{lat} in (3) can be neglected. The maximum number of access time is $N_{acs} = N_{cam} \times N_\theta \times N_\phi$ which occurs in case when the cameras contribute in all directions for the linear interpolation technique. For high number of cameras and high camera resolutions, the F_{clk} is the dominant demand. The aggregate of the two demands is translatable to the memory bandwidth requirement of the system using the multiplying factor for number of pixels (N_{pix}). As the output resolution increases, memory bandwidth and clock frequency increases accordingly. Processing demand becomes major bottleneck, and distributing the algorithm becomes inevitable.

3.2   Effects of Pixelation Schemes

The pixel gridding scheme for the omnivision application has an effect on the load imposed on each camera module of the Panoptic system when implemented distributively.

The pixel directions ω shown in Fig. 2(a) derive from an equi angular segmentation of longitude and latitude coordinates of a unit sphere into N_ϕ and N_θ segments, respectively. This pixelation enables the rectangular presentation of the reconstructed image suitable for ordinary displays, but results in a non-equal contribution of the Panoptic cameras. The density of the pixel directions close to the poles of the sphere is higher compared to the equator of the sphere in the equi angular pixelation scheme. Hence, the cameras positioned closer to the poles of the sphere contribute to more pixels in comparison to the other cameras of the system. The equi angular pixelation derives mathematically from (4):

$$\phi_\omega(i) = \frac{2\pi}{N_\phi} \times i, \quad 0 \leq i < N_\phi$$
$$\theta_\omega(j) = \frac{\pi}{2N_\theta} \times (j + \frac{1}{2}), \quad 0 \leq j < N_\theta \qquad (4)$$

The equi angular pixel gridding scheme depicted in Fig. 2(a) does not yield an equal number of ω pixel direct camera to construct. For the nearest neighbour interpolation of the distributed and parallel approach, computational load is not equally distributed among the camera modules. For example, the camera which is placed in the north pole of the system, is responsible for more than 10 % of ω pixel directions. The workload among the cameras are not distributed evenly, which is not suitable for implementation of the omnidirectional vision reconstruction algorithm in parallel.

An equal density pixelation scheme depicted in Fig. 2(b) resulting in an approximately even contribution of the cameras is devised for the Panoptic system. The scheme is based on enforcing a constant number of pixels per area, as expressed in (5) and (6). Compared to the equi angular pixelation, the change is observed in latitude angles.

$$\phi(i) = \frac{2\pi}{N_\phi} \times i, \qquad\qquad 0 \le i < N_\phi \qquad (5)$$

$$\theta(j) = \arccos(1 - \frac{j}{N_\theta}), \qquad\qquad 0 \le j \le N_\theta \qquad (6)$$

The equi angular pixelation leads to an evenly distributed workload among the camera modules, that makes distributing and parallelizing the algorithm more feasible. Detailed discussion on how the different pixelation scheme effects the distributed algorithm and corresponding memory demand for increased resolution and number of the cameras can be seen in [29].

4   Interconnected Network of Cameras

An interconnection network is a programmable system capable of transporting data between terminals. The system illustrated in Fig. 4 shows N terminals, $C_1 \ldots C_N$ connected to a network. For example, when terminal C_2 wishes to exchange data with terminal C_5, C_2 sends a message containing the data to the network and the network delivers the message to C_5. The terminals C_i resemble the camera nodes with processing and networking features in addition to basic imaging.

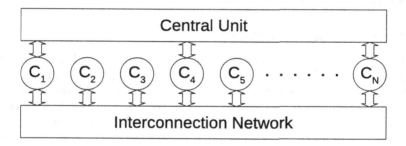

Fig. 4. High level model of an interconnected network of cameras. All cameras C_i are connected via interconnection network and some cameras have direct access to central unit.

Having a distributed camera system does not imply the omission of a central unit. For example a central unit is required for the cameras to send their processed information for the purpose of display. Also a hybrid approach for the application deployment can be considered, where some of the processing is distributed at the camera level and the rest of the processing is conducted in the central unit. For this purpose it is preferred that all the distributed cameras also have a direct access to a central unit. This feature is not feasible or optimal in most cases. A central unit may not have enough ports to interface with all the cameras of the system. In a case where all the cameras are connected to the central unit with distinct interfaces, and the respective bandwidth of these connections are not fully utilized, an inefficient usage of resources is taking place. Hence it is more efficient to provide some of the cameras with direct accessing capability to the central unit and share these connections with the cameras that do not have a direct interface to the central unit. The availability of an interconnection network permits the utilization of this strategy. The latter concept is depicted for the Panoptic system with N cameras in Fig. 4.

In multi-camera applications, information exchange mostly takes part among the neighbouring cameras. Thus, during the creation of an interconnection network, neighbourhood relations of camera modules should be preserved as much as possible. The neighbourhood relation for the cameras in Panoptic System can be seen in Fig. 5(b). It is an irregular graph-based topology. However, in most of the systems, this irregular graph-based topology is hard to implement and control on hardware level. A regular graph-based topology can be used to simplify the implementation of the interconnection network. Instead of creating an irregular graph-based network shown in Fig. 5(b), a regular graph-based, 7×7 mesh topology is chosen in order to realise interconnected network of cameras.

A regular network topology is relatively simple to implement and control. It is scalable and easy to extend, add or subtract nodes. Flow control mechanisms and packet structures are easier to construct at the hardware level. Furthermore, it generalizes the problem regardless of the source network topology and the camera arrangement in the physical hemisphere dome. However, mapping cameras into the network nodes creates new problems.

4.1   Camera Assignment Problem

In order to obtain the neighbourhood relation graph of the Panoptic system, the surface of the Panoptic device hemisphere is partitioned into a set of cells centered on the camera locations. Each cell is defined as the set of all points on the hemisphere which are closer to the camera location contained in the cell than to any other camera positions. The boundaries of the cells are determined by the points equidistant to two nearest sites, and the cell corners (or nodes) to at least three nearest sites. This particular partitioning falls into the category of a well-established geometry concept known as the Voronoi diagram (or Voronoi tessellation [30]). The Voronoi diagram of a 5 floors and 49 cameras Panoptic system can be seen in Fig. 5(a). The geometrical neighbourhood relation of 5 floors and 49 cameras extracted from the Voronoi diagram is shown in Fig. 5(b).

This assignment strategy is known in the context of a facility allocation problem called the Quadratic Assignment Problem (QAP). The QAP models the following real-life problem: In a graph-based topology, for each pair of locations a distance is specified and for each pair of facilities a weight or flow (e.g. the amount of supplies transported between two facilities) is specified. The problem is to assign all facilities to different locations with the goal of minimizing the sum of the distances multiplied by the corresponding flows. A planar graph representing the neighbouring of the cameras is extracted in Fig. 5(b) where the nodes of the extracted graph represent the cameras and its edges resembles the neighbouring of the cameras. Hence, in the latter graph two nodes are connected

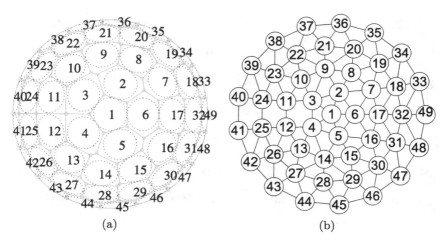

Fig. 5. (a) Top view of the Voronoi diagram of a five-floor Panoptic system containing 49 camera locations (b) The planar graph extracted from the Voronoi diagram.

if their respective cameras are geometrical neighbours. The adjacency matrix of this graph can be used as the flow matrix of the QAP.

The QAP is an NP-hard problem; which means there is no known algorithm for solving this problem in polynomial time, and even small instances may require long computation time. Among different proposed solutions, sparse version of the GRASP algorithm [31] has given the best result solving the QAP. The assigned camera numbers of Fig. 5(b) is represented on the mesh graph shown in Fig. 6(a). The assignment allocates the cameras such that all geometrical neighbouring cameras are not more than three hops away from each other in the new topology. The number of nodes in the target topology and the cameras of the Panoptic system are the same in the demonstrated example. The same method is applicable if the number of the nodes in the target topology is larger than the number of cameras of the Panoptic system, by assuming to have cameras with no flow exchanges with other cameras. This solution is considered when no regular based graph topology is selectable to support the exact number of cameras of the Panoptic system.

4.2   Central Unit Access

As stated previously, having a distributed camera system does not imply the omission of a central unit. However, we have explained that connecting all units to the central unit is also problematic. We need to find candidate cameras that will have direct access to central unit. In order to decide which cameras will have direct access, the problem to solve is which p candidate cameras to select to have access to the central unit so that the rest of the cameras can access the central unit with minimum number of hops. This feature is desired for reducing access time between the central unit and any camera of the interconnected

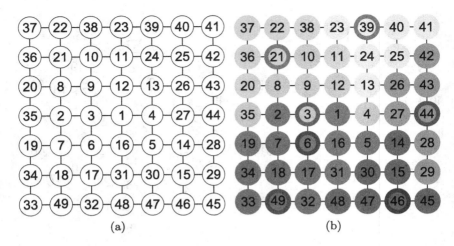

Fig. 6. (a) The assigned 7×7 mesh topology interconnected network (b) The 7×7 Mesh topology with 7 vertex p-centers.

network, assuming sufficient channel bandwidth is available. The latter problem can also be mapped into a facility allocation problem known as the vertex p-center problem. The basic p-center problem consists of locating p facilities and assigning clients to them so as to minimize the maximum distance between a client and the facility it is assigned to. This problem is also known to be NP-hard [32]. In order to distribute forty-nine cameras' load equally, the p value is chosen as seven. As an example, a vertex 7-center problem has been solved for the mesh graph topology depicted in Fig. 6(b) assuming that each camera with access to central unit can support up to 7 clients. The problem is solved using an exact algorithm for the capacitated vertex p-center problem [33]. The solution is depicted in Fig. 6(b). All the cameras acting as p-center (*i.e.*, with access to central unit) shown with a bold edge. The cameras belonging to the same p-center are also filled with similar colors. All cameras are at most two hops away from their supporting facility camera. This strategy aims to minimize the network load caused by the transmission of central unit access packets.

4.3   Verification

The designed interconnection network is simulated under real or close-to-real conditions. The "BookSim" simulator [34] is used for the purpose of performance analysis of the interconnection network of cameras. The BookSim simulator is a C++ based cycle-accurate interconnection network simulator. The simulator is extended to support custom-defined traffic patterns which are configured by a custom text file. This development was accomplished to support any traffic pattern for target networks under test. A MATLAB-based routine is developed in order to simulate different injection rates with several different test patterns. Optimal parameters for router unit such as number of virtual channels, buffer

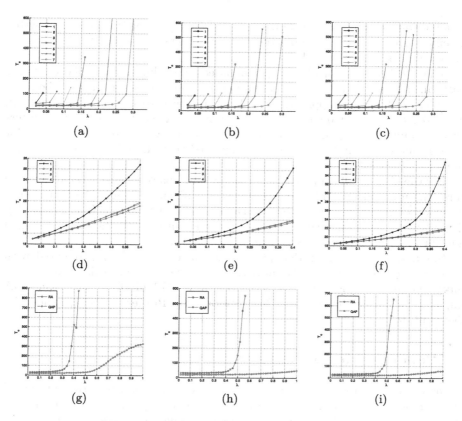

Fig. 7. Average packet latency (T_c) vs average throughput (λ) (i.e., packet injection rate) graphs. The (a), (b), (c) and graphs demonstrate the latency vs throughput for routers with flit buffer size equal to 8, 32 and 64, respectively. The (d), (e) and (f) graphs demonstrate the latency vs throughput for routers for a 7×7 mesh network with QAP assigned camera locations comparing number of virtual channels, flit buffer sizes equal to 8, 32 and 64, respectively. The (g), (h) and (i) graphs demonstrate the comparison in between QAP camera assignment versus random camera assignments, flit buffer sizes equal to 8, 32 and 64, respectively. Several different random assignments have been conducted and the average latency values obtained through BookSim simulations

size etc. are extracted in terms of latency (T_c) versus throughput (λ) with custom created Panoptic traffic pattern. Injection rate is indicating how frequently a new packet is injected into network while latency indicates how many clock cycles it takes for a network packet to traverse to the destination node. All the injection rates are normalized to channel bandwidth and latency is expressed in number of cycles.

The graphs in Fig. 7(a), (b) and (c) depicts the latency vs. injection rate for different number of vertex p-centers selected for direct access to the central unit. It is observed that for the nearest neighbour technique traffic pattern, the demands on the interconnection network tend to reduce as the number of vertex p-centers grows. As the number of vertex p-centers grows, the traffic becomes more balanced and localized.

The 7×7 mesh network is also simulated under linear interpolation traffic pattern. The number of vertex-p centers is chosen as seven. The assignment provided by the QAP approach and shown in Fig. 6(b) is used. The graphs in Fig. 7(d), (e) and (f) demonstrate the latency versus throughput for routers with flit buffer size equal to 8, 32 and 64, respectively. The results are given for throughput values of $\lambda < 0.4$, as it is expected that the injection rate will not be higher than 0.4.

For the purpose of comparison, a set of average packet latency versus average throughput graphs under linear interpolation traffic pattern for a 7×7 mesh network with random and QAP assigned camera locations. Figure 7(g), (h), and (i), demonstrate the latency versus throughput for routers with one virtual channel and flit buffer size equal to 8, 32 and 64, respectively.

Simulations prove that Panoptic traffic pattern can be implemented with expected injection rate and latency. Extracted parameters utilized during the implementation of the router mechanism in an FPGA platform. For the FPGA implementation, an open source Network-on-Chip Router in RTL provided by [34] is utilized.

5 Panoptic Media Platform

A custom-made FPGA platform is designed for the practice of the concept of an interconnected network of cameras. The developed platform is referred to as the Panoptic Media. A Panoptic system comprising 49 cameras is interfaced to this platform. The design and implementation of the parallel and distributed approach of the omnidirectional vision reconstruction algorithm of the Panoptic camera is elaborated for the Panoptic Media platform. The Panoptic Media Board (PMB) is an FPGA-based development board. The PMB includes eight Xilinx XC5VLX110 Virtex5 FPGAs. One FPGA is targeted for the implementation of the central unit and the other seven are slaves and used for emulating an interconnected network of cameras. The FPGA hosting the central unit is referred to as the central/master FPGA and FPGAs hosting cameras is referred to as the slave FPGAs. The top view of the designed platform is shown in Fig. 1(b).

5.1 Central FPGA

The central FPGA hosts the central unit of the system. It is designed to be in charge of initialization, synchronization among the FPGAs and camera nodes, camera router nodes configuration and control, display and external host communications of the system. For external communications, the central unit has access to a USB-2.0 device and 1 Gb/s Ethernet physical controller device.

At system power up the central unit enters an initialization phase. In this phase, the external physical channel ports of the central FPGA which are connected to that of the slave FPGAs are synchronized. This synchronization is conducted on all FPGAs to achieve a fully synchronous interconnected network. The synchronization is a phase alignment process in which the data bus connections are adjusted at the receiver side for optimum clock sampling. The phase alignment is adjusted using the dynamic time delay adjustment feature of the Virtex-5 FPGA IO buffers. For this purpose, a synchronization pattern is first transmitted on all transmitting bus connections (*i.e.*, outward bus connections) while the receiver bus connections IO buffer time delays are adjusted for optimum clock sampling by their host MicroBlaze processor, on all FPGAs.

The central unit can communicate with all camera router nodes of the interconnection network through packet transmission and reception. Two types of packet exist in the system, named control and data packets. Control packets are used for configuring camera router modules or monitoring and status check purposes. The central FPGA's MicroBlaze processor can access all the register banks of the SmartCam IPs via the interconnection network using packet based messages. The data packets contain image information data which are used for display or for transfer to an external host. Each packet type and subtype is identified using a specific packet ID.

Each data packet contains a pixel information of an image frame. The data packets can be sent by all the cameras simultaneously. Therefore the pixels of an image are receivable in a shuffled order by the central unit. Hence all the data packets pertaining to an image frame are temporarily stored by the RCTRL IP in the ZBT-SRAM first. The shuffled order of the receiving data packets implies a random write access nature to a memory. To this aim, the ZBT-SRAM is chosen for the temporary storage of the data packets pixel information part. When a full frame is received the RCTRL IP transfers the received frame to the SDRAM. The SDRAM is used as the video memory for external display interfaces like monitors or projectors.

The Central unit has access to a USB-2.0 device through a Xilinx external peripheral controller (EPC) IP. The Central unit identifies the USB-2.0 device as an asynchronous FIFO memory. The EPC IP is configured for correct access times with the USB-2.0 device. The USB-2.0 device is used as the primary path for external host communication. The ordered image data in the ZBT SRAM can be transferred to an external host.

5.2   Slave FPGAs

The role of a slave FPGA is to emulate a portion of a 7×7 mesh interconnected network of cameras. Each slave FPGA is responsible for seven imagers, hosts seven camera modules and seven ASRAM memories, application control unit (ACU) and channel synchronisation (CHSYNC) modules for inter fpga communication and synchronization. The SoC architecture for Slave unit can be seen in Fig. 8. Each imager is interfaced to a custom-designed smart camera IP (Smart-Cam). The SmartCam IP is a camera module with router connectivity, memory

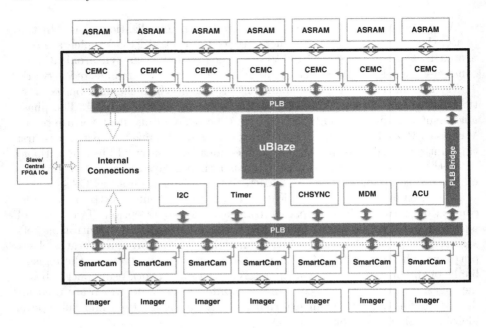

Fig. 8. SoC architecture of the slave FPGA.

and application processing units. The internal blocks of the custom-designed SmartCam IP is shown in Fig. 9. Each SmartCam IP interfaces with a custom external memory controller (CEMC). SmartCam IPs are provided access to an ASRAM via its interfacing CEMC IP.

The SmartCam IP comprises five sub-blocks. The applications intended for the SmartCam IP are implemented into the Image Processing Unit sub-block. The Image Processing (IP) sub-block is designed to perform image processing applications. There are three modes of operation, named as video stream, nearest neighbour and linear interpolation. In the video stream, the SmartCam IP transfers the video stream generated by the camera to the central unit for visual display or external host transfer. This mode is necessary for calibration purposes. In the nearest neighbour and linear interpolation modes, it is responsible for creating network demand packets for pixel values obtained by the other contributing cameras and performing the first and second steps of interpolations of the reconstruction algorithm. Each SmartCam IP provides its portion of omnivision of the panoptic system to the central unit.

The Imager Interface sub-block is responsible for image acquisition and transfers the video stream generated by the imager to the ASRAM memory. The IP sub-block communicates with the central unit and other SmartCam IPs in the panoptic system through the Router sub-block. The Router sub-block comprises five-ports (*i.e.*, north, south, east, west and an input/output port in order to

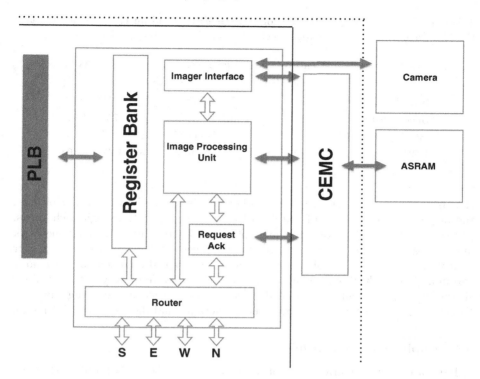

Fig. 9. Internal blocks of the SmartCam IP used in the slave FPGAs

enter or flush out of the network ports). The router sub-blocks' main aim is to create the communication medium among the SmartCams.

The Request Acknowledge sub-block responds to the incoming demand packets from other SmartCam IPs. It creates respond packets that contains the necessary intensity values and coefficients that are used in the second step of interpolation. Register Bank sub-block is for the IP's mode configuration, monitoring and status checks. It can be reached by the central unit via the interconnection network to perform overall control of the system.

Forty-nine SmartCams distributed over seven FPGAs are operate in parallel for omnidirectional vision reconstruction. Throughout the interconnection network, pixel intensity values are interchanged among the modules and each camera constructs its assigned portion of the omnidirectional vision. The central unit is responsible for obtaining all reconstructed pixels and displaying them.

5.3   Inter FPGA Communication

Each FPGA has twelve sets of 24-bit bus connections. Each two set of 24-bit bus connections are bundled to form a physical channel port for an FPGA. Each FPGA contains six physical channel ports. The direction of one bus connec-

Table 1. FPGA Device Utilization for Central FPGA and an example of the Slave FPGAs, for both nearest neighbour technique and linear interpolation techniques

Resources	Central FPGA		Slave NN		Slave LIN		Avail.
	Used	Util.	Used	Util.	Used	Util.	
Slice LUTs	19495	28 %	54360	78 %	61416	88 %	69120
Slice registers	20617	29 %	32326	47 %	40038	57 %	69120
BlockRAM/FIFO	93	72 %	89	69 %	89	69 %	128
DSP48Es	3	4 %	26	40 %	61	95 %	64

tion is chosen as outward while the other one is selected as inward. However, the physical channel ports of the FPGAs can contain multiple logical channels. For the presented partitioning scheme of a 7×7 mesh interconnected network among the slave FPGAs of the PMB, it is sufficient to have a maximum of four logical channels within a physical channel port. Logical channels are realizable through time multiplexing while operating at higher frequency rates within a single physical channel. Four logical channels are realized by doubling the slave FPGA clock frequency and sending the packets in dual data rate (DDR) mode.

5.4 Implementation Results

A Panoptic multi-camera sphere of diameter $2r_\odot = 30$ cm is built by stacking circular PCB rings on top of each other as shown in Fig. 1(a). VGA camera modules are operated at 25 fps. The camera module requires to be programmed for activation through a two-wire I2C serial interface. At start-up, the central FPGA resets all the slave FPGAs and hence the interconnection network. At first, a calibration phase of the physical interconnect channels that exist among the FPGAs of the system is conducted. After the synchronization among the FPGAs is accomplished, the slave FPGAs' MicroBlaze processors start initializing the ASRAM memories. The central FPGA is designed as a control unit and its MicroBlaze processor can access all the register banks of the camera IPs of any slave FPGA via the interconnection network using packet-based messages. The system was found to support the real-time operation of a 7×7 interconnected network of VGA cameras and providing an omnidirectional vision with a 25 frame per second rate an XGA (1024×768 pixel) resolution with the linear interpolation method. The resource utilization percentage of the central FPGA and one of the slave FPGAs can be seen in Table 1.

6   Visualization of Omnidirectional Data

The Panoptic Camera can be used as a perfect example of a telepresence system. Unlike the virtual reality systems, where users are transported to a virtual scene, telepresence allows users to be in another location in real world. Videoconferencing is one example of telepresence. Among the benefits of videoconferencing, we can say it lowers the travel requirements, improves dialog efficiency and allows mobility impaired people to visit distant places. Instead of using narrow angle field of view cameras, we can achieve a better telepresence with the Panoptic Camera.

Early omnidirectional imagers were mainly using extreme fish eye lenses or hyperboloidal mirrors, such as described in [35]. These imaging systems are limited by the resolution capabilities of a single sensor and feature strong distortions. The resolution can be increased by using more modern image sensors, as described in [36], however the distortions remain. Additionally a big portion of the image is covered by the reflection of the camera lens. In [37] a multi-camera approach is proposed for omnidirectional video generation for telepresence. However this particular solution cannot be used for real-time video streaming, because the video generation is achieved in post processing.

In this section, we will present a novel telepresence system, which allows users to naturally observe the remote location. Omnidirectional data will be created with the Panoptic Media Platform, and remapping of omnidirectional data through observed direction will be created by using the wide field of view head mounted display (HMD) Oculus Rift.

As explained in Sect. 5.4, Panoptic camera has two different operation modes. For the telepresence system, full XGA resolution (1024×768) of the [29] will be used. The system can be divided into two parts, one is the server application and the second one is the client application.

6.1 Server Application

The omnidirectional XGA output generated by the Panoptic Camera is transmitted via the DVI output. A capture card connected to the server PC is utilized to transfer omnidirectional data into the server PC. The main task of the server PC is to distribute the whole omnidirectional image via TCP to clients. The application automatically adapts to input resolution changes and can therefore also be used with other camera systems and future versions of the Panoptic camera. The server application is able to stream video to multiple clients at the same time via TCP.

6.2 Client Application

The client application receives the TCP stream originating from the server application and generates the views for the head-mounted display. Optionally it can also directly receive the images from the DVI capture card, when the camera system is close to the user.

In order to display the hemispherical image on the client side of the telepresence system, a virtual environment is created. This virtual environment is created using the OpenGL API and consists of a user controlled camera and a large overhead hemisphere, onto which the image is mapped. The camera rotates according to the sensor data received from the head-mounted display. The omnidirectional image is used as a texture for the virtual hemisphere. To retrieve the correct dimensions of the captured objects, the equal density mapping scheme expressed in (5) and (6) needs to be reversed.

Using the inverse mapping functions (7) and (8) the original angular directions are restored. In these equations, $\frac{i}{N_\phi}$ and $\frac{j}{N_\theta}$ correspond to the OpenGL texture coordinates s and t respectively.

$$s(\phi) = \frac{i(\phi)}{N_\phi} = \frac{\phi}{2\pi} \qquad 0 \le \phi < 2\pi \qquad (7)$$

$$t(\theta) = \frac{j(\theta)}{N_\theta} = 1 - \cos(\theta) \qquad 0 \le \theta \le \frac{\pi}{2} \qquad (8)$$

(a)   (b)

Fig. 10. (a) The textured OpenGL hemisphere showing a captured image, viewed from the side. (b) The client application generating the left and right eye view for the head-mounted display.

Figure 10(a) shows the textured virtual hemisphere from the side. When using the application with the head mounted display, the user Viewpoint is in the middle of the sphere. Figure 10(b) shows the application in normal use with the HMD.

In order to ensure a high frame rate at all times, the application receives new omnidirectional images in a secondary thread. Thanks to the multi-threaded implementation the rendering frame rate is independent from the USB or network connection speed, as well as the camera frame rate. This is important for the network streaming functionality, in which the frame rate can vary.

6.3   Future Work

Panoptic Camera can broadcast the omnidirectional image and clients with head mounted display can observe the surroundings of the system remotely. Thanks to the natural behaviour of the system, each user can observe different direction at the same time. The Oculus Rift tracks the direction and angle of the users head, thus enables to render the observerd location from the obtained real-time omnidirectional data. An example video can be seen in [38]. We believe the system can be used to broadcast the concerts or sports events and allow people to visit distant places. Currently, it is planned to develop a new Panoptic Camera system, which will increase the output resolution of the system as the resolutions of the head mounted displays increase. Furthermore, video compression and decompression will be implemented, in order to allow higher frame rates via internet.

7   A Real-Time HDR Panorama with Panoptic Camera

High dynamic range (HDR) images are usually obtained by capturing several images of the scene at different exposures. Previous HDR video techniques adopted the same principle by stacking HDR frames in time domain. We have modified Panoptic Camera Platform in order to construct and render HDR panoramic video in real-time, with 1024×256 resolution and a frame rate of 25 fps. We exploit the overlapping fields-of-view between the cameras in the bottom row of the Panoptic Camera with different exposures to create an HDR radiance map. We have proposed a method for HDR frame reconstruction which merges the previous HDR imaging techniques with the algorithms for panorama reconstruction. The developed FPGA-based processing system is able to reconstruct the HDR frame using the proposed method and tone map the resulting image using a hardware-adapted global operator. Detailed explanation of the implementation of the HDR Panoptic System can be seen in [39] and [40].

Dynamic range in the digitally acquired images is defined as the ratio between the brightest and the darkest pixel in the image. Most modern cameras cannot capture sufficiently wide dynamic range to truthfully represent radiance of the natural scenes, which may contain several orders of magnitude from light to dark regions. This results in underexposed or overexposed regions in the taken image and the lack of local contrast. The underexposed and overexposed images show fine details in very bright and very dark areas, respectively. These details cannot be observed in the moderately exposed image.

High dynamic range (HDR) imaging technique was introduced to increase dynamic range of the captured images. HDR imaging is used in many applications, such as remote sensing [41], biomedical imaging [42] and photography [43], thanks to the improved visibility and accurate detail representation in both dark and bright areas.

Besides capturing the natural scenes, another problem occurs when displaying them. The modern displays are limited to the low dynamic range, which causes inadequate representation of even standard LDR images. In order to avoid such problems, a tone mapping operation is introduced to map the real pixel values to the ones adapted to the display device. The purpose of tone mapping is to compress the full dynamic range in the HDR image, while preserving natural features of the scene.

In this section we present a new imaging system for HDR video construction and rendering. The key idea is to use a multi-camera Panoptic Camera setup to create a composite frame, where cameras with the overlapping field-of-view (FOV) are set to different exposure times. Such system reduces the motion blur, as there is no inter-frame gap time (which can be several hundreds milliseconds in the standard HDR cameras). Additionally, the frames are captured at the same moment by all cameras, which reduces the intra-frame motion of the scene objects to the difference interval of cameras' exposure times. We developed a hardware prototype customized for real-time video processing, utilizing the multi-camera setup. It is a high performance field programmable gate array (FPGA) based system which provides capability for real-time HDR frame construction and tone mapping.

The pixel streams coming from the cameras are processed in real-time; hence, HDR video is created as a stack of HDR frames in time domain. Construction of each frame can be divided into two independent processes: (1) construction of HDR composite frame, and (2) tone mapping the composite frame to achieve realistic rendering.

7.1   HDR Composite Frame

Thanks to the circular arrangement of the cameras on this prototype, we adopted the similar approach as in [25], simplified to a two-dimensional case. The installed cameras were calibrated for their intrinsic and extrinsic parameters: focal length, frame center position, lens distortion and angular position in space (yaw, pitch, roll) with geometric center of the prototype as the origin point. To be able to reproduce the HDR image, the cameras are also color calibrated. The camera's response curve is recovered using a set of shots of the same scene with different exposure settings. The response curve is recovered by applying the algorithm proposed by Debevec and Malik [4]. Only one camera is color calibrated, as we assumed that the response curve is identical for all installed cameras. Both calibrations are done only once, as the parameters do not change over time.

FOVs of the cameras overlap such that each point in space is observed by at least two cameras. We exploit this property and set the camera exposures to different values. During the camera initialization phase, all cameras are set to the auto-exposure mode. The camera with the longest exposure time, $i.e.$, the one observing a dark region, is taken as a reference. In the following step, half of the cameras are set to the reference exposure t_{ref}, while other half is set to $t_{ref}/4$, such that two cameras with overlapping FOVs have different exposure times.

Even though after the calibration process, the registration errors and visible seams are unavoidable. Hence, an additional blending process is required. The Gaussian blending method proposed in [25] is based on a weighted average among the cameras contributing to the observed direction. The result of applying Gaussian blending on the acquired data provides the composite HDR radiance map, which should be tone mapped for realistic display (Table 2).

Table 2. FPGA Device Utilization for Central FPGA and an example of the Slave FPGAs, for High Dynamic Range Image Reconstruction

Resources	Central FPGA		Slave FPGAs		Avail.
	Used	Util.	Used	Util.	
Slice LUTs	18376	26 %	63732	92 %	69120
Slice registers	17498	25 %	40509	58 %	69120
BlockRAM/FIFO	88	69 %	89	69 %	128
DSP48Es	58	90 %	61	95 %	64

7.2 Tone Mapping

Yoshida et al. [44] made an extensive comparison of the tone mapping operators. The comparison was realized by human subjects grading several aspects of the constructed image, such as contrast, brightness, naturalness and detail reproduction. One of the best graded techniques in this review was the local operator by. Therefore, this operator will be taken as a base for the development of an FPGA-suitable operator. Even though this mapping is created for interactive applications, its speed is very slow for video applications. The reported frame rate is below 10 fps, for 720×480 pixels image, without any approximations which decrease the image quality [45].

Drago et al. [45] proposed changing logarithm base and calculating only natural and base-10 logarithms. In this approach, fast calculation of generic power functions, is not possible. Hence, we adopted the parameters to relax the hardware implementation, without losing any image quality. In [40], the new tone mapping operator suitable for hardware implementation is described in detail. The set of required mathematical operations is reduced to only addition, multiplication and division, which are suitable for fast implementation.

7.3 FPGA Implementation

Smart Camera IP in Fig. 9 is now responsible for calculation of the final HDR pixel value. Using the calibration data, the block reads the appropriate pixel from memory, multiplies it with the weight, and requests the weighted pixel from the secondary camera. The secondary pixel has already been multiplied by the HDR blending weight in the Secondary pixel block, thus only final addition is required. The resulting HDR pixel is further provided to the central unit.

In Omnidirectional implementation of the Panoptic Camera, the Central Unit was solely responsible for reordering the pixel packets coming from Slave FPGAs and displaying the output data from DVI display. In HDR reconstruction, the Central Unit also responsible for tone mapping algorithm. The tone mapping implementation consists of two parts: finding the maximum pixel luminance L_{max} and tone mapping curve implementation. Finding L_{max} consists of finding the maximum value in a sequence of the read luminances. L_{max} value is needed for the core tone mapping operation. When HDR video stream is processed, L_{max} is taken from the previous frame, under the assumption that the scene illumination does not vary faster than response time of the human visual system. The parameter is updated at the end of each frame.

7.4   Discussion and Future Work

Our HDR construction method does not provide as significant increase in dynamic range as some of the other methods, due to the use of only 2 f-stops. However, up to our knowledge, it is the only system which uses multiple cameras to create and render HDR radiance map simultaneously, and provides real-time HDR video signal at the output. The next step is to additionally improve the dynamic range by increasing the number of cameras, and using more than two different exposures per reconstructed pixel. Furthermore, image quality can be improved by using a more complex blending algorithm, such as [46]. However, real-time implementation of such algorithm requires a more powerful hardware setup.

8   Conclusion and Future Work

A novel parallel and distributed technique for the omnidirectional vision reconstruction of the Panoptic camera in an interconnected network of cameras arrangement is presented. A methodology for camera's assignment into regular network node and selecting candidate cameras for central unit communication is shown. A custom-made FPGA-based platform termed the Panoptic Media Board (PMB) was implemented and introduced for the emulation of a 7×7 mesh interconnected network of smart cameras. The system-level design of the PMB was elaborated. The SoC architecture of the FPGAs of the PMB was presented. The PMB prototype provides a real-time 25 frame per second omnidirectional vision at XGA resolution. For a second operation mode in addition to the XGA output resolution, Panopticmedia also be found to support a 256×1024 output resolution with nearest neighbour interpolation method. During the display of 256×1024 resolution, a chosen camera in VGA resolution can also be displayed below the 360 omnidirectional output. Reader is referred to [38] for examples of such videos taken by the PanopticMedia Platform. Furthermore, we have presented a visualization technique for Omnidirectional Camera in order to make the created 360° view suitable for telepresence applications. Finally, by utilizing the overlapped angle of views of the cameras in the bottom row of the Panoptic System, we have created and rendered a real-time multiple camera HDR video. The distributed and parallel implementation of multi-band blending technique [46] is considered for the next real-time application deployment of the Panoptic device. Moreover, a new version of the Panoptic System is under development, for providing higher output resolutions than XGA. Future work and application areas of the Panoptic device are not limited to omnidirectional reconstruction. Depth-map estimation, super-resolution and multi-view imaging are open research topics.

References

1. Kubota, A., Smolic, A., Magnor, M., Tanimoto, M., Chen, T., Zhang, C.: Multiview imaging and 3DTV. IEEE Sig. Process. Mag. **24**(6), 10–21 (2007)
2. Szeliski, R.: Image mosaicing for tele-reality applications. In: Proceedings of the Second IEEE Workshop on Applications of Computer Vision, pp. 44–53, Dec 1994
3. Mann, S., Picard, R.W.: On being undigital with digital cameras: extending dynamic range by combining differently exposed pictures. In: Proceedings of IS&T, pp. 442–448 (1995)
4. Debevec, P.E., Malik, J.: Recovering high dynamic range radiance maps from photographs. In: Proceedings of the 24th Conference on Computer Graphics and Interactive Techniques, New York, NY, USA, pp. 369–378 (1997)
5. Tanimoto, M., Tehrani, M., Fujii, T., Yendo, T.: Free-viewpoint TV. IEEE Sig. Process. Mag. **28**(1), 67–76 (2011)
6. Yagi, Y.: Omni directional sensing and its applications. IEICE Trans. Inform. Syst. **E82–D**(3), 568–579 (1999)
7. Levoy, M., Hanrahan, P.: Light field rendering. In: Proceedings of the 23rd Annual Conference on Computer Graphics and Interactive Techniques, New York, NY, USA, pp. 31–42 (1996)
8. Schechner, Y., Nayar, S.: Generalized mosaicing. In: IEEE International Conference on Computer Vision (ICCV), vol. 1, pp. 17–24 (2001)
9. Taylor, D.: Virtual camera movement: the way of the future? Am. Cinematographer **77**(8), 93–100 (1996)
10. Rander, P., Narayanan, P.J., Kanade, T.: Virtualized reality: constructing time-varying virtual worlds from real world events. In: IEEE Visualization 1997, pp. 277–284 (1997)
11. Zhang, C., Chen, T.: A self-reconfigurable camera array. In: Eurographics Symposium on Rendering, pp. 243–254 (2004)
12. Yang, J.C., Everett, M., Buehler, C., McMillan, L.: A real-time distributed light field camera. In: Proceedings of the 13th Eurographics Workshop on Rendering, Aire-la-Ville, Switzerland, pp. 77–86 (2002)
13. Wilburn, B., Joshi, N., Vaish, V., et al.: High performance imaging using large camera arrays. ACM Trans. Graph. **24**, 765–776 (2005)
14. Yuan, X., Qinghai, Z., Liwei, G., Mingcheng, Z., Xiaohong, D., Teng, R.: High speed simultaneous image distortion correction transformations for multi-camera cylindrical panorama real-time video system using FPGA. IEEE Trans. Circuits Syst. Video Technol. **24**(6), 1061–1069 (2013)
15. Ladybug, Point Grey Research Inc. http://ww2.ptgrey.com
16. Schreer, O., Feldmann, I., Weissig, C., Kauff, P., Schafer, R.: Ultrahigh-resolution panoramic imaging for format-agnostic video production. Proc. IEEE **101**(1), 99–114 (2013)
17. Anguelov, D., Dulong, C., Filip, D., Frueh, C., Lafon, S., Lyon, R., Ogale, A., Vincent, L., Weaver, J.: Google street view: capturing the world at street level. Computer **43**(6), 32–38 (2010)
18. Cogal, O., Akin, A., Seyid, K., Popovic, V., Schmid, A., Ott, B., Wellig, P., Leblebici, Y.: A new omni-directional multi-camera system for high resolution surveillance. In: SPIE Sensing Technology Applications. International Society for Optics and Photonics (2014)
19. Brady, D., Gehm, M., Stack, R., Marks, D., Kittle, D., Golish, D., Vera, E., Feller, S.: Multiscale gigapixel photography. Nature **486**(7403), 386–389 (2012)

20. Song, Y.M., Xie, Y., Malyarchuk, V., Xiao, J., Jung, I., Choi, K.-J., Liu, Z., Park, H., Lu, C., Kim, R.-H., et al.: Digital cameras with designs inspired by the arthropod eye. Nature **497**(7447), 95–99 (2013)
21. Afshari, H., Jacques, L., Bagnato, L., et al.: The PANOPTIC camera: a plenoptic sensor with real-time omnidirectional capability. J. Sig. Process. Syst., 1–24 (2013)
22. Neumann, J., Fermuller, C., Aloimonos, Y.: Polydioptric camera design and 3d motion estimation. In: 2003 Proceedings, 2003 IEEE Computer Society Conference on Computer Vision and Pattern Recognition, vol. 2, pp. II-294-301, June 2003
23. Levoy, M., Hanrahan, P.: Light field rendering. In SIGGRAPH 1996, Proceedings of the 23rd Annual Conference on Computer Graphics and Interactive Techniques, pp. 31–42. ACM (1996)
24. Afshari, H., Akin, A., Popovic, V., et al.: Real time FPGA implementation of linear blending vision reconstruction algorithm using a spherical light field camera. In: IEEE Workshop on Signal Processing Systems (2012)
25. Popovic, V., Afshari, H., Schmid, A., Leblebici, Y.: Real-time implementation of Gaussian image blending in a spherical light field camera. In: 2013 IEEE International Conference on Industrial Technology (ICIT), pp. 1173–1178, Feb 2013
26. Popovic, V., Seyid, K., Akin, A., Cogal, Ö., Afshari, H., Schmid, A., Leblebici, Y.: Image blending in a high frame rate FPGA-based multi-camera system. J. Sig. Process. Syst., pp. 1–16
27. Cogal, O., Popovic, V., Leblebici, Y.: Spherical panorama construction using multi sensor registration priors and its real-time hardware. In: 2013 IEEE International Symposium on Multimedia (ISM), pp. 171–178, Dec 2013
28. Afshari, H., Popovic, V., Tasci, T., Schmid, A., Leblebici, Y.: A spherical multi-camera system with real-time omnidirectional video acquisition capability. IEEE Trans. Consum. Electron. **58**(4), 1110–1118 (2012)
29. Seyid, K., Popovic, V., Cogal, O., Akin, A., Afshari, H., Schmid, A., Leblebici, Y.: A real-time multiaperture omnidirectional visual sensor based on an interconnected network of smart cameras. IEEE Trans. Circuits Syst. Video Technol. **25**(2), 314–324 (2015)
30. de Berg, M., van Kreveld, M., Overmars, M., Schwarzkopf, O.: Computational Geometry: Algorithms and Applications, 2nd edn. Springer, Heidelberg (2000)
31. Pardalos, L., Resende, M.: A greedy randomized adaptive search procedure for the quadratic assignment problem. In: Quadratic Assignment and Related Problems. DIMACS Series on Discrete Mathematics and Theoretical Computer Science, vol. 16, pp. 237–261 (1994)
32. Kariv, O., Hakimi, S.L.: An algorithmic approach to network location problems. I: the p-centers. SIAM J. Appl. Math. **37**, 513–538 (1979)
33. Pinar, M.C., Ozsoy, F.A.: An exact algorithm for the capacitated vertex p-center problem. Comput. Oper. Res. **33**(5), 1420–1436 (2006). http://dx.doi.org/10.1016/j.cor.2004.09.035
34. Jiang, N., Becker, D., Michelogiannakis, G., et al.: A detailed and flexible cycle-accurate network-on-chip simulator. In: Proceedings of the 2013 IEEE International Symposium on Performance Analysis of Systems and Software (2013)
35. Onoe, Y., Yamazawa, K., Takemura, H., Yokoya, N.: Telepresence by real-time view-dependent image generation from omnidirectional video streams. Comput. Vis. Image Underst. **71**(2), 154–165 (1998). http://www.sciencedirect.com/science/article/pii/S1077314298907056
36. Yamazawa, K., Takemura, H., Yokoya, N.: Telepresence system with an omnidirectional HD camera. In: Proceedings of the 5th Asian Conference on Computer Vision (ACCV 2002), vol. 2, pp. 533–538 (2002)

37. Ikeda, S., Sato, T., Yokoya, N.: Panoramic movie generation using an omnidirectional multi-camera system for telepresence. In: Bigun, J., Gustavsson, T. (eds.) SCIA 2003. LNCS, vol. 2749, pp. 1074–1081. Springer, Heidelberg (2003)
38. LSM. Real-time panoptic video by EPFL-LSM. http://www.youtube.com/user/LSMPanoptic/videos
39. Popovic, V., Seyid, K., Pignat, E., Cogal, O., Leblebici, Y.: Multi-camera platform for panoramic real-time HDR video construction and rendering. J. Real-Time Image Process., 1–12 (2014). http://dx.doi.org/10.1007/s11554-014-0444-8
40. Popovic, V., Pignat, E., Leblebici, Y.: Performance optimization and FPGA implementation of real-time tone mapping. IEEE Trans. Circuits Syst. II Express Briefs **61**(10), 803–807 (2014)
41. Chander, G., Markham, B.L., Helder, D.L.: Summary of current radiometric calibration coefficients for Landsat MSS, TM, ETM+, and EO-1 ALI sensors. Remote Sens. Environ. **113**(5), 893–903 (2009)
42. Jungmann, J.H., MacAleese, L., Visser, J., Vrakking, M.J.J., Heeren, R.M.A.: High dynamic range bio-molecular ion microscopy with the timepix detector. Anal. Chem. **83**(20), 7888–7894 (2011)
43. Bloch, C.: The HDRI Handbook 2.0: High Dynamic Range Imaging for Photographers and CG Artists. Rocky Nook, Santa Barbara (2013)
44. Yoshida, A., Blanz, V., Myszkowski, K., Seidel, H.-P.: Perceptual evaluation of tone mapping operators with real-world scenes. In: SPIE Human Vision and Electronic Imaging X, pp. 192–203 (2005)
45. Drago, F., Myszkowski, K., Annen, T., Chiba, N.: Adaptive logarithmic mapping for displaying high contrast scenes. Comput. Graph. Forum **22**(3), 419–426 (2003)
46. Brown, M., Lowe, D.: Automatic panoramic image stitching using invariant features. Int. J. Comput. Vision **74**(1), 59–73 (2007)

Transmission Channel Noise Aware Energy Effective LDPC Decoding

Thomas Marconi[1]($\boxtimes$), Christian Spagnol[2], Emanuel Popovici[2], and Sorin Cotofana[1]

[1] Computer Engineering Lab, TU Delft, Delft, The Netherlands
{T.Marconi,S.D.Cotofana}@tudelft.nl
[2] Electrical and Electronic Engineering, University College Cork, Cork, Ireland
c.spagnol@ue.ucc.ie, e.popovici@ucc.ie

Abstract. In communication systems channel quality variation, mostly induced by interferences, mobility, and environmental factors, is an unhindered physical phenomenon, which is usually perceived as a threat in pursuing reliable communication. There is a direct relation between the channel condition and the amount of computational resources and energy that have to be spend in order to reconstruct the correct messages at the reception side. When the quality is good, the decoding requires less resources and energy to identify and correct channel condition induced message errors, while when the channel noise level is high more resources and energy are needed to correct the errors. To be able to properly handle high noise levels while keeping the QoS requirements satisfied, telecom platforms are built upon largely over-designed hardware, i.e., they rely on worse case designs, which results in a substantial energy waste during most of their operation. In this chapter we introduce a methodology to dynamically adapt the platform operation mode to the channel noise level. The main objective is to keep QoS requirements satisfied regardless of the actual channel conditions while minimizing the energy consumption footprint. In particular, we propose a technique to exploit channel noise variability towards energy effective LDPC decoding amenable to adaptable low-energy operation. Endowed with the instantaneous channel noise level knowledge, our technique dynamically adjusts the operating voltage on-the-fly, aiming to achieve the optimal tradeoff between decoder performance and energy consumption without ignoring the fulfillment of the QoS requirements expressed in terms of frame/bit error rate. To demonstrate the capabilities of our proposal we implemented it and other state of the art energy reduction methods in the framework of a fully parallel LDPC decoder mapped on a Virtex-6 FPGA. Our experiments indicate that the proposed technique outperforms state of the art counterparts, in terms of energy reduction, with 71 % to 76 % and 15 % to 28 %, w.r.t. early termination without and with DVS, respectively, while maintaining the targeted decoding robustness. Moreover, the measurements suggest that in certain conditions Degradation Stochastic Resonance occurs, i.e., timing faults caused by unpredictable underpowered components in the circuit unexpectedly become supporters rather than enemies of the decoding process.

© IFIP International Federation for Information Processing 2015
L. Claesen et al. (Eds.): VLSI-SoC 2014, IFIP AICT 464, pp. 198–219, 2015.
DOI: 10.1007/978-3-319-25279-7_11

Keywords: LDPC decoding · Low energy · Dynamic Voltage Scaling · FPGAs · Communication systems

1 Introduction

To communicate messages from senders to recipients channels are indispensable required. In one hand, we need channels to convey our messages. In the other hand, we want to avoid the channels from corrupting our messages. Channel quality variation is an unhindered physical phenomenon which is usually perceived as a threat in pursuing reliable communication. It is well known that channel quality variation may occur in communication systems as a result of, e.g., multi-path, interferences, mobility, and environmental conditions [1] as illustrated in Fig. 1. When the quality is low a large number of errors might occur during the transmission and high performance error correctors are required to recover the original message. However, if the quality is good, the system experiences less errors case in which decoders with lower decoding capabilities are enough to fulfill the Quality of Service (QoS) requirements. Since the systems are designed to meet a target acceptable error rate even in the worst-case scenario, e.g., the highest expected channel noise level, the decoders are over-designed. Thus decoders have excess performance during good channel conditions and as the worst-case, i.e., bad condition, rarely occurs, significant energy consumption is wasted during most of their operation.

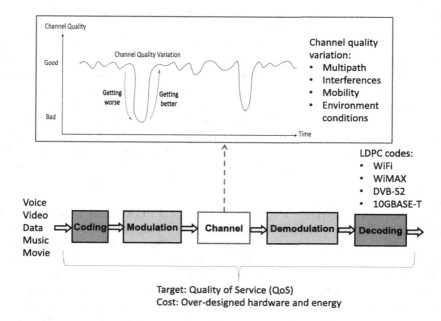

Fig. 1. Illustration of communication systems

In view of this observation, the main question that we are addressing in this work is "Can we adapt the decoder performance to the channel status to prevent energy over-consumption?" We positively answer this question by proposing a technique to trade off performance with energy while fulfilling error rates requirements by exploiting channel noise variability towards energy effective Low Density Parity Check (LDPC) decoding [2]. Decoding at the required performance is the key idea behind our method to diminish energy consumption and we determine the operation conditions resulting in the highest energy savings by actively monitoring the channel noise. More specifically, we diminish the supply voltage value when the channel is in a good condition to save energy and vice versa we increase it when the channel is getting worse for meeting the target error rate. To be able to properly adjust at run time the power supply voltage to the channel status we perform at design time a decoder pre-characterization, i.e., we measure decoder's Frame Error Rate (FER), Bit Error Rate (BER), and energy/bit under voltage scaling on a variety of noisy channels. The main objective is to minimize the energy consumption while preserving the decoder performance in terms of FER and BER. The operating voltage adaptation is done based on the estimated Signal-to-Noise Ratio (SNR) of an Additive White Gaussian Noise (AWGN) channel with Binary Phase Shift Keying (BPSK) modulation.

Although our technique is applicable to any electronic system for which the power supply vs performance relation can be pre-characterized, in this work, we experimentally evaluate it for an LDPC decoder implemented on Field-Programmable Gate Array (FPGA). We utilize as discussion vehicle an LDPC decoder based on Log Likelihood Ratio (LLR) Belief Propagation (BP) algorithm implemented with fully parallel architecture. The reasons for choosing the LDPC decoder [2] for evaluating our proposed technique are (i) the superiority of its decoding performance, which is very close to the Shannon limit [3], and (ii) its popularity, being adopted by many communication standards, e.g., WiFi [4], WiMAX [5], DVB-S2 [6], 10GBase-T [7]. The decoder is automatically generated and the energy consumption is measured directly on the FPGA board by accessing the PMBus through the USB interface adapter. In contrast to [8], we adjust the supply voltage value by directly controlling the board internal power supply, thus we do not rely on an external power supply or need to operate board modifications for effective and efficient voltage scaling experiments. We note that we report measured data, gathered from experiments on a Virtex-6 FPGA, and not from theoretical analysis, e.g., density evolution, EXIT charts, or from, e.g., Monte-Carlo simulation.

For comparison purpose we mapped into the FPGA three versions of the considered LDPC decoder as follows: (i) equipped with our technique, (ii) with powering off capability/early termination (ET) technique, e.g., [9], operated at nominal supply voltage value, and (iii) with a hybrid scheme combining ET and the Dynamic Voltage Scaling (DVS) techniques in [8]. Our experiments indicate that the proposed technique outperforms the other schemes, resulting in 71 % to 76 % and 15 % to 28 % energy reduction w.r.t. ET without and with DVS, respectively, while maintaining the required decoding performance. Moreover, we observe that in certain condition Degradation Stochastic Resonance (DSR) [10,11] occurs, i.e., timing errors caused by voltage scaling improve the decoding performance, and by implication diminish the energy consumption, due to the fact that unpredictable underpowered components facilitate rather than impede the decoding process.

Many approaches have been proposed to reduce energy consumptions of LDPC decoders. Generally speaking voltage scaling has been frequently applied in Complementary Metal-Oxide-Semiconductor (CMOS) integrated circuits as by reducing the supply voltage we can gain energy efficiency at the expense of a longer circuit delay. However, as timing violation may occur if the circuit delay gets longer than the clock period, existing approaches either avoid this situation by tuning the operating frequency accordingly or correct potential errors by means of additional hardware.

To reduce LDPC decoders energy consumption, Dynamic Voltage Frequency Scaling (DVFS) based on the estimation of the maximum number of iterations was proposed in [12,13]. In [14] a Signal to Noise Ratio (SNR) estimator is utilized to guide the operating frequency scaling based on the target throughput and channel conditions. Subsequently, assisted by an error detector and a critical path replica, the suitable voltage that ensures no timing violation is determined. In [15] Reduced-Precision Replicas (RPR) of the bit and check nodes are utilised to detect and correct voltage scaling induced errors while in [16], Voltage Over-Scaling (VOS) and RPR are combined.

In our proposal, the best operating voltage is chosen based on knowledge of the underpowered LDPC decoder behavior. The operation supply voltage is chosen such that the decoding performance of the decoder operated at the typical voltage, measured in terms of FER/BER, is maintained or a specific target decoding performance is achieved. Similar to [14], we utilize the SNR estimator of existing communication systems but we do not modify the frequency in order to maintain the throughput and we allow for timing violation as long as the target performance is still achievable. We do not make use of additional hardware for error detection/correction or reduced precision replicas thus our approach results in smaller hardware overhead. In [15,16], the supply voltage is fixed at runtime while our method adjusts the supply voltage according to the channel conditions at runtime. Last but not least our technique does not require any decoder modifications hence it can be easily combined with other techniques.

In summary, the main contributions of this work are: (i) A technique for exploiting channel noise variability, (ii) Measured results from FPGA based experiments demonstrating the energy savings capabilities of the proposed method, (iii) A new way to perform voltage scaling on commercial FPGAs without relying on an external power supply, and (iv) Evidence of DSR occurrence in LDPC decoder implementations. This chapter is an extended version of our previous conference paper in [17].

The rest of the chapter is organized as follows. It starts with a short introduction of Sum-Product LDPC Decoding in Sect. 2. In Sect. 3, we present the proposed technique in the context of an LDPC decoder and evaluate it in Sect. 4. In Sect. 5, we close the discussion with some conclusions.

2   Sum-Product LDPC Decoding

Before we introduce Sum-Product (SP) LDPC decoding, we start with a brief introduction within the LDPC concept and decoding methodology. Generally speaking, adding parity bits to source information bits, i.e., creating a codeword, is a way to achieve reliable communication through unreliable channels between two parties located at the two channel ends. Each codeword should satisfy a set of pre-determined parity check equations and parties need to send only codewords on the channel. By doing so, the receiving party gets the means to check if the received message is right and if this is not the case to apply error corrective changes. For example, $[BN_1 BN_2 BN_3 BN_4 BN_5 BN6] = [101110]$ is a codeword that satisfies the following set of pre-determined parity check equations:

$$BN_1 \oplus BN_2 \oplus BN_4 = 0 \tag{1}$$

$$BN_2 \oplus BN_3 \oplus BN_5 = 0 \tag{2}$$

$$BN_1 \oplus BN_5 \oplus BN_6 = 0 \tag{3}$$

$$BN_3 \oplus BN_4 \oplus BN_6 = 0 \tag{4}$$

These parity check equations, taken from [18], can be written as a parity check matrix H presented in Fig. 2(a). Each row and each column of the H matrix represent a parity check equation and a codeword bit, respectively. This H matrix corresponds to a Tanner graph [19] visualized in Fig. 2(b), which describes an iterative decoding process. The Tanner graph in Fig. 2(b) consists of two sets of vertices: 6 bottom vertices for visualizing 6 Bit Nodes (BNs) and 4 top vertices for visualizing 4 Check Nodes (CNs). Bit node n is connected to check node m if the element of column n row m of the parity-check matrix H is '1'. We use this figure to introduce general idea of decoding and SP LDPC decoding as a particular example.

Now, we start with general idea of decoding. Let say we sent a message $[BN_1 BN_2 BN_3 BN_4 BN_5 BN6] = [101110]$ from the Moon to the Earth using the code in Fig. 2. When it reaches the Earth, due to the noisy channel BN_4 flips from '1' to '0', the received message becomes $[BN_1 BN_2 BN_3 BN_4 BN_5 BN6] = [101010]$. Since the incoming message is not a codeword, the receiving decoder knows that this message is not the message transmitted by the sender. Subsequently the decoder tries to correct the error, e.g., comparing the received message with the closest valid codeword. In this case, the closest codeword is [101110] at a Hamming distance 1 away from the received message [101010]. The identification of the closest codeword is guided by the parity check equations which we can perceive as an agreement between two parties to conduct reliable communications. If the agreement is violated, it means that something went wrong during the transmission on the unreliable noisy channel and corrective actions are required.

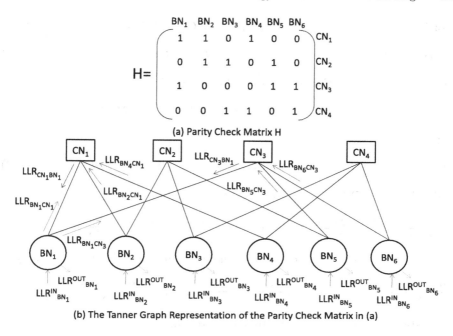

(a) Parity Check Matrix H

(b) The Tanner Graph Representation of the Parity Check Matrix in (a)

Fig. 2. An example of parity check matrix (a) and its Tanner graph representation (b)

To get more insight into the decoding process we assume as a discussion vehicle the Sum-Product (SP) LDPC decoder which is a soft decision decoder based on the message-passing algorithm, as visualized in Fig. 2(b). In soft decision decoding, each received bit x is represented as $P(x = 1)$, i.e., the probability that x is logic '1'. The probability is expressed as a Log-Likelihood Ratio (LLR) in SP decoding to reduce the implementation complexity by turning multiplications into additions. LLR of x is defined as:

$$LLR_x = log_e \left[\frac{P(x = 0)}{P(x = 1)} \right] \tag{5}$$

$LLR_{BN_n}^{IN}$ stands for a message received from channel in form of the LLR of the bit node n. Messages are iteratively passing by between Bit Nodes (BNs) and Check Nodes (CNs) along the edges of the Tanner graph as illustrated in Fig. 2(b). A message from a bit node n to a check node m in LLR form is written as $LLR_{BN_n CN_m}$. In the opposite direction, a message from a check node m to a bit node n in LLR form is denoted as $LLR_{CN_m BN_n}$. Each output decoding in LLR form for a bit node n, expressed as $LLR_{BN_n}^{OUT}$, is utilized for (i) making hard decision at the end of each iteration for decoders with early termination and (ii) the determination of the final output at the end of the decoding process.

Let us focus our attention to CN_1 in Fig. 2(b). Given that $BN_2 CN_1 \oplus BN_4 CN_1 = 0$ is true if both $BN_2 CN_1$ and $BN_4 CN_1$ have the same value either

'0' or '1', the probability of $(BN_2CN_1 \oplus BN_4CN_1 = 0)$ can be computed as:

$$P(BN_2CN_1 \oplus BN_4CN_1 = 0) = P(BN_2CN_1 = 0)P(BN_4CN_1 = 0) + P(BN_2CN_1 = 1)P(BN_4CN_1 = 1) \quad (6)$$

Since $P(x = 0) = 1 - P(x = 1)$, Eq. (6) becomes:

$$P(BN_2CN_1 \oplus BN_4CN_1 = 0) = \tfrac{1}{2} + \tfrac{1}{2}\{[1 - 2P(BN_2CN_1 = 1)][1 - 2P(BN_4CN_1 = 1)]\} \quad (7)$$

and:

$$P(BN_2CN_1 \oplus BN_4CN_1 = 1) = \tfrac{1}{2} - \tfrac{1}{2}\{[1 - 2P(BN_2CN_1 = 1)][1 - 2P(BN_4CN_1 = 1)]\} \quad (8)$$

By dividing Eq. (7) by Eq. (8), we obtain:

$$\frac{P(BN_2CN_1 \oplus BN_4CN_1=0)}{P(BN_2CN_1 \oplus BN_4CN_1=1)} = \left(\frac{\tfrac{1}{2}+\tfrac{1}{2}\{[1-2P(BN_2CN_1=1)][1-2P(BN_4CN_1=1)]\}}{\tfrac{1}{2}-\tfrac{1}{2}\{[1-2P(BN_2CN_1=1)][1-2P(BN_4CN_1=1)]\}} \right) \quad (9)$$

and by multiplying the numerator and the denominator of Eq. (9) by 2, we get:

$$\frac{P(BN_2CN_1 \oplus BN_4CN_1=0)}{P(BN_2CN_1 \oplus BN_4CN_1=1)} = \left(\frac{1+\{[1-2P(BN_2CN_1=1)][1-2P(BN_4CN_1=1)]\}}{1-\{[1-2P(BN_2CN_1=1)][1-2P(BN_4CN_1=1)]\}} \right) \quad (10)$$

To satisfy check node 1, we need to submit to Eq. (1):

$$LLR_{CN_1BN_1} = log_e \left[\frac{P(BN_2CN_1 \oplus BN_4CN_1=0)}{P(BN_2CN_1 \oplus BN_4CN_1=1)} \right] \quad (11)$$

By substituting Eq. (10) to Eq. (11) we obtain:

$$LLR_{CN_1BN_1} = log_e \left(\frac{1+\{[1-2P(BN_2CN_1=1)][1-2P(BN_4CN_1=1)]\}}{1-\{[1-2P(BN_2CN_1=1)][1-2P(BN_4CN_1=1)]\}} \right) \quad (12)$$

and since $log_e \left(\frac{1+x}{1-x} \right) = 2tanh^{-1}(x)$, Eq. (12) becomes:

$$LLR_{CN_1BN_1} = 2tanh^{-1}\{[1 - 2P(BN_2CN_1 = 1)][1 - 2P(BN_4CN_1 = 1)]\} \quad (13)$$

Since $tanh \left[\tfrac{1}{2}log_e \left(\frac{1-x}{x} \right) \right] = 1 - 2x$, thus Eq. (13) is transformed into:

$$LLR_{CN_1BN_1} = 2tanh^{-1} \left\{ tanh \left[\tfrac{1}{2}log_e \left(\frac{1-P(BN_2CN_1=1)}{P(BN_2CN_1=1)} \right) \right] tanh \left[\tfrac{1}{2}log_e \left(\frac{1-P(BN_4CN_1=1)}{P(BN_4CN_1=1)} \right) \right] \right\}$$
$$(14)$$

Given the LLR definition in Eq. (5), Eq. (14) becomes:

$$LLR_{CN_1BN_1} = 2tanh^{-1} \left[tanh \left(\frac{LLR_{BN_2CN_1}}{2} \right) tanh \left(\frac{LLR_{BN_4CN_1}}{2} \right) \right] \quad (15)$$

By separating signs and magnitudes of $LLR_{BN_2CN_1}$ and $LLR_{BN_4CN_1}$, Eq. (15) can be written as:

$$LLR_{CN_1BN_1} = 2tanh^{-1} \left[tanh \left(\frac{sign(LLR_{BN_2CN_1})|LLR_{BN_2CN_1}|}{2} \right) tanh \left(\frac{sign(LLR_{BN_4CN_1})|LLR_{BN_4CN_1}|}{2} \right) \right]$$
$$(16)$$

Separating sign and magnitude of $LLR_{CN_1BN_1}$ in Eq. (16) results:

$$sign(LLR_{CN_1BN_1}) = sign(LLR_{BN_2CN_1})sign(LLR_{BN_4CN_1}) \qquad (17)$$

and:

$$|LLR_{CN_1BN_1}| = 2tanh^{-1}\left[tanh\left(\frac{|(LLR_{BN_2CN_1})|}{2}\right)tanh\left(\frac{|(LLR_{BN_4CN_1})|}{2}\right)\right] \qquad (18)$$

Since $log_e(xy) = log_e(x) + log_e(y)$, therefore Eq. (18) also can be restructured into:

$$|LLR_{CN_1BN_1}| = 2tanh^{-1}log^{-1}\left(\left\{log\left[tanh\left(\frac{|(LLR_{BN_2CN_1})|}{2}\right)\right] + log\left[tanh\left(\frac{|(LLR_{BN_4CN_1})|}{2}\right)\right]\right\}\right) \qquad (19)$$

Let us define $\phi(x)$ as:

$$\phi(x) = -log[\tanh(x/2)] = log\left(\frac{e^x + 1}{e^x - 1}\right) \qquad (20)$$

If we find the inverse of $\phi(x)$ through very simple mathematics, we get:

$$\phi^{-1}(x) = log\left(\frac{e^x + 1}{e^x - 1}\right) = \phi(x) \qquad (21)$$

Using the definition of $\phi(x)$, Eq. (19) becomes:

$$|LLR_{CN_1BN_1}| = 2\tanh^{-1}\log^{-1}\{-[\phi(|LLR_{BN_2CN_1}|) + \phi(|LLR_{BN_4CN_1}|)]\} \qquad (22)$$

If we find the inverse of Eq. (20) through very simple mathematics, we obtain:

$$\phi^{-1}(x) = 2\tan^{-1}\log^{-1}(-x) \qquad (23)$$

Substitute Eq. (23) to Eq. (22):

$$|LLR_{CN_1BN_1}| = \phi^{-1}[\phi(|LLR_{BN_2CN_1}|) + \phi(|LLR_{BN_4CN_1}|)] \qquad (24)$$

Using $\phi^{-1}(x) = \phi(x)$ in Eq. (21), Eq. (24) is transformed into:

$$|LLR_{CN_1BN_1}| = \phi[\phi(|LLR_{BN_2CN_1}|) + \phi(|LLR_{BN_4CN_1}|)] \qquad (25)$$

By doing the same computation for CN_3, we get:

$$|LLR_{CN_3BN_1}| = \phi[\phi(|LLR_{BN_5CN_3}|) + \phi(|LLR_{BN_6CN_3}|)] \qquad (26)$$

and:

$$sign(LLR_{CN_3BN_1}) = sign(LLR_{BN_5CN_3})sign(LLR_{BN_6CN_3}) \qquad (27)$$

Using $LLR_{CN_1BN_1}$ and $LLR_{CN_3BN_1}$, we can compute $LLR_{BN_1CN_1}$, $LLR_{BN_1CN_3}$, and $LLR_{BN_1}^{OUT}$ as:

$$LLR_{BN_1CN_1} = LLR_{BN_1}^{IN} + LLR_{CN_3BN_1}, \qquad (28)$$

$$LLR_{BN_1CN_3} = LLR_{BN_1}^{IN} + LLR_{CN_1BN_1}, \tag{29}$$

and:

$$LLR_{BN_1}^{OUT} = LLR_{BN_1}^{IN} + LLR_{CN_1BN_1} + LLR_{CN_3BN_1} \tag{30}$$

This $LLR_{BN_1}^{OUT}$ is used for making a hard decision for bit 1 using this equation:

$$BN_1^{OUT} = \begin{cases} 0, & \text{if } LLR_{BN_1}^{OUT} \text{ is positive} \\ 1, & \text{if } LLR_{BN_1}^{OUT} \text{ is negative} \end{cases} \tag{31}$$

This hard value BN_1^{OUT} is used with other bits for parity check to determine whether the vector $[BN_1^{OUT} BN_2^{OUT} BN_3^{OUT} BN_4^{OUT} BN_5^{OUT} BN_6^{OUT}]$ is a codeword or not using Eqs. (1) to (4). If the vector is a valid codeword, the decoder with early termination stops decoding and then sends this vector as the final output of decoding. $LLR_{BN_1CN_1}$ and $LLR_{BN_1CN_3}$ are used for next iteration using the same computation of bit 1. In the previous derivations we concentrated on the calculation of bit 1, computation of all the other bits can be done in the same way. The computation is stopped either when the decoder finds a codeword (for decoder with early termination) or the decoder gives up, i.e., the decoder could not find the codeword after a pre-defined maximum number of iterations.

3 Proposed Technique

The main concept behind the proposed technique is presented in Fig. 3. Maintaining the decoding performance (in terms of FER/BER) to its required value by actively monitoring the channel noise is the key idea to prevent energy over-consumption. More precisely, we turn the supply voltage up when the channel is getting worse for meeting the target error rate and vice versa we turn it down when the channel is in a good condition to save energy. The question is "How far can we turn the supply voltage down in good channel conditions or up in bad channel conditions?" If we increase the voltage too much when the channel is getting worse, we may spill energy, while if the voltage is not big enough, the target error rate cannot be satisfied. Similar situations may also occur when turning down the voltage in good channel conditions. To determine the appropriate decoder operating voltage at a specific channel condition, we need to know the decoder behavior by means of a *pre-characterization* process as detailed in Subsect. 3.1. The pre-characterization results are then used to compute the decoding operating voltage for any specific channel condition. These values are stored in an LUT and utilized in guiding the decoder to meet the required target error rate while consuming as low energy as possible in the *adaptation* process detailed in Subsect. 3.2.

3.1 Pre-characterization

It is clear that the decoder has to be aware of the channel condition for taking the best runtime decisions. Another important information the decoder needs to

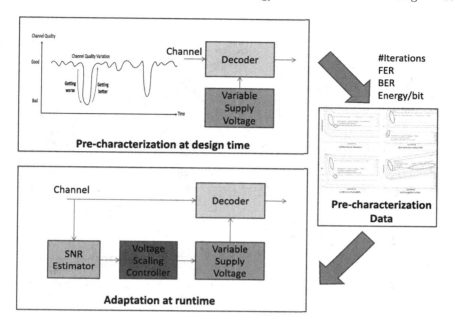

Fig. 3. Transmission channel noise aware energy effective decoding

have is its own behavior when operating at different supply voltages and for various channel conditions in terms of performance/correction capability and energy efficiency. For this reason, in order to equip the decoder with the required knowledge, we need to make real measured data known to the decoder. Thus, during *pre-characterization*, we need to measure decoder FER, BER, and energy/bit on a variety of noisy channels and voltage conditions. There are 3 steps to do *pre-characterization*: (1) *generation*, (2) *setup*, and (3) *run* as depicted in Figs. 4, 5, and 6, respectively.

Generation (see Fig. 4) is the process of creating the decoder for *pre-characterization*. The decoder VHDL code is produced by a tool designed for the automatic generation of LDPC decoder fully parallel IP cores starting from an H matrix, regular or irregular, and the number of bits to represent the channel message. The presented results are obtained using a MacKay A matrix [3] with dimensions n = 1000, k = 500, and 4-bit 2's complement fixed point number representation of the message. Each fixed point number consists of 1 sign bit, 2 integer bits, and 1 fractional bit. The implemented decoder is based on Log Likelihood Ratio (LLR) Belief Propagation (BP) or the sum-product algorithm [2]. The parallel implementation consists in a one to one mapping of the bit and check nodes in the Tanner graph to the respective bit and check modules. The edges in the graph become physical buses of width equal to the chosen precision. In a fully parallel implementation the number and complexity of the interconnections may result in implementations where the area is dominated

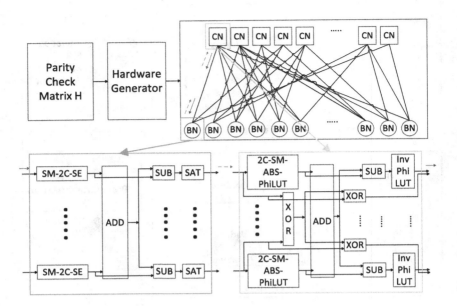

Fig. 4. Step 1 of Pre-characterization: Generation

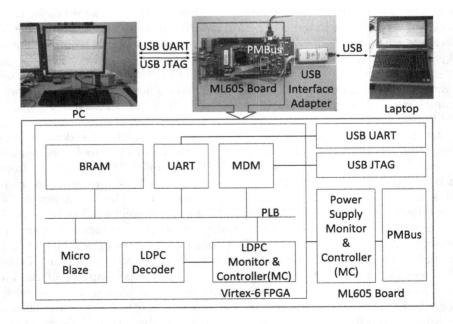

Fig. 5. Step 2 of Pre-characterization: Setup

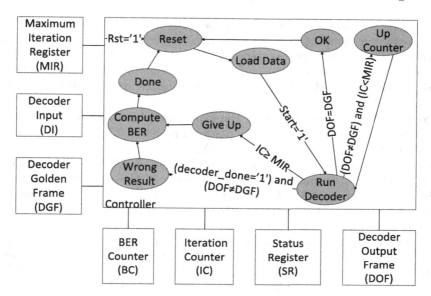

Fig. 6. Step 3 of Pre-characterization: Run

by the routing. However it is highly efficient from a power and speed point of view. For these reasons and given the high density and connection capability of modern FPGA chip, a fully parallel architecture has been chosen as the testcase for the research presented here. The maximum number of iterations is set at 100. Two clock cycles are needed for each iteration. LLRs represented by two's complement fixed point numbers are the inputs to the CN while its outputs are represented as Sign Magnitude (SM) numbers. The Check Node (CN) converts each 2's Complement (2C) number to a Sign Magnitude (SM) number using its 2C-SM converter. The absolute value of this SM number is then computed by ABS. This absolute value is further processed to obtain its $\phi(x) = -log(\tanh(x/2)) = log(\frac{e^x+1}{e^x-1})$ function. The function ϕ is even and has the property that $\phi^{-1}(x) = \phi(x)$ for $x > 0$. In this work, each ϕ or ϕ^{-1} function is approximated by a 4-bit Look-Up Table (LUT) denoted as phiLUT or invphiLUT in the figure. This choice allows to take advantage of the structure of FPGA slices and the free availability of LUTs. To ease automatic hardware generation in a parametric way, all related $\phi(x)$ values are added (using ADD). The output of ADD is then subtracted (using SUB) by each specific $\phi(x)$ value. The subtraction result is then fed to $\phi^{-1}(x)$ function to obtain the magnitude bits as part of sign magnitude representation at the output of CN. In similar way like processing absolute value, each sign bit is processed separately using XOR. The input(output) of BN is represented as sign magnitude number(2's complement number). Each SM number at the input is converted to 2's complement number (denoted as SM-2C) and then sign extended (presented as SE) by $\frac{N+2}{2}$ before being processed further, where N is the number of connected CNs.

The same reason like CN for making an easy automation of hardware generation, all related input values of each Bit Node (BN) are added (using ADD) and then subtracted (using SUB) by each specific output value of the SM-2C-SE. Since the result can be a number that cannot be represented by the number of bits of representation, we need to process it further by taking its saturated value using SAT operation.

Setup is the process of building the experimental platform in Fig. 5. A PC is used for synthesizing the hardware platform targeting Xilinx Virtex-6 FPGA: XC6VLX240T-1FFG1156 using Xilinx CAD tools version 13.4. The PC is also used for downloading the bitstream file to the Xilinx ML605 board through the USB JTAG interface and for monitoring/capturing the number of iterations, FER, and BER through the USB UART. The energy/bit is obtained using the Fusion Digital Power Designer from Texas Instrument running on the Laptop through Texas Instrument USB Interface adapter by reading PMBus, accessing Power Supply Monitor and Controller inside the board. This technique allows for separately controlling and monitoring each on-board specific internal power supply. The measurements are done only for the internal circuits of the FPGA. The supply voltage is adjusted by directly controlling the internal power supply of the FPGA of the targeted board, keeping other supply voltages unchanged. In contrast to [8], no additional external power supply is needed. To simulate realistic scenarios we use an AWGN channel with BPSK modulation (with mapping $0 \rightarrow 1$ and $1 \rightarrow -1$) for our experiments. The generated input vectors are fed to the decoder by the MicroBlaze processor resident on the FPGA. BRAM is used to store software and data for Microblaze execution.

Run is the process of running the decoder on the experimental platform for *pre-characterization* purpose as depicted in Fig. 6. This functionality is mainly operated by LDPC Monitoring and Controller (MC). The MC monitors the condition of decoding, feeds LLRs to the decoder, and computes BER. The Maximum Iteration Register (MIR) stores the maximum number of iterations allowed for decoding. This register is initialized by the MicroBlaze. If the decoder reaches the maximum number of iterations without reaching a valid code word, i.e., correcting the errors, MC goes to "Give Up" state. Soft messages in form LLRs are fed by MC to the LDPC decoder through the register Decoder Input (DI). This register can be accessed by the MicroBlaze through the PLB bus. The Decoder Golden Frame (DGF) is the original frame sent by the transmitter and conveyed by the MicroBlaze to the MC for evaluating purposes. By comparing this frame with the Decoder Output Frame (DOF), the controller determines the decoding success rate for computing FER and BER. The computed BER is stored in the BER Counter (BC) and can be accessed by the MicroBlaze. The Status Register (SR) indicates the decoder status and it is accessible by the MicroBlaze. The possible states are: (1) successful decoding denoted as "OK" state, (2) giving up decoding stored as "Give Up" state, or (3) wrong result decoding written as "Wrong Result" state means that the decoder can satisfy all check nodes but it is not the right frame as it was sent by the LDPC encoder. This can happen if the severity of noisy channel alters the frame to another valid codeword, which is considered as an error. The MC enters "Compute BER" state and starts to compute BER when errors occur.

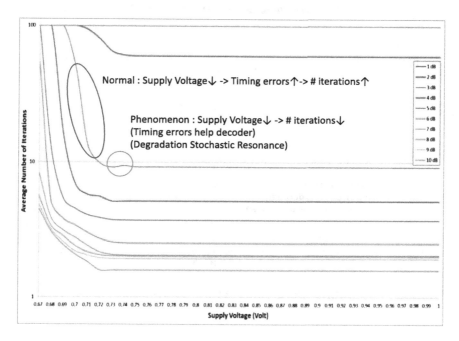

Fig. 7. Pre-characterization Results: Number of Iterations

Based on Post-PAR Static Timing Report of Xilinx tools, the minimum clock period is 19.992 ns (i.e., the maximum frequency is 50.020 MHz). The actual implementation is clocked at 50 MHz. Therefore, the throughput at its maximum iterations is 250 Mbps for all experiments. The complete experimental platform including the decoder requires 31433 FFs, 117231 LUTs, and 16 BRAMs whereas the decoder itself needs 29281 FFs and 114968 LUTs. The *pre-characterization* results of average number of iterations, FER, BER, and Energy/bit (nJ/bit) when varying the power supply value from 1 V to 0.67 V and the channel SNR from 10 dB to 1 dB are presented in Figs. 7, 8, 9, and 10, respectively. Each SNR has its own minimum supply voltage after which the number of iterations starts to increase sharply as one can observe in Fig. 7. In general, the increase starts earlier for lower SNR channels and this behavior can be related to the fact that the decoder can do self-correction easier for higher SNR channels where there is not much noise involved. Each SNR has its own specific minimum supply voltage after which its number of iterations goes to the maximum number of iterations which is 100. For the majority of the results it can be seen that when the supply voltage is lowered, the number of iterations stays constant for a while and then increases for the decoder to tackle timing errors. It is unexpected but interesting

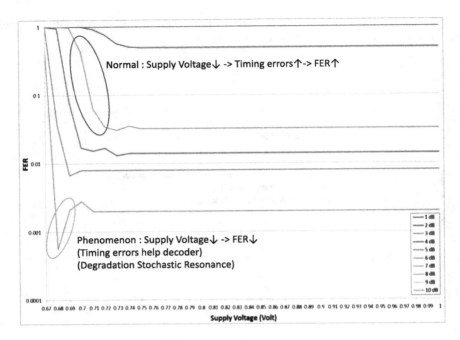

Fig. 8. Pre-characterization Results: FER

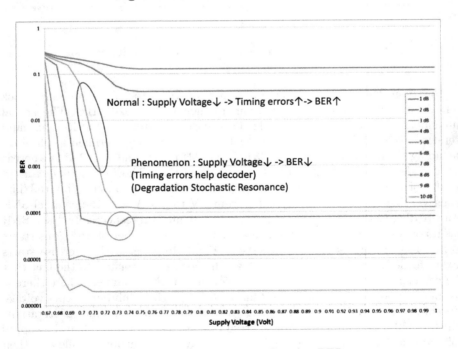

Fig. 9. Pre-characterization Results: BER

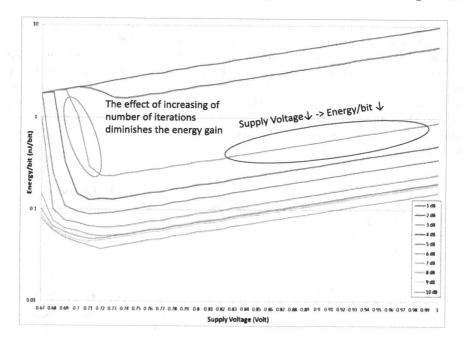

Fig. 10. Pre-characterization Results: Energy/bit (nJ/bit)

to note that sometimes, the average number of iterations decreases even if the supply voltage is reduced, which suggests that sometimes the timing errors can help the decoder converging to the correct codeword. This phenomenon is called Degradation Stochastic Resonance (DSR) [11] or Stochastic Resonance (SR) [10] and it can be also observed in Figs. 8 and 9 where we present the measured results for FER and BER, respectively. This suggests that voltage reduction can sometimes help improving the decoder performance. Finally, in Fig. 10, the measured energy/bit for various SNRs is presented. This figure shows the effect of the law of diminishing returns. The energy/bit decreases by scaling the voltage, however, after a certain point, an increase in energy/bit is visible. This is due to the effect of increasing of number of iterations that diminishes the energy gain we get from reducing the voltage.

3.2   Adaptation

The voltage scaling controller for the targeted LDPC decoder depicted in Fig. 11 operates as follows. It gets SNR information from the SNR estimator and changes the operating supply voltage at runtime based on the knowledge it has from the measured information gathered during the *pre-characterization* stage. We note that given that in communication systems with adaptive coding and modulation, the SNR estimator is a standard system component. The basic principle of the adaptation is to trade off over-needed performance for energy saving through active channel quality monitoring. More precisely, we turn down the supply voltage when the channel is in good condition, hence allowing energy saving. However, for preserving target performance, it is required to turn the voltage up when the channel SNR is getting worse. The objective is to minimize the energy not the voltage while ensuring the decoder achieves its needed performance. Note that minimizing the voltage may not always improve the energy efficiency, because the number of iterations of the decoder may increase due to induced timing errors. Thus, this diminishing returns effect needs to be considered when choosing the operating voltage.

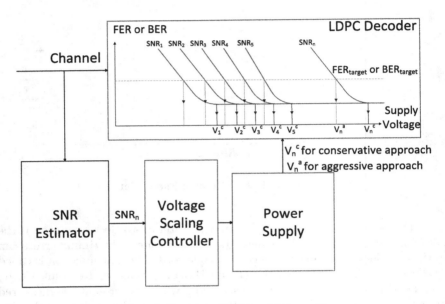

Fig. 11. Hardware Design of Adaptation

We developed two different adaptation strategies as follows: (i) the conservative approach which guaranties that the original decoder performance is always preserved and (ii) the aggressive approach which only concentrates on achieving the required target performance. To maintain identical performance while ensuring higher energy efficiency for the channel condition characterized by SNR_n, the operating voltage V_n is moved towards the point where the energy/bit is minimized and at the same time the FER and BER remain identical to those of the decoder operated at the typical voltage $V_{Typical}$. By its conservative nature this approach may still sometimes result in energy waste as it tries to mimic the worse case designed decoder and not to just fulfill the target performance requirements. In view of this the aggressive strategy is designed to enable the decoder to adapt itself such that it delivers the required correction capability while minimizing the energy consumption.

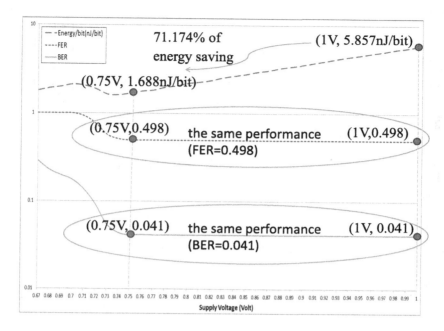

Fig. 12. An Example Result of Conservative Approach

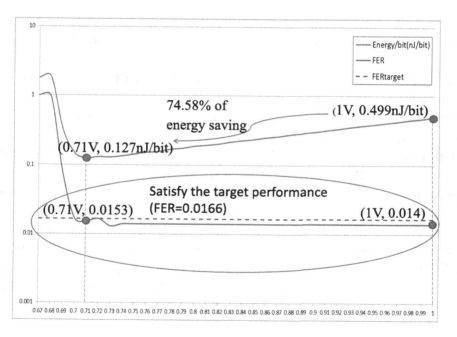

Fig. 13. An Example Result of Aggressive Approach

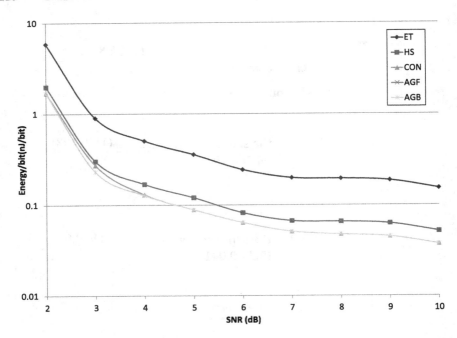

Fig. 14. Experimental Results

To discuss how the Voltage Scaling Controller (VSC) determines the operating voltage of the decoder formally, some definitions are introduced as follows.

Definition 1: $FER_{Typical}$ ($BER_{Typical}$) is the FER (BER) corresponding to the supply voltage $V_{Typical}$.

Definition 2: $V_{min}^{FER_{Typical}}$ $\left(V_{min}^{BER_{Typical}}\right)$ is the minimum supply voltage for which FER $\leq FER_{Typical}$ (BER $\leq BER_{Typical}$) is satisfied.

Definition 3: $V_{min}^{FER_{Target}}$ $\left(V_{min}^{BER_{Target}}\right)$ is the minimum supply voltage for which FER $\leq FER_{Target}$ (BER $\leq BER_{Target}$) holds true.

Definition 4: $V_{best}^{(Energy/bit(x,y))}$ is the voltage corresponding to the minimum energy/bit value within the voltage range $[x,y]$, $x < y$.

Based on these definitions, the conservative approach required operating voltage at signal-to-noise ratio SNR_n denoted as $V_n^c(SNR_n)$ can be computed as $V_{best}^{Energy/bit\left(max\left(V_{min}^{FER_{Typical}},V_{min}^{BER_{Typical}}\right),V_{Typical}\right)}$. Similarly the aggressive approach operating voltage targeting FER_{Target} or BER_{Target} at signal-to-noise ratio SNR_n denoted as $V_n^{a_{FER}}(SNR_n)$ and $V_n^{a_{BER}}(SNR_n)$ can be calculated as $V_{best}^{Energy/bit\left(V_{min}^{FER_{Target}},V_{Typical}\right)}$ and $V_{best}^{Energy/bit\left(V_{min}^{BER_{Target}},V_{Typical}\right)}$, respectively.

For example, using the above equations, the conservative approach can operate the decoder at $V_n^c = 0.75V$ preserving the performance (i.e., FER = 0.498 and BER = 0.041) of the original LDPC decoder operated at $V_{Typical} = 1$ V. In this situation much less energy is consumed (i.e., 71 % of energy saving) as illustrated in Fig. 12. According to the aggressive scaling we adjust the power supply value to $V_n^a = 0.71$ V while maintaining FER $\leq FER_{Target}$ (i.e., FER = 0.0166), reducing the energy by 74 % as illustrated in Fig. 13. Note that to minimize the adaptation process energy overhead all of these computations are performed at design time and their results are placed in an LUT mapping SNR_n to V_n.

To sum up, although our conservative approach runs at lower supply voltage for saving energy, it insures of having an identical decoding quality like the one operated at standard voltage thanks to its endowed knowledge during design time and its smart adaptation at runtime. Awareness of its target performance is the added value of our aggressive approach to surpass the conservative one in terms of energy efficiency at the cost of performance degradation while still satisfying the required error rate.

4   Evaluation

To evaluate our technique, we utilize the platform and LDPC decoder as in the pre-characterization stage augmented with the following energy reduction schemes: (i) powering off capability using Early Termination (**ET**) technique operated at the original supply voltage as presented in [9], (ii) a Hybrid Early Termination Scheme (**HS**) which includes the DVS technique in [8], (iii) our Conservative Approach (**CON**), (iv) our Aggressive Approach targeting FER (**AGF**), and (v) our Aggressive Approach targeting BER (**AGB**).

We evaluated the energy consumption of all the approaches when changing the channel SNR from 2 dB to 10 dB and the results are plotted in Fig. 14. The energy/bit is obtained by accessing Power Supply Monitor and Controller inside the ML605 board through PMBus. Because AGF and AGB result in identical energy consumptions their plots are overlapped in the figure.

One can observe in Fig. 14 that: (i) Regardless of SNR value ET always consumes more energy than the other approaches and this can be explained by the fact that it has no capability to adapt to channel conditions. Energy consumed by ET decreases when the channel quality is getting better due to its early termination capability. At good channel quality, number of flipped bits decreases. Fewer flipped bits make decoding faster to converge and as a result, ET turns it power off earlier, reducing the consumed energy. (ii) Our technique always outperforms both ET and HS. However at low SNRs (2 to 3 dB) the energy reduction is limited (only 10–15 % and 15–23 % reductions over HS, for CON and AGF/AGB, respectively) by the fact that there is not that much excess performance to exploit. However, for less noisier channels, i.e., SNRs from 3 to 10 dB, more excess performance is available and CON achieves a 22–28 % energy reduction over HS thanks to its adaptability to exploit channel noise variability; (iii) Because of its additional DVS technique, HS consumes 66 % less energy than ET. CON (AGF/AGB) consumes around 71 % (73 %) and 76 % (76 %) less energy than ET, for bad and good channel quality, respectively; and (iv) At high SNR values CON, AGF, and AGB consume almost the same energy due to diminishing returns effect, while at low SNR values both AGF and AGB provide 15 % energy reduction over CON.

We note that given that our technique does not alter the operating frequency it results in a better performance in terms of decoding throughput when compared to other decoders utilizing dynamic frequency scaling technique.

5   Conclusions

In this chapter, a technique towards energy effective LDPC decoding by exploiting channel noise variability to transform excess performance for energy saving was proposed. The proposed technique adaptively tunes the operating voltage on-the-fly based on the knowledge of the instantaneous channel noise level at run-time by utilizing its pre-characterization results, aiming to achieve the optimal tradeoff between decoder performance and power consumption, while fulfilling the QoS requirements. To demonstrate the capabilities of our proposal we implemented it and other state of the art energy reduction methods in the framework of a fully parallel LDPC decoder on a Virtex-6 FPGA. Based on the experimental results, when applied to a Sum-Product LDPC decoder our conservative approach improves energy efficiency by 71 % to 76 % and 15 % to 28 % compared to early termination without and with DVS, respectively, while preserving the decoder performance in terms of bit/frame error rate. With respect to the conservative version, our aggressive approach meets a given target error rate with up to 15 % additional energy reduction thanks to its robustness-on-demand capability. In addition, since our technique maintains the operating frequency regardless of the utilized power supply voltage value, the frame throughput is preserved. Moreover, the FPGA-based experiments suggest that in certain conditions Degradation Stochastic Resonance occurs, i.e., the energy consumption is unexpectedly diminished due to the fact that unpredictable underpowered components facilitate rather than impede the decoding process.

Acknowledgments. This work was supported by the Seventh Framework Programme of the European Union, under the Grant Agreement number 309129 (i-RISC project).

References

1. Tse, D.: Fundamentals of Wireless Communication. Cambridge University Press, Cambridge (2005)
2. Gallager, R.: Low-density parity-check codes. IRE Trans. Inf. Theory **8**(1), 21–28 (1962)
3. MacKay, D.J., Neal, R.M.: Near shannon limit performance of low density parity check codes. Electron. lett. **32**(18), 1645–1646 (1996)
4. IEEE: The IEEE 802.11n working group std. http://www.ieee802.org/11/

5. IEEE: The IEEE 802.16 working group std. http://www.ieee802.org/16/
6. ETSI: The digital video broadcasting standard. https://www.dvb.org/standards/dvb-s2
7. IEEE: IEEE p802.3an (10gbase-t) task force. http://www.ieee802.org/3/an/
8. Chow, C., Tsui, L.S.M., Leong, P.W., Luk, W., Wilton, S.J.E.: Dynamic Voltage Scaling for commercial FPGAs. In: 2005 Proceedings of the 2005 IEEE International Conference on Field-Programmable Technology, pp. 173–180, December 2005
9. Darabiha, A., Carusone, A., Kschischang, F.: Power reduction techniques for LDPC decoders. IEEE J. Solid-State Circuits **43**(8), 1835–1845 (2008)
10. Gammaitoni, L., Hänggi, P., Jung, P., Marchesoni, F.: Stochastic resonance. Rev. Mod. Phys. **70**, 223–287 (1998)
11. Aymerich, N., Cotofana, S., Rubio, A.: Degradation stochastic resonance (DSR) in AD-AVG architectures. In: 2012 12th IEEE Conference on Nanotechnology (IEEE-NANO) pp. 1–4, August 2012
12. Wang, W., Choi, G., Gunnam, K.: Low-power VLSI design of LDPC decoder using DVFS for awgn channels. In: 2009 22nd International Conference on VLSI Design, pp. 51–56, January 2009
13. Zhang, X., Cai, F., Shi, C.J.: Low-power LDPC decoding based on iteration prediction. In: 2012 IEEE International Symposium on Circuits and Systems (ISCAS), pp. 3041–3044, May 2012
14. Ahn, Y., Park, J.Y., Chung, K.S.: Dynamic voltage and frequency scaling scheme for an adaptive LDPC decoder using SNR estimation. EURASIP J. Wireless Comm. Networking **2013**, 255 (2013)
15. Kim, E., Shanbhag, N.: Energy-efficient LDPC decoders based on error-resiliency. In: 2012 IEEE Workshop on Signal Processing Systems (SiPS), pp. 149–154, October 2012
16. Cho, J., Shanbhag, N., Sung, W.: Low-power implementation of a high-throughput LDPC decoder for IEEE 802.11n standard. In: 2009 IEEE Workshop on Signal Processing Systems, pp. 040–045, October 2009
17. Marconi, T., Spagnol, C., Popovici, E., Cotofana, S.: Towards energy effective LDPC decoding by exploiting channel noise variability. In: 2014 22nd International Conference on Very Large Scale Integration (VLSI-SoC), pp. 1–6, October 2014
18. Johnson, S.J.: Introducing low-density parity-check codes. Technical report, Department of Electrical and Computer Engineering, University of Newcastle, Australia (2006)
19. Tanner, R.: A recursive approach to low complexity codes. IEEE Trans. Inf. Theory **27**(5), 533–547 (1981)

Laser-Induced Fault Effects
in Security-Dedicated Circuits

Vincent Beroulle[4], Philippe Candelier[7], Stephan De Castro[3,6],
Giorgio Di Natale[3], Jean-Max Dutertre[6], Marie-Lise Flottes[3(✉)],
David Hély[4], Guillaume Hubert[5], Regis Leveugle[1], Feng Lu[3],
Paolo Maistri[2], Athanasios Papadimitriou[4], Bruno Rouzeyre[3],
Clement Tavernier[7], and Pierre Vanhauwaert[1,2]

[1] Univ. Grenoble Alpes, TIMA, 38000 Grenoble, France
[2] CNRS, TIMA, 38000 Grenoble, France
[3] LIRMM, Université Montpellier/CNRS UMR 5506, Montpellier, France
flottes@lirmm.fr
[4] LCIS, Université Grenoble Alpes, 26000 Valence, France
[5] ONERA, Toulouse, France
[6] CMP, LSAS, École nationale supérieure des mines de Saint-Étienne,
Gardanne, France
[7] STMicroelectronics, Grenoble, France

Abstract. Lasers have become one of the most efficient means to attack secure integrated systems. Actual faults or errors induced in the system depend on many parameters, including the circuit technology and the laser characteristics. Understanding the physical effects is mandatory to correctly evaluate during the design flow the potential consequences of a laser-based attack and implement efficient counter-measures. This paper presents results obtained within the LIESSE project, aiming at defining a comprehensive approach for designers. Outcomes include the definition of fault/error models at several levels of abstraction, specific CAD tools using these models and new counter-measures well-suited to thwart laser-based attacks. Actual measures on components manufactured in the new 28 nm FDSOI technology are also presented.

Keywords: Hardware security · Fault attacks · Lasers · Fault models · Security evaluation · Counter-measures

1 Introduction

Hardware attacks on secure integrated systems can be done by several means, including side-channel observation (measuring e.g., computation time, power consumption or electromagnetic emissions) and faulty behavior exploitation. We will focus here on fault-based attacks aiming at retrieving some confidential information such as a private cryptographic key stored in the circuit. One of the most efficient techniques to induce faults in a circuit is to use a laser [1].

Since the pioneer work by Skorobogatov and Anderson [2], many experimental works have been done on laser-based attacks on various types of circuits, including smartcards but also FPGAs. However, a clear view of laser effects is still lacking [1].

© IFIP International Federation for Information Processing 2015
L. Claesen et al. (Eds.): VLSI-SoC 2014, IFIP AICT 464, pp. 220–240, 2015.
DOI: 10.1007/978-3-319-25279-7_12

From a designer point-of-view, it is therefore difficult to understand the exact protections ("counter-measures") to implement in a circuit, and also to identify the most critical parts in a given design.

The work presented here aims at providing a more comprehensive framework to designers. One part of the proposal concerns the definition of models representing the effects of laser attacks with several levels of abstraction. The second part concerns specific counter-measures that can be selected to increase the robustness. The designer work is also supported by specific design tools.

In this chapter, Sect. 2 is dedicated to laser-silicon interaction. Section 3 gives an overview of the global modeling and design flow from a laser-based attack perspective. Section 4 summarizes results obtained by actual laser attacks, especially on components in the new 28 nm FDSOI technology. Section 5 discusses the fault and error models. Section 6 is dedicated to the CAD tools and Sect. 7 shows new counter-measures adapted to the effects of laser-based attacks.

2 Laser/Silicon Interaction

2.1 Photoelectric Effect

When light emitted by a laser hits a CMOS device, its energy is turned into electrical current thanks to the photoelectric effect. Provided that the energy of the photons emitted by the laser is sufficient, these photons create electron/hole pairs along their path through the silicon (the so-called photoelectric effect).

A current is the result of charges moving. As a consequence of the photoelectric effect, two mechanisms put the charges created by the laser in movement and therefore induce a transient current. A reverse biased PN junction (drain tied to Vdd, P-substrate tied to Gnd) is taken as example in Fig. 1 to present these mechanisms.

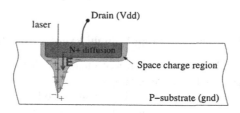

Fig. 1. The mechanism responsible for optical beam induced current [3]

The biasing enlarges the space charge region at the interface between P and N regions. As the laser beam goes through the PN junction and the silicon, it creates electron/hole pairs. Then the charges that are close enough to the junction are moved (attracted or repulsed depending on the charge) by the effect of both the electric field and the diffusion effect. The charges that are far from the junction recombine themselves without any effect on the induced current at the drain of the junction.

Figure 2 shows the typical shape of the induced transient current at the drain node created by the laser. The electric field and the diffusion effects can be differentiated on the shape. The prompt collection corresponding to the electric field effect induces a high current during a short time. The diffusion-induced current has low amplitude that lasts longer than the prompt collection. This is due to the speed of the diffusion phenomenon in silicon.

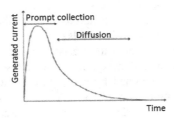

Fig. 2. Typical shape of nodal current at a p-n junction [4]

Equation (1) [5] represents the general equation of the current shape observed in Fig. 2.

$$I(t) = \frac{Q}{\tau a - \tau b}\left(e^{-\frac{t}{\tau a}} - e^{-\frac{t}{\tau b}}\right) \tag{1}$$

With Q the charge deposited by the laser strike, τa the collection time constant which is a process-dependent collection time constant of the junction and τb is the ion-track establishment time constant which is relatively independent of the technology. Typical value of τa and τb can be found in [6].

The induced current can be high enough to temporarily invert the output of a logic cell, thus possibly generating an error in the circuit. The following subsection details how faults can be generated within a digital circuit, by means of a laser injection.

2.2   Single Event Transient (SET) and Single Event Upset (SEU)

The mechanism by which the induced current changes a logic value is presented in Fig. 3. An inverter gate is taken as an example.

Let assume the input of the inverter being equal to the logic value '0', therefore its output being '1'. By assuming to be in stationary conditions, the equivalent output capacitance Cload (i.e., the sum of all gate capacitances of cells connected to this output) is fully charged.

If a laser beam reaches the drain of the NMOS transistor in OFF mode (i.e. a reverse biased PN junction as exemplified in Sect. 2.1), then a transient current is generated between the drain and the bulk node. This current makes electrons move from both Vdd and the equivalent output capacitance toward Gnd.

As a consequence, the output capacitance may be discharged provided that the photocurrent is higher than the current flowing through the PMOS transistor. The duration of this effect depends on the injection time. If the illumination duration is large

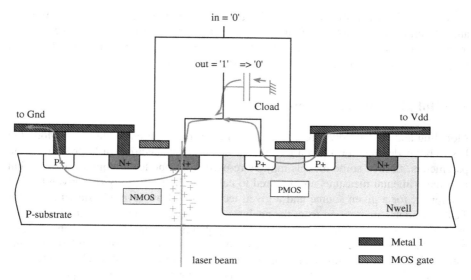

Fig. 3. Effect of the laser-induced photocurrent (red arrows) on an inverter gate (Color figure online)

enough, the output capacitance can be discharged at the point where its voltage falls under the threshold voltage of the next logic gates, thus causing a logic fault.

Logic faults can have different effects based on the target cell. If the laser illuminates a combinational gate (e.g. Fig. 4(a)), the erroneous transient value generated at the output of the gate must reach the downstream memory cell during the memorization time-window of that cell in order to affect the circuit behavior and propagate through the circuit at the next clock cycle. This kind of effect is called Single Event Transient (SET).

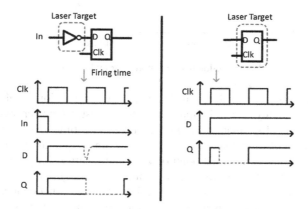

Fig. 4. (a) SET, and (b) SEU mechanisms

Conversely, when the laser bean directly affects the memory cell (Fig. 4(b)), there are no timing constraints to induce an error. Indeed, the logic value stored in the memory cell can be directly flipped (the so-called Single Event Upset: SEU) and propagates through the logic during the next clock cycle.

3 Global Flow: Overview

Modeling and design flows are illustrated in Fig. 5, resp. left and right sides. Modeling has to be made once for a given technology and a given spectrum of laser sources and parameters. In fact, some models may be re-used from one technology to another, but new experimental measures are required to calibrate the probability of a given type of fault/error, for a given source and a given technology. Low-level physical models (or TCAD models) are derived from the analysis of the interaction between the laser beam and the circuit material. Such models are very long to simulate, so more abstract models based on current curves must be derived in order to perform simulations at the electrical level. Abstraction can then be raised again at the logical level for gate-level netlist simulation. Finally, behavioral error models corresponding to data perturbations can be proposed for early design analysis. This bottom-up process, validated by the experiments performed on real circuits, lead to a set of models adapted to several design steps.

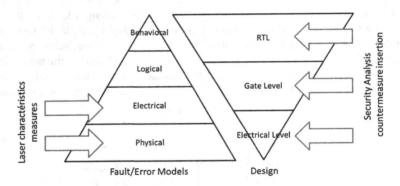

Fig. 5. Global flow: modeling and design

Once the models are available, a designer can perform various analyses at several design steps. Early analyses can be made after the Register-Transfer level description, using either behavioral simulation or emulation, and injecting errors corresponding to the behavioral models. This first analysis may allow him to quantify the probability of a successful attack from a functional point of view and identify some weak points in the design (including or not some functional counter-measures). On this basis, counter-measures may be added to the design at several levels, from functional checks down to e.g., placement and routing constraints or sensor insertions. Further analyses can then be performed once the gate-level netlist is available, and then when the placement and routing has been done, with potentially electrical-level simulations using the previously developed fault models. All these steps must maximize the probability that the final qualifications made on the first product prototypes confirm a satisfying level of resilience against attacks.

4 Measures on Bulk and FDSOI Components

Measures from actual experiments using a laser are mandatory to develop and assert the validity of physical and electrical models. Previous related work was done in order to derive models of laser shots on CMOS Bulk ICs, especially on SRAM cells [7]. The model validity was assessed by a very good correlation with an experimental laser sensitivity map.

Our current modeling work is focused on the emerging 28 nm Fully Depleted Silicon On Insulator (FDSOI) technology. FDSOI is mainly dedicated to low-power applications and provides thanks to well biasing techniques the ability to optimize dynamically the circuit's speed versus its power consumption [8]. FDSOI is also expected to bring reduced sensitivity to laser attacks due to the thin oxide box that isolates the channel of transistors from their wells [9]. This feature of FDSOI transistors is illustrated in Fig. 6, in which the cross sectional view of both NMOS and PMOS is drawn.

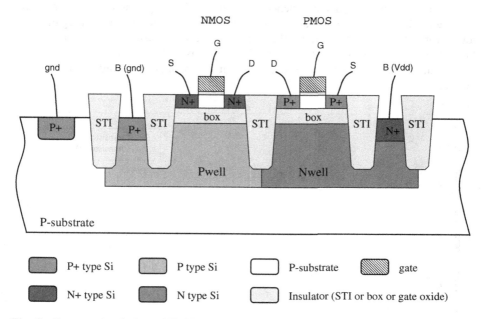

Fig. 6. Cross sectional view of NMOS (left) and PMOS (right) regular V_t transistors in 28 nm

FDSOI technology (note that dimensions are not drawn at scale for readability purposes).FDSOI transistors are built on a thin isolation box (less than 30 nm) that isolates their channel and diffusions (both source and drain) from the corresponding well. The channel of 28 nm FDSOI transistors is made of intrinsic silicon; its thickness is less than 10 nm. As a consequence, because of the isolation box, charge carriers induced by a laser shot outside the transistor cannot contribute to a transient current at the origin of a SET or SEU. Only charge carriers induced inside a transistor, which has a reduced volume, may create a transient current. The related phenomenon is significantly different from that described in Fig. 1 for bulk CMOS, for which charge carriers induced outside the transistor itself may contribute to the photocurrent. As a result, the induced photocurrent should be reduced both in magnitude (fewer charges are collected) and in time (because the diffusion component of a photocurrent, as drawn in Fig. 2, will not be collected due to the isolation box).

For the purpose of validating the assumption of reduced laser sensitivity of FDSOI technology and of building a simulation model we measured the laser-induced photocurrent on FDSOI test patterns (transistors of various types and sizes). We used the following laser settings: 1064 nm wavelength, 20 μs pulse duration, 5 μm spot diameter and backside illumination.

We report here the experiments carried out on two thick oxide high voltage NMOS transistors denoted #1 and #2 hereafter. Transistor #2's area is three times that of transistor #1. The transistors were biased in OFF state: $V_{drain} = 1.8$ V, $V_{source} = V_{gate} = V_{Pwell} = 0$ V. The laser pulse power was set to 855 mW. We measured the peak magnitude of the photocurrent pulse induced by a laser shot in the drain of the transistor as a function of the distance between the laser spot and the center of the transistor. The corresponding curves are given in Fig. 7. The maximum magnitude is found for a laser spot located on the transistor's center (distance equals to zero in Fig. 7): 8 μA for transistor #1 and 27 μA for transistor #2. Then, as the distance is increased, the current magnitude decreases. It tends almost toward zero after ten micrometers.

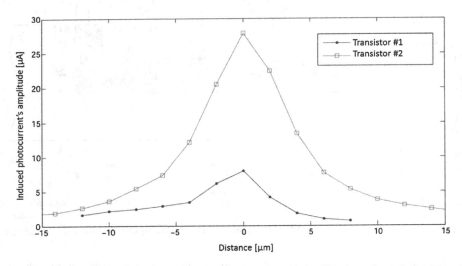

Fig. 7. Laser induced photocurrent magnitude [μA] in the drain diffusion of transistors #1 and #2 in OFF state as a function of the distance [μm] between the laser spot and the transistor's center

These results illustrate perfectly the main features of laser-induced photocurrents in FDSOI: (a) the photocurrent magnitude is significantly lower than that induced in Bulk CMOS transistors which would be close to the mA range for these laser settings [10], and (b) as a consequence of the isolation box, the photocurrent is halved for a distance of approximately 4 µm (the laser spot diameter is 5 µm), while it takes several tens of µm to halve the photocurrent in the case of a transistor in the Bulk technology [10].

According to these results, a lower sensitivity of FDSOI technology to laser attacks may be expected. However, an experimental validation on complex ICs is still needed.

5 Models: From Physical-Level to Behavioral-Level

5.1 Physical-Level

Laser effects on electronics are very similar to effects induced by radiations in the sense that both laser and radiations generate electron-hole pairs in the semi-conductor; the charges are transported into the media and are collected at the electrodes of the device. In order to model these phenomena, a tool called "MUSCA SEP3" (MUlti-SCAles Single Event Phenomena Predicted Platform) has been developed and is detailed in [11]. It is based on a Monte Carlo approach, and consists in sequentially modeling all the physical and electrical mechanisms.

In the laser attack framework, but also for heavy ion effects in nano-scales technologies, a very important contribution concerns the accounting for the carrier/charge track structure. Pulsed lasers generate electron-hole pairs by photo-ionization process; the ionizing mechanisms are addressed in detail in [12]. If linear absorption in semi-conductor is considered (low doping level), the linear transfer energy (LET) can be de-fined by the Eq. (2):

$$LET(z) = \frac{\alpha \cdot \lambda \cdot E_{e/h}}{\rho \cdot h \cdot c} \cdot E_{laser} \cdot e^{-\alpha \cdot x} \tag{2}$$

α is the absorption coefficient in cm^{-1}, λ is the pulsed laser wavelength in nm, E_e/h is the energy required to induce an electron-hole pair in eV, ρ is the Si density in mg/cm^3, h is the Planck constant, c the light velocity and E_{laser} the laser energy. Equation (2) allows for calculating the LET as a function of the depth penetration z. Since, differently from particles, laser beam does not have a punctual effect, it is necessary to define the radial deposition of the charges. Thus, the Eq. (3) describes the radial profile of the deposited charge:

$$I(r, z) = I_0(z) \cdot e^{\frac{2 \cdot r^2}{\omega(z)^2}} \cdot E_{lazer} e^{-\alpha z} \tag{3}$$

with:

$$\omega(z)^2 = \omega_o^2 \cdot \left(1 + \left(\frac{\lambda \cdot (z - z_o)}{\pi \cdot n \cdot \omega_o^2}\right)^2\right) \tag{4}$$

ω_o is "beam waist" i.e. the beam width for the focalization point ($z = z_o$) and n is the refraction index. Thanks to Eqs. (2) and (3), it is possible to describe the 3-dimensional charge deposition on the semi-conductor material. The next step consists in modeling the transport-collection physical mechanisms to deduce the transient pulse. Carrier generation and transport in the silicon active area is the most important part of the simulation flow and significantly influences the accuracy of collection-charge assessment. The transport/collection physical model is based on the dynamic coupled ambipolar diffusion and collection velocity. The approach is based on charge sharing rules, which depend on the distance from strike location to collection volume, the local electric field, and the process parameters (substrate/well doping).

Required information is directly extracted from layout files in GDS format and mainly includes areas and positions of the active layer. The representative 3D structure for Monte-Carlo simulation only contains N and P active junctions (drains and sources) of the design. The global collection volume takes into account the depletion capacitance of Drain and Source-Substrate junction. Figure 8 illustrates the GDS extractor applied to a NAND cell (0.35-μm technology). The GDS extractor allows deducing from the GDS file, the STI, the well locations and all active junctions.

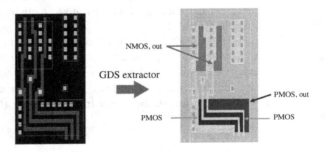

Fig. 8. GDS extractor applied to academic NAND cell

Transient currents issued from physical model can be injected on each collection node, i.e., the drain of each transistor. Doing so, the electrical model of the transient pulses can be associated with the circuit netlist. The link between the layout and the netlist is performed in our flow thanks to the "Calibre" tool [13].

5.2 Electrical –Level

Transient currents issued from physical model can be injected on each illuminated collection node (transistor drains or sources). Doing so, the electrical model of the transient pulses can be associated with the circuit netlist. The link between the layout and the netlist is performed in our flow thanks to the "Calibre" tool from Mentor Graphics. According to this physical-level model, the laser effect is modeled at electrical level as a plug-in current source for each illuminated junction. The model is depicted in Fig. 9.

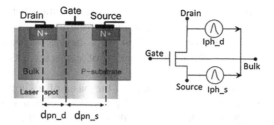

Fig. 9. Simple electrical model for a large spot laser-induced fault

In order to link the physical-level models and the electrical-level models for simulation purpose, a database was developed; each file corresponds to a standard cell in a given library and to a laser configuration data (energy, spot size). In each file, the transient current pulses I(t) are enumerated for each collection zone according to the position of the laser (dpn_d, dpn_s) for each logic state of the standard cell.

5.3   Logical Level

The eventual effect of a current injection at electrical level in a digital circuit is a modified logic signal during a period of time related to the exposure time, the so-called transient fault. The propagation of the fault and the final consequences on the circuit behavior can then be analyzed using logic-level simulations. A multi-level fault simulator has therefore been implemented and will be described in Sect. 6.

5.4   Behavioral Level

Finding design flaws late in the design flow is costly and strongly impairs the global development time. Evaluating the resilience of a given architecture at early design steps is therefore suitable. In most cases, such evaluations start at Register-Transfer Level (RTL) in order to benefit from a precise view of the registers in the design; higher-level descriptions are too abstract to clearly identify the real hardware that will be implemented in the circuit.

Early identification of design flaws can be achieved by using fault injection techniques [14]. At that level, the final design structure is not known so only errors in registers can be injected. The evaluation is meaningful only if errors injected at design time are actually representative of errors induced during a real attack. Also, evaluation time is limited so it is mandatory to trigger fault injection campaigns on reduced but significant sets of errors, including single-bit and multiple-bit error models.

Single-bit Errors. A very usual assumption consists in modeling the effect of laser shots as bit-flips. However, some previous work reported that bit-flips are not necessarily an adequate model.

Previous work [15] has shown that, at least in some experimental conditions, errors are unidirectional. Bits are in that case always modified in the same manner, setting them to either zero or one. Such effects lead to the error models called bit-reset or bit-set. It means that more or less bits will be sensitive to the perturbation, depending on the current state during the attack. The choice of the model may therefore have an impact on the resilience evaluation. Part of our work therefore aimed at identifying the impact of a given error model on the accuracy of early security evaluations w.r.t. differential fault attacks.

Fault injection experiments were defined on the basis of a simple circuit example, implementing a 16-bit sequential integer multiplier. This circuit is part of those currently manufactured in 28 nm technologies within the project LIESSE, and will be used in further work to compare in details early analyses with the consequences of real laser attacks. No error detection or tolerance mechanism is implemented in this circuit. Errors can therefore either be silent, or lead to computation errors (or crashes). The external communication protocol is based on handshake so the differences in computation time are not taken into account for the classification; only the result value is checked. Crashes were very few so they will not be explicitly discussed.

Exhaustive single-bit error injections have been performed (in all flip-flops, at each clock-cycle, so a total of 11,410 injections) using the functional test bench used for validation of the circuit, then several similar test benches with random multiplication operands.

The first outcome is clearly the impact of the circuit state on the difference in the percentage of computation errors for the 3 models (bit-flip, bit-set, bit-reset). For this particular example with the validation test bench, bits are more often at zero than one so the bit-reset model leads to noticeably more "non-injected" errors, i.e. injections that do not modify the flip-flop contents. About 3500 single-bit error injections have no impact for the bit-set model, while near 8000 injections have no impact for the bit-reset model.

The second outcome is related to the use of the fault injection results. Considering the total number of injected errors, bit-flips are the most critical errors with 40.1 % computation errors, while the bit-reset model only leads to 5.9 % computation errors and the bit-set model leads to 34.3 % computation errors. However considering only the actual bit modifications obtained during the campaign, the most critical injections correspond to bits forced at one, with 49.5 % computation errors in that case (while the percentage is 19.6 % for bits forced at zero).

When using random multiplication operands, the percentages are different, but the qualitative comparison of the three models is the same.

Table 1 illustrates a more detailed view, analyzing each register independently. The register criticality level is obtained with respect to the percentage of computation errors recorded after an exhaustive fault injection campaign with each of the error models. The percentage of computation errors noticeably differs from one model to the other. However, the classification in terms of criticality only slightly differs for the functional test bench. In all cases the state register (storing the current state of the Finite State Machine) is the most critical. After that, two groups of registers can be identified (Acc/MQ and Counter/B) with some inversions between bit-set and bit-reset. With random operands, results are similar for bit-flip and bit-reset, but slightly different for bit-set since the counter becomes the most critical register when "non-injected" errors are not considered.

Table 1. Classification of internal register criticality for single-bit error injections (excluding "non injected" errors) – multiplier, functional validation testbench

Criticality level	Bit-flip	Bit-reset	Bit-set
1	State	State	State
2	Acc	Acc	Acc
3	MQ	MQ	MQ
4	Counter	B	Counter
5	B	Counter	B

The choice of the right model to select for early fault injections therefore depends a lot on the designer intents. The bit-flip model creates more actual errors in the circuit but is more independent of the application characteristics. If those characteristics have to be taken into account, and if experiments have shown the feasibility of bit-set or bit-reset errors for a given technology, those models may lead to more accurate results, with in some cases significant differences in the error percentages. If the goal is to identify the most critical registers, the three models may lead to very similar results, at least for our case study, and in that case the bit-flip model may lead to more efficient fault injection campaigns.

Multiple-bit Errors. One of the key benefits of a laser source, as a tool to perform fault-based attacks, is its high precision locality, although a single laser shot may generate either single or multiple faults inside an integrated circuit. These characteristics must be taken into account by an RTL laser fault model assuming multiple-bit errors. Usual methods based only on fault injections for a given maximum error multiplicity are quite time-consuming and do not take into account the locality characteristics. Although at RT-Level it is not possible to precisely know the final placement of the element, it is possible to evaluate proximity on the basis of functional relationships.

There are two different categories of faults that can finally affect the circuit and potentially create an error. A fault may originate either from the combinational part or it can be directly injected inside a flip-flop (FF). Our proposed approach is attempting to unify these two different ways of introducing faults by modeling faults injected into the FFs of the design.

Our approach, as described in [16], makes use of a logic cone partitioning methodology, capable of introducing the notion of locality to an early RTL analysis including the ability to model multiple faults. The developed tool uses the elaborated RTL netlist of a behavioral (VHDL) description. The elaborated netlist and its analysis are obtained thanks to the Verific front-end API [17]. As shown in Fig. 10, the circuit under analysis is partitioned into intersecting functional blocks of combinational logic, called logic cones. Each cone starts from FFs of the circuit and/or primary inputs, and ends to another FF and/or a primary output.

Given a subset of the circuit, assumed as the area under attack, we are thus able to determine the sequential elements that may potentially contain an error.

Initially each attack is assumed to impact an entire logic cone and the application generates for each cone under attack a set of FFs that may potentially capture a fault.

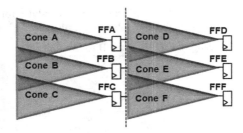

Fig. 10. Logic cone partitioning of the elaborated netlist

In a second step, depending on the results, this assumption can be modified to better focus laser attacks in suppressing some logic dependencies. Since we are able to know the functional relationship between the FFs of the design, we can also deduce information about the FFs that are likely to be attacked concurrently by a single laser shot, because of their potentially adjacent placement later in the design flow.

The method leads to the creation of a fault space with varying multiplicities for each attack depending on the functional relationship between the cone under attack and all the remaining cones of the circuit [18]. For example in Fig. 11, when Cone 2 is under attack, its fault set includes FFs: 1, 2 and 3; when Cone 3 is affected, the corresponding set includes FFs: 2, 3 and 4. These sets are also referred to as "cone-attack sets".

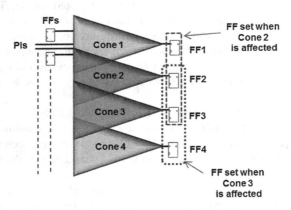

Fig. 11. Determination of FFs in a "cone-attack set"

Then, multiple-bit errors are injected into each cone-attack set. Our results show that the approach achieves a noticeable reduction of the size of the fault space, compared to random exhaustive multi-bit fault approaches, without even considering a maximum multiplicity for each attack. This way we can save computational resources for a fault injection campaign and, at the same time, take into account faults that are more realistic when we model a localized laser attack. Errors are injected into the FFs of the design so the approach is compatible with fast emulation techniques that can be very useful for an RTL evaluation.

As an example, Fig. 12 shows the sets obtained for the 128-bit datapath of an AES crypto-processor. The largest cone-attack sets include 62 FFs so errors with a maximum multiplicity of 62 may be injected for those sets. On the opposite, for all sets with only one FF, single-bit error injections are sufficient. In the classical approach, the maximum multiplicity would be defined more arbitrarily and errors would be injected randomly in the global set of 512 FFs.

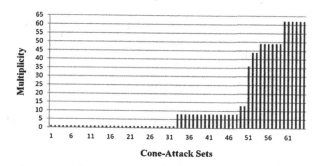

Fig. 12. Size of AES data path cone-attack sets

6 CAD Tools

The proposed security-evaluation flow is supported by several tools dealing with different abstraction levels. First, the databases of induced currents is generated using the MUSCA SEP3 tool on every standard cell, then the Calibre tool is used to transfer this information on the netlist of the circuit under evaluation as presented in Sects. 5.1 and 5.2.

Developed on the basis of the 0-delay simulator LIFTING [19], tLIFTING (timing LIFTING) [20] is an open-source fault simulator for single/multiple stuck-at faults, single/multiple upsets and single/multiple transients faults. The tool allows 0-delay/delay-annotated logic-level simulations and transistor-level fault simulation for digital circuit described in Verilog. Cooperating with a set of sub-tools, this simulator is able to perform transistor-level simulations based on the laser-induced fault model (current curves) and then further logic-level simulation for the whole circuit in order to analyze propagations of transient misbehaviors. As an open-source tool, it was expanded to read the database generated by MUSCA SEP3. Figure 13 shows how these tools interact with each other to produce simulation reports of laser-induced faults.

The simulation process is illustrated in Fig. 14: starting from the laser's parameters (size, position, power) and circuit layout information, affected PN junctions are located as sub-circuit in the design, and corresponding I(t) curves are extracted from the database. The corresponding electrical fault models are injected into the affected sub-circuit at transistor-level description. Then the whole system is simulated at logic-level in order to compute the sub-circuit input waveforms during the whole external perturbation. This information is then provided to the electrical-level simulator in charge of the simulation of the sub-circuit in order to simulate the electrical perturbation. After electrical simulation of the affected gates, if the perturbation changes

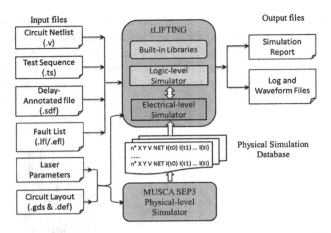

Fig. 13. From physical-level to logic-level laser-induced faults simulation

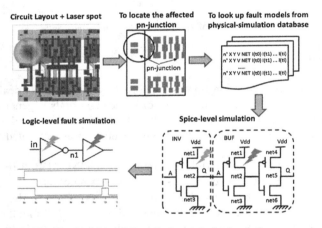

Fig. 14. The multi-level laser-induced fault simulation process

the state of circuit nodes, these new values are translated to logic-level for finishing the fault simulation at logic-level.

At higher level, prototyping platforms are used in order to evaluate early in the design flow the functional consequences of errors. These platforms are based on commercial FPGA development boards, but specific tools have been developed in order to manage the injection process. Platform examples are cited in [21].

7   Counter-Measures

Several types of hardware counter-measures are developed in order to improve the circuit resilience to laser-based attacks. The existing counter-measures can be classified as technological counter-measures (such as metal shield), redundancy-based counter-measures for error detection (e.g. [22–24]), detector-based counter-measures which focus on fault detection (e.g. [25, 26]). In this chapter, we detail a counter-measure based on laser beam detection, i.e. a detector-based approach. The principle consists in designing a cell with higher sensibility to laser attack than any other cell in the library, and then to spread several instances of that cell over the device in order to trigger an alarm wherever the laser beam hits the circuit.

7.1 Structure of the Detector

We choose an inverter as detector because of its small size compared to other cells. When both its NMOS and PMOS transistors are affected by a laser spot, the amplitude of the transient current pulse Iph_out on the inverter output is the difference between the photocurrents generated in both transistors: Iph_out = Iph_dp - Iph_dn (Fig. 15 (left)). When the inverter input is set to 1, transistor PMOS is OFF, transistor NMOS is ON, a positive current pulse Iph_out can be observed at the cell's output due to the laser attack. When Iph_out is large enough, the inverter output switches temporary from 0, the fault-free state, to 1, and this transition can be used to propagate an alarm signal (laser attack detection).

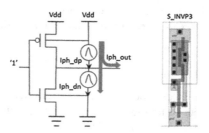

Fig. 15. (left) Laser-induced effect in an inverter, and (right) Inverter-based detector cell S_INVP3

In order to improve the detection of a laser shot thanks to such inverter-based light sensor, and make the sensor more sensible than any other gate in the design, we must increase Iph_out on the sensor output. We thus propose to design a new inverter from the regular INV2 cell of the working library (AMS C35 technology) such that Iph_dp increases, Iph_dn decreases, and thus Iph_out increases.

For that, we combined a large PMOS transistor with a small NMOS one. We designed a new cell from these two transistors, the S_INVP3 inverter shown in Fig. 15 (right). The ratio of the P+/N- and N+/P- junction areas in this new cell is now 48:5 instead of 8:5 as in the original standard inverter INV2 of the target library. As detailed in [27] for logic gates, and in [7] for SRAM cells, the photocurrents Iph_dp and Iph_dn being proportional to the area of the junctions, this new area ratio between the inverter's PMOS and NMOS transistors allows us to increase Iph_dp compared to Iph_dn and thus to increase Iph_out. The proposed invertor-based sensor is thus more sensible than the original cells (see Fig. 16 for comparison between several cells).

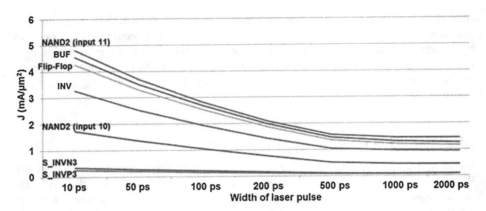

Fig. 16. Minimum current density for transmissible or detectable transient pulse (mA/μm2)

Similarly, we elaborated another sensor named S_INVN3 for which the ratio of the P +/N-well area and N+/P-sub is 8:30. Conversely to the S_INVP3 detector, the S_INVN3 input must be set 0 (P transistor ON, N transistor OFF) so that a laser beam provokes a negative pulse on the detector output that switches temporary from 1 (fault-free state) to 0 (transient fault used to detect the laser attack). Since detector cells have the same height as other standard cells, they can be easily integrated into the design.

7.2   Detector Sensitivity

Figure 16 shows for several cells the minimum current density required for different laser pulse duration in order to temporarily switch the cell output. These results were obtained from models and tools developed in the framework of the LIESSE project.

Clearly, the two proposed detectors are more sensitive to laser illumination than other standard cells thanks to the proposed (over)sizing of the PMOS (resp. NMOS) network compare to the NMOS (resp. PMOS) network in the proposed S_INVP3 (resp. S_INVN3) sensor. On average, the S_INVP3 is 6.5 times more sensitive than a NAND2 gate with input values set to "10", and 18.9 times more sensitive than this NAND2 gate when its input values are set to "11". For S_INVN3, these ratios are 5.1:1 and 15.1:1.

7.3   Insertion of Detectors in the Design

The principle is to spread detectors in the layout such that any spot location is detected by one or several detectors, and the detection signal is not masked by other detectors. For gathering all detector signals to a single detection flag, the detectors are combined into a chain-based structure as shown in Fig. 17. In this example, 4 chains have been built and connected to the flag FF thanks to a NOR gate.

As an example, when this detector-based countermeasure is applied for protecting a substitution-box of an AES co-processor, the area overhead is of 4.17 % of the original

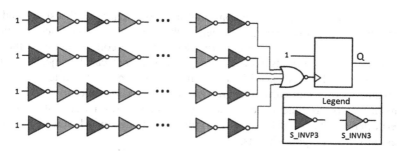

Fig. 17. The detector chain structure for injected fault detection

substitution-box. We performed 2000 laser-induced-fault simulations on that example. In each experiment, the location of the laser spot and the circuit input patterns was randomly chosen. The laser spot diameter was assumed to be 40 μm, i.e. covering 20 standard cells, and the current density was set to 0.08 mA/μm². From these simulations we obtained 3.1 % of error rate on the substitution-box and 100 % of detection rate (non-detected error: 0 %) thanks to the extra INV-based detectors.

8 Conclusions

This paper summarizes the main results obtained so far in the LIESSE project. Work is on-going to refine the tools and compare their outcomes with actual attacks on bulk and FDSOI prototypes.

FDSOI is often introduced as a technological answer to radiation effects and also to laser-based fault attacks [8, 28] due to the thin box that isolates the CMOS transistors from their wells. To date, an experimental validation of these expectations is still pending. We brought to the reader attention the first results we have obtained on isolated NMOS transistors (at 28 nm technology node) that tend toward proving this assumption. The magnitude of the laser-induced photocurrents in FDSOI transistors was found significantly lower than that induced in bulk transistors. However, we also find out that the effect area of a laser spot is reduced for FDSOI. This may be worrying because it may help an attacker to restrict fault injection to a few bits, thus making it easier to fulfill the fault models required for differential fault attacks [29]. However, these first results and assumptions must be corroborated on ICs at the state-of-art complexity: our next research work will be to compare the laser-fault sensitivity of two CMOS 28 nm circuits embedding a hardware implementation of the AES crypto-algorithm respectively in FDSOI and bulk technologies. If full immunity seems out of scope, we nonetheless expect a reduced laser sensitivity of the FDSOI devices.

Models and tools are now available for simulation of laser-silicon interactions from low levels, for better precision on the interaction, to high levels, for dealing with large devices.

A laser-induced transient pulse model was proposed at physical level including the laser interaction in Silicon step, the carrier transport and charge collection mechanisms. This physical model calculates the transient-current response based on the underlying physics phenomena (field modulation, multiple-node charge, diffusion) and laser characteristics as the wavelength, the energy, the focalization properties and the size beam. A GDS extraction process allows for identifying the collection area in the circuit design, and transient-currents issued from physical model can be injected at circuit level. The first results on isolated N and PMOS transistors at 28 nm technology node were obtained. Transient-current characteristics were compared for modelling and experiment results (as function of laser properties), first results are satisfactory. The short-term perspectives will be to use the physical model for FDSOI and bulk technologies on more complex circuits.

Results obtained on RT-level fault injections based on emulation show that the choice of the error model has noticeable effects on the early predictions made at design time. Bit-flip injections lead to more injected errors, but bit-set or bit-reset injections can have more impact when effective. The choice of the model therefore depends on the injection campaign objectives (qualitative or quantitative) and also on the knowledge of the technology and on the application execution, leading to more or less 0's and 1's in registers. Laser-based experiments on the LIESSE demonstrators will allow to better decide about the model to select.

For designers, performing fault effect analysis early in the design flow is a must. This early analysis can avoid time consuming and very expensive design re-spins. We thus propose a way to extract security-related information from RTL descriptions, particularly a list of Flip-Flop sets potentially affected at the same time by a laser shot according to the laser locality characteristics. This high-level fault injection approach is more realistic than the usual random multi-bit fault injection approach used in the literature. However our approach assumes that each laser spot impacts concurrently one entire single RTL cone and, therefore, all its intersecting cones. In our next work we will show the extent of the validity of this assumption by comparing the sets of Flip-Flops extracted from the RTL circuit description, and supposedly affected by the same laser shot, with the Flip-Flop sets arising from local attacks on the finalized layout of a circuit.

Acknowledgment. This work has been supported by the French National Research Agency project "LIESSE" (ANR-2012-INSE-0008). The counter-measure development has also been partially supported by the contract FUI CALISSON 2 (DGCIS AAP10). TIMA is Partner of the Labex PERSYVAL Lab (ANR-11-LABX-0025).

We would like to thank Verific Design Automation Inc. for providing the SystemVerilog and VHDL front-end used for the implementation of our RTL methodology.

References

1. Leveugle, R., Maistri, P., Vanhauwaert, P., Lu, F., Di Natale, G., Flottes, M.-L., Rouzeyre, B., Papadimitriou, A., Hely, D., Beroulle, V., Hubert, G., De Castro, S., Dutertre, J.-M., Sarafianos, A., Boher, N., Lisart, M., Damiens, J., Candelier, P., Tavernier, C.: Laser-induced fault effects in security-dedicated circuits. In: IEEE 22nd International Conference on Very Large Scale Integration, VLSI-SoC 2014 (2014). doi:10.1109/VLSI-SoC.2014.7004184

2. Skorobogatov, S.P., Anderson, R.J.: Optical fault induction attacks. In: Kaliski, B.S., Koç, çK, Paar, C. (eds.) CHES 2002. LNCS, vol. 2523, pp. 2–12. Springer, Heidelberg (2002)
3. Dutertre, J.M., De Castro, S., Sarafianos, A., Boher, N., Rouzeyre, B., Lisart, M., Damiens, J., Candelier, P., Flottes, M.L., Di Natale, D.: Design and technology of integrated systems in nanoscale era. In: DTIS 2014 (2014)
4. Baumann, R.C.: Radiation induced soft errors in advanced semiconductor technologies. IEEE Trans. Device Mater. Reliab. 5(3), 305–316 (2005)
5. Messenger, G.C.: Collection of charge on junction nodes from ion tracks. IEEE Trans. Nucl. Sci. 29(6), 2024–2031 (1982)
6. Carreno, V., Choi, G., Iyer, R.K.: Analog-digital simulation of transient-induced logic errors and upset susceptibility of an advanced control system. In: NASA Technical Memo 4241 (1990)
7. Sarafianos, A., Roscian, C., Dutertre, J.-M., Lisart, M., Tria, A.: Electrical modeling of the photoelectric effect induced by a pulsed laser applied to an SRAM cell. Microelectron. Reliab. 53(9–11), 1300–1305 (2013)
8. Golanski, D., et al.: First demonstration of a full 28 nm high-k/metal gate circuit transfer from bulk to utbb fdsoi technology through hybrid integration. In: Symposium on VLSI Technology (VLSIT), pp. T124–T125, June 2013
9. Ferlet-Cavrois, V., et al.: Direct measurement of transient pulses induced by laser and heavy ion irradiation in deca-nanometer devices. IEEE Trans. Nucl. Sci. 52, 2104–2113 (2005)
10. Sarafianos, A., Llido, R., Dutertre, J.-M., Gagliano, O., Serradeil, V., Lisart, M., Goubier, V., Tria, A., Pouget, V., Lewis, D.: Building the electrical model of the photoelectric laser stimulation of a NMOS transistor in 90 nm technology. In: Conference Proceedings from the 38th International Symposium for Testing and Failure Analysis, Phoenix, États-Unis (2012)
11. Hubert, G., Artola, L.: Single-event transient modeling in a 65 nm bulk CMOS technology based-on multi-physical approach and electrical simulations. IEEE Trans. Nucl. Sci. 60(6), 4421–4429 (2013)
12. Schmid, P.E.: Optical absorption in heavily doped silicon. Phys. Rev. B 23, 5531–5536 (1981)
13. http://www.mentor.com/
14. Leveugle, R.: Early analysis of fault-based attack effects in secure circuits. IEEE Trans. Comput. 56(10), 1431–1434 (2007)
15. Roscian, C., Dutertre, J.-M., Tria, A.: Frontside laser fault injection on cryptosystems - application to the AES' last round. In: International Symposium on Hardware-Oriented Security and Trust (HOST), pp. 119–124 (2013)
16. Papadimitriou, A., et al.: A multiple fault injection methodology based on cone partitioning towards RTL modeling of laser attacks. In: Design, Automation and Test in Europe Conference (DATE), 24–28 March 2014
17. www.verific.com
18. Vanhauwaert, P., et al.: On error models for RTL security evaluations. In: International Conference on Design and Technology of Integrated Systems in Nanoscale Era (DTIS) (2014)
19. Bosio, A., Di Natale, G.: LIFTING: a flexible open-source fault simulator. In: 17th Asian Test Symposium, Sapporo, pp. 35–40, November 2008
20. Lu, F., Di Natale, G., Flottes, M.-L., Rouzeyre, B.: Laser-induced fault simulation. In: DSD, pp. 609–614 (2013)
21. Ben Jrad, M., Leveugle, R.: Comparison of FPGA platforms for emulation-based fault injections using run-time reconfiguration. In: 27th Conference on Design of Circuits and Integrated Systems (DCIS), pp. 184–188, 28–30 November 2012

22. Moore, S., Anderson, R., Cunningham, P., Mullins, R., Taylor, G.: Improving smart card security using self-timed circuits. In: Proceedings of the Eighth International Symposium on Asynchronous Circuits and Systems, Manchester, UK, pp. 211–218, 9–11 April 2002

23. Rajendran, J., Borad, H., Mantravadi, S., Karri, R.: SLICED: slidebased concurrent error detection technique for symmetric block ciphers. In: 2010 IEEE International Symposium on Hardware-Oriented Security and Trust (HOST), pp. 70–75 (2010)

24. Di Natale, G., Doulcier, M., Flottes, M.-L., Rouzeyre, B.: A reliable architecture for parallel implementations of the advanced encryption standard. J. Electron. Test. (JETTA) 25(4–5), 269–278 (2009). doi:10.1007/s10836-009-5106-6

25. Bastos, R.P., Torres, F.S., Dutertre, J.-M., Flottes, M.-L., Di Natale, G., Rouzeyre, B.: A bulk built-in sensor for detection of fault attacks. In: 2013 IEEE International Symposium on Hardware-Oriented Security and Trust (HOST), pp. 51–54 (2013)

26. Lisart, M., Sarafianos, A., Gagliano, O., Mantelli, M.: Device for protecting an integrated circuit chip against attacks. Publication N°: FR2976722, December 2012

27. Feng, L., Di Natale, G., Flottes, M.-L., Rouzeyre, B.: Customized cell detector for laser-induced-fault detection. In: IEEE 20th International On-Line Testing Symposium (IOLTS 2014), pp. 37–42 (2014). doi:10.1109/IOLTS.2014.6873669

28. Alles, M., Schrimpf, R., Reed, R., Massengill, L., Weller, R., Menden-hall, M., Ball, D., Warren, K., Loveless, T., Kauppila, J., Sierawski, B.: Radiation hardness of fdsoi and finfet technologies. In: 2011 IEEE International in SOI Conference (SOI), pp. 1–2, October 2011

29. Barenghi, A., Breveglieri, L., Koren, I., Naccache, D.: Fault injection attacks on cryptographic devices: theory, practice, and countermeasures. Proc. IEEE 100, 3056–3076 (2012)

Author Index

Printed in the United States
By Bookmasters